Embattled Saints

View of the Bara Valley looking southeast toward Pakistan.

Embattled Saints

My Year with the Sufis of Afghanistan

Kenneth P. Lizzio

QUEST BOOKS
Theosophical Publishing House
Wheaton, Illinois * Chennai, India

First Quest Edition 2014

Quest Books
Theosophical Publishing House
PO Box 270
Wheaton, IL 60187-0270

www.questbooks.net

Cover images:
Afghan village: karssar/iStock/Thinkstock.
Fresco: Edward Kim/Bigstock.com
Cover design by Kirsten Hansen Pott
Typesetting by Datapage, Inc.

Chapter 3 and chapter 7 appeared in different form in *Central Asian Survey* and the *Muslim World*, respectively.

Library of Congress Cataloging-in-Publication Data

Lizzio, Kenneth P.
Embattled saints: my year with the Sufis of Afghanistan / Kenneth P. Lizzio.
pages cm
Includes index.
ISBN 978-0-8356-0923-4
1. Naqshabandiyah—Afghanistan. 2. Naqshabandiyah members—Afghanistan. 3. Sufism—Afghanistan—History—21st century. 4. Sufis—Afghanistan—Biography. 5. Lizzio, Kenneth P. I. Title.
BP189.7.N35L59 2014
297.4'8—dc23 2013040038

5 4 3 2 1 * 14 15 16 17 18 19 20

Printed in the United States of America

Contents

Note on Transliteration

Transliteration of words in Arabic, Persian, and Pashtu generally follows the conventions of the *International Journal of Middle Eastern Studies*. Thus, I have omitted diacritical dots and long vowel markings. For the sake of simplicity I have shortened *nisba* endings so that, for example, the term *Naqshbandiyyah* is instead *Naqshbandi*. When quoting another writer, I have been obliged to use his or her system. I have tried to remain consistent in the spelling of personal names but did not feel justified in rewriting an author's name for that purpose. I have also made an exception in transliteration of personal names where it would have substantially altered the manner in which it is pronounced in the subcontinent. Generally, this applies to names in which the Arabic article *al* is elided; thus, while the name *Saif ur-Rahman* properly transliterated is *Saif al-Rahman* or *ar-Rahman*, I have retained the spoken form of the name.

Map of Afghanistan and Northwest Pakistan

Prologue

Interest in Islam has intensified in the West since the attacks of 9/11 and the uprisings of the Arab Spring. In the media, an array of think-tank specialists, academics, policy analysts, journalists, military strategists, and even Evangelical preachers have all expounded on the "true nature" of Islam. Books have proliferated on Islamic radicalism, Muslim terrorists, Middle East history and politics, tensions between Sunni and Shi'a, and dozens of related topics.

Behind this torrent of information are many competing agendas that are more likely to confuse than enlighten; some portrayals are informed and accurate while others amount to little more than partisan attacks. On balance, the image of Islam—and of the complex civilization that it inspired—emerges as alien, exotic, conflicted, and prone to violence. Islam has replaced Communism as the new bugbear.

Other distortions are created less by what is said and written than by what is overlooked. In the public discourse on Islam, very little has been said about Sufism, the mystical dimension of Islam. Perhaps this omission is because Sufism, like all mysticisms, is perceived as ethereal and otherworldly. Or it may simply be dismissed out of hand as nonsense, the delusions of an irrational and backward people. Either way, it has little to do with "real-world" concerns of national security, access to oil, and political stability that any mention of Islam tends to evoke.

This book is an attempt to correct such misperceptions. It is an account of the history of a major branch of the Naqshbandi order of Sufism in South Asia, the Mujaddidi, and the year I spent living and studying with the then head of the order. At the time, these Sufis, primarily Afghans, were based in Pakistan's unruly rural tribal region. As violence has increased there, they have been forced in recent years to relocate to the safety of the urban sprawl of the ancient city of Lahore.

The Naqshbandis, like other schools of Sufism, maintain that in addition to sensory and intellectual modes of cognition, a third mode exists: gnosis. Based on the principle that modes of knowing and being are linked, gnosis is attained when the disciple follows a path (*tariqa*) of moral purification and mental contemplation under the initiation and guidance of a spiritual master. The process is intended to undermine narcissistic and exclusive identification of consciousness with self. With the aid of the shaikh, the disciple progresses through more advanced stages and states of consciousness, culminating in realization of the disciple's conscious identity with spirit as the fundamental ground of existence.

Though I did not fully appreciate it at the time, the Naqshbandi way of life I observed is facing threats to its very existence. Such threats are nothing new. The British and Russian empires, for instance, in their "Great Game" of colonial rivalry that once included central Asia, each tried to subdue them but failed in the end. Today, the Naqshbandis face new perils that are less overt but just as lethal.

One peril lies in the creeping secularization of Islamic society, a process set in motion more than a century ago by colonization and industrialization. Another is emerging from within Islam itself as one radical fundamentalist sect after another morphs into existence to assert, often forcibly, its own exclusive and narrow interpretation of Islam in which there is no place for Sufis.

Amid the welter of competing claims for Islamic truth, Sufis may provide the key to resolving the differences. Historically, Sufism has been the well from which Islam has drawn for spiritual revival during troubled or irreligious times. Whatever other roles they choose to play—and they are diverse—mystics are essentially technicians of the transcendent. And because Sufis traffic in matters that are timeless and cross-cultural, they help outsiders understand not only the true nature of Islam but the deeper meaning of all religions.

Prologue

This book is a rare historical and ethnographic account of a vibrant Sufi order in all its complex dimensions—social, economic, political, and, most important, spiritual—at a pivotal moment in its history. In my account I try to privilege the Naqshbandi worldview over the Western one. To be sure, every representation is a form of interpretation, but this one, I would hope, Naqshbandis themselves would endorse as their own.

Before master Muhammad Sadiq went to Saudi Arabia, he had been initiated into the line of Tariqat by Dr. Abdul Hamid Qureshi, a renowned physician of Jhelum. It so happened that one day . . . Sadiq had gone to see Dr. Qureshi. He knew him to be a very pious and God-fearing person, but that day a strange sight fascinated him. While he was conversing with the doctor, he noticed the visible flutter of his shirt on the left. It was the heavy pounding of a heart busy at 'Zikr'. He inquired from where he had got that and he said: "from Mian Muhammad Din" [his shaikh].

—Sayed Ishfaq 'Ali

Knowledge is of two kinds: Divine and Human.

—'Ali Uthman al-Hujwiri

Introduction

I first met Pir Saif ur-Rahman on a scorching summer afternoon in 1991 at his hospice in the turbulent tribal region of Pakistan's Northwest Frontier Province. The pir, known as *Mubarak Sahib* (Blessed Master) to his disciples, was head of the Naqshbandi order of Sufis. Afghan by birth, he had sought sanctuary in Pakistan's tribal region after the Soviet invasion of his country in 1979.

Seemingly fortuitous, our meeting had not been entirely accidental. After three attempts at a doctoral program in Sufism, which were rooted in a personal search for spiritual knowledge, I had become disillusioned with academia's preoccupation with ancient texts to elucidate a tradition that is primarily direct and oral. I felt a need to study Sufism from Sufis themselves rather than through Western interpreters. I was disillusioned not just with academia but also with a society that, for all its material and intellectual achievements—indeed, *because* of them—left little cultural space for the sacred. I was hoping to find that sense of the sacred in Sufism.

I began to seek passage to Afghanistan. Just why Afghanistan, instead of the dozens of other Islamic countries where Sufi orders could be found, had as much to do with my own imperfect understanding of the orders as it did with a vague sense that I would find what I was seeking in a country least affected by modernity. By utter chance, soon after deciding on Afghanistan as my destination, I landed a job in 1990 as research director for a US-government-funded project to curb opium production in Afghanistan. The Soviets had already withdrawn from that country the previous year, and a vicious civil war was breaking out in the power vacuum they had left. Because of the ongoing conflict, Americans working in Afghanistan were based in Peshawar, the capital of Pakistan's Northwest Frontier Province, or the NWFP, as it is known.

When I had studied Sufism in graduate school some twenty years earlier, professors said Sufis were relics of the past. The Sufis' greatest days, it was taught, had occurred between the twelfth and fourteenth centuries, a moment that scholars dubbed the "classical period" of Islamic mysticism. During that era, Sufism and Islam underwent an unprecedented literary and cultural flowering in virtually every sphere of life: poetry, mysticism, philosophy, art, architecture, and painting. A period of general decline followed, which was accelerated with the arrival of the European powers in the eighteenth century. The final blow came with modernization in the twentieth century. What then remained of the rich Sufi mystical tradition was dismissed as essentially "a club of old men who smoked pipes."[1]

So the scenario went. But the secular process that modern-minded academics of the 1960s and 1970s believed was inexorable gave way to the postmodern 1980s. Sufis were suddenly in evidence everywhere in the Islamic world, as Islam itself went through a resurgence generally. An Egyptian government survey in the 1980s revealed no fewer than twenty-eight Sufi orders in Cairo alone. Sufis were also flourishing in Turkey, despite Kemal Ataturk's closure of the lodges in 1925. Indeed, President Turgut Ozal, who served both as Turkey's prime minister and president in the 1980s, had formal ties to Naqshbandis, as did a number of other Turkish heads of state. In Senegal, an order of Sufis known as the Muridi was a powerful political and economic force, producing most of the country's foreign exchange through peanut cultivation. Even in Soviet central Asia, where Sufis had experienced prolonged systematic repression, the orders had begun to resurface.

Despite this growing awareness that the Sufi orders were again thriving, surprisingly little had been written about contemporary Sufism. Islamic scholars remained preoccupied with the texts of the classical period, as if Sufism had ended in the fourteenth century. Clearly for some it did. Popular accounts of mysticism—usually in the form of memoirs or travelogues—centered mostly on Hinduism or Buddhism.

For their part, anthropologists did travel to Islamic countries to investigate the Sufi orders, especially in the 1960s and 1970s. While their ethnographies were often fascinating and informative, too often Sufi spirituality was reduced to latent social, political, or economic imperatives. In some cases, this was a function of the prevailing worldview; in others it was because as non-Muslims, anthropologists were usually prohibited access to the sacred precincts of Sufism. As a result, the image of Sufis in the anthropological literature is decidedly negative: they are essentially political and social parasites. In this way, Western interpretations held sway over those of Sufis themselves.

Unlike other countries, very little was known about Sufism in Afghanistan. Apart from some translations of poetry, almost nothing had been written in a European language about Sufis there. This was a surprising omission, given that the Naqshbandi and other orders were central to the ten-year war against the Soviets. If nothing else, their role in the resistance was proof that Sufism, whatever its contemporary form, had survived centuries of colonization, modernization, secularization, civil war, and other threats to its existence.

So when I arrived in Peshawar in the spring of 1990, it seemed a propitious time to explore the state of this neglected fifteen-hundred-year-old mystical tradition.

At the time of my arrival, the Afghan economy was teetering on the brink of total collapse. Two decades of war had destroyed most of the native *kanat* irrigation systems essential for the country's primary economic activity, agriculture. Also, farm fields were riddled with some thirty million land mines planted by the Soviets. Where cultivation was possible, fertilizer and seed for wheat and rice production were scarce.

In this dire environment, opium production had become an important means of survival for many farmers and their families. With an average land holding of about two acres, small farmers could produce enough opium to earn about $300 a year. In the south, where there were larger holdings and more arable land, opium production had become big business, some farmers receiving advances from drug traffickers on the next season's harvest.

Opium has been produced in Afghanistan since at least the fifteenth century. Its treacly amber resin is harvested from the bulbs of the poppy plant, fashioned into a paste, and dried into a flat cake. The cake is smoked as a pain killer. The seeds can also be used to make "poppy tea." What remains of the tall flowering plant, its stalk, becomes fodder for draught animals and mulch for the soil. Nothing goes to waste. In every town or village there was inevitably a derelict addict, but for the most part the substance was not widely abused by Afghans.

That situation changed dramatically following the Islamic revolution in neighboring Iran in 1979. The revolution's leader, Ayatollah Khomeini, cracked down on drug traffickers who were processing raw opium from across the region into heroin, which increased its value tenfold while vastly reducing its bulk. The heroin processors fled into the Pashtun tribal belt that straddles Afghanistan and Pakistan, where government barely existed. There they could operate labs with virtual impunity. Makeshift heroin labs were set up in homes where they could easily be dismantled in the event of a police raid. Some producers had even operated under the protection of *mujahiddin* leaders, who demanded a share of the profits to finance their war against the Soviets.

The war against the Soviets unexpectedly provided the heroin traffickers with a means to transport the drug out of Afghanistan to Western markets with devastating efficiency. The United States, through its Central Intelligence Agency (CIA), was funneling tons of arms, including Stinger missiles, to the Afghan mujahiddin to fight the Soviets. The CIA worked through the Pakistan army's intelligence unit known as Inter-Services Intelligence (ISI). Pakistani Army cargo trucks carried American weapons into Afghanistan and returned with processed heroin ready to ship to Western markets. The CIA turned a blind eye to this illicit activity. Its goal was to defeat the Soviets, a Cold War obsession that trumped the need to stem the flow of Afghan heroin into the United States and other countries.

Afghans, meanwhile, were falling victim to the ravages of heroin, which was largely new to them and far more vicious than the opium they used occasionally as a natural remedy. An increasing number of Afghans began engaging in a practice called "chasing the dragon," in which a small amount of heroin is placed on a square of tin foil, heated, and its fumes inhaled. The result is instant intoxication and near-instant addiction.

By the time I arrived in Peshawar, estimates of the number of heroin addicts had soared from none in 1979 to nearly one million in less than a dozen years, and the number was growing. The addicted included Afghans and Pakistanis alike. Although poppy production had largely been eradicated by the Pakistani government in the 1980s, profits from its cultivation were so high that impoverished farmers had reestablished it as a cottage industry.

With a team of thirty Afghan researchers, I studied local attitudes toward the use of opiates. Based on the raw data they collected, I estimated that 1,500 metric tons of opium was being produced annually. This was more than twice the official US government's then estimate of six hundred metric tons. Eventually, I would study the most dangerous element in the narcotics equation: the heroin trade.

In my free time, I concentrated on Sufism. I asked colleagues and local staff if they knew of any Sufis. No one did. Some said there were no Sufis left; others said the only true mystics were *malang*, wandering mendicants in South Asia who dressed in tatters and behaved in outrageous ways. I once saw one on the highway between Islamabad and Peshawar. Dressed in a pleated blue skirt and a woman's blouse, he was dancing insouciantly amid speeding cars and trucks. When I stopped to take his photo, he mimicked me by holding up an imaginary camera. A female anthropologist at a university in Islamabad said I would find Sufis in Sindh province in the south of Pakistan. She claimed to have seen an ancient man in the town of Multan sitting on a bed of nails in a courtyard filled with human excrement.

From these comments I concluded that neither Afghans nor Pakistanis had an interest in, or appreciation for, a major part of their own religious heritage. Indeed, so anxious were they to effect a modern outlook that they seemed to want to distance themselves from what they viewed as an embarrassing vestige of their backward past. At best, Sufism was little more than quaint folklore. I had begun to wonder if my professors were right after all.

One day, a member of my staff entered the office. Looking behind himself conspiratorially, he closed the door. It was Sayyid Bacha. Though he was of average size and not particularly muscular, enormous block-like fists betrayed his pugilistic prowess. Bacha had been former national boxing champion of Afghanistan, so he was something of a celebrity. He possessed a great deal of self-confidence, not only because of his athletic fame but because he was a sayyid, a descendant of the Prophet. He had attended a French lycée in Kabul and, like me, spoke French fluently. I spoke halting Persian, so we usually conversed in French.

Over time I noticed Bacha was using our common language to forge personal ties with me. Increasingly, he was bypassing his immediate supervisor, Izzatullah. I was becoming concerned that his behavior would be viewed as favoritism by the rest of the staff. I was about to broach the subject when he cut me off.

"Agha [Mr.] Ken," he began, his voice low and guarded. "Don't talk openly about Sufism in this office or anywhere else for that matter. There are many Afghans around here who don't like Sufis . . . like Izzatullah."

In any other case, I might have dismissed his remark as an attempt, so common in this tribal culture, at simple slander. But Izzatullah had once been a commander in the Hezb-i Islami (Party of Islam). The HI, as it was known, was an Islamic party that had earned a reputation during the war as the most ferocious of the several Afghan mujahiddin parties that had sprung up after the Soviet invasion. The CIA had funneled the lion's share of one billion dollars in weapons for the Afghan resistance to the HI. Only later was it learned that the HI's reputation was due chiefly to the public relations skill of its head, Gulbuddin Hekmatyar, who for a time had joined ranks with the Taliban after the war's end. The HI was, however, ferocious in its opposition to one thing—Sufism. Because Sufism did not figure explicitly in the Qur'an or in accounts of the Prophet's life, fundamentalist groups like the HI regarded it as an accretion and a heresy (*bid'a*).

Afghans are among the most gracious and congenial people on earth. They are also a warrior people quick to act out grievances. It was conceivable that a member of the HI would harm me for my Sufi sympathies. Already the staff was issuing veiled threats to burn down the office—a disturbingly common Pashtun tribal practice called *lashgar*—in protest over a tryst between the front-office secretary, an Afghan woman named Jamila, and a Pakistani employee. Indeed, the Afghan staff of CARE had razed their office in Peshawar in protest over just such an affair the year prior. More worrisome was the fatal shooting of an Afghan-American two weeks earlier in a street not far from my office. Though the reasons for it were unclear, all of this violence was worrisome. So as I turned these things over in my mind, I thanked Bacha for his advice and moved to open the door lest the staff think a cabal was being hatched. As I reached for the door, Bacha put his hand on my shoulder reassuringly.

"If you want to meet some Sufis, I'll take you, but don't talk about these things around here anymore."

A few weeks later Sayyid Bacha took me to meet Shaikh Ismael Khan, an Afghan shaikh of the Suhrawardi order of Sufis. Shaikh Ismael was living in Nasir Bagh, one of the largest refugee camps set up for some three million Afghans who had fled to Pakistan during the Soviet occupation. New waves of refugees were now fleeing the civil war in Afghanstan. Located north of town, the camp was home to thousands of Afghans huddled together and living in squalor. Widowed women could be seen wandering the nearby streets, begging with one hand and clutching a baby with the other. These Afghans had been living as refugees so long that an entirely new generation was being raised in the camps. And it was in these camps that the Taliban were being groomed.

When we arrived, Shaikh Ismael was standing in front of his house. It was a simple mud structure. After the formal greeting—shaking with both hands clasped and touching the right to the heart—he led us into a prayer room adjoining the house. The room also served as the neighborhood mosque. Ismael was tall and erect with a long grey beard. He appeared to be in his sixties. He was clad in a khirqa, a cloak that Sufis wear, of a type believed to have been worn by the Prophet. A long white turban covered his head. Inside the mosque there was no furniture, save some cushions against the walls and reed mats to cover the clay floor. Ishmael called out, a young boy appeared, and the shaikh instructed him to fetch us food and water.

We sat at the end of the mosque that faced the *qibla*, the direction of Mecca, two thousand miles away to the southwest. On the wall hung a plaque with the inscription "*Allahu Akbar*" (God is Great). Speaking in

Persian, the shaikh said he was from the Gardez region of Afghanistan. He had emigrated to Peshawar in 1982, three years after the Soviet invasion of his country. He brought his wife, six children, and several members of his extended family. The conditions in the camp were difficult, but, God willing, the shaikh and his family would one day return to Afghanistan, where life was once good and where shari'a (Islamic law) would one day prevail again.

Ismael had a warm, avuncular manner, and I immediately felt at ease in his presence. The boy reappeared with a platter of cucumber salad, yoghurt, a flat bread called nan, and some beef kebabs, setting it out on a plastic mat. Ismael ate little himself, preferring to tear a piece of nan or slide a piece of grilled meat from the skewer and hand it to me.

Eventually we got around to Sufism. He said he was a shaikh initiated in all four of the orders in Afghanistan. Sufism, he lamented, had been weakened not only by the Soviet invasion but also by corrupt practices within Islam. He said that there was the son of a leading Qadiri shaikh who practiced with women in the nude. (This sounded wildly implausible, but I chose not to pursue it as I had questions about other things.) When I asked about his own Sufi teaching, he said that he had discontinued practice after repeated threats from the HI. When we finished our meal, bowls of water were brought out and we washed our hands. Ismael then recited a short prayer. As we rose to leave, I asked if I could return. Ismael said I was welcome in his home any time.

Ismael had struck me as deeply pious. But his fear of the HI seemed uncharacteristic of Sufis. Since its inception in the seventh century, Sufism had faced opposition from many quarters, but courageous defiance had always been its hallmark. I wondered if all Sufis in Peshawar were cowering under the menace of the HI or if Ismael was merely an exception.

A few weeks later, Bacha came to my house to tell me he had learned of another Sufi, this one a master in the Chishti order, living nearby on the Grand Trunk Road. But the shaikh, I discovered when I visited, had actually died some years earlier. His disciples, one of whom was the former president of Peshawar University, were meditating on a set of photos of the deceased shaikh. Like Ismael, they seemed deeply pious. But their shaikh was dead, and it all seemed too abstract. In any case, I wanted to encounter a *living* Sufi.

One Saturday afternoon Bacha showed up unannounced at my house. He was on his way to the market to buy groceries and asked if I wanted to join him. I asked why his wife did not accompany him, even though I knew the answer. Bacha said that he did not want his wife to leave the house. The traditional place for a woman, he said, was in the home. "You know," he remarked proudly, "only three men have seen my wife's face: her brother, her father, and I."

On the way to the market we talked about Sufism. I expressed my disappointment with the Sufis I had thus far met. Bacha was perplexed. Had I not met genuine Sufis, he asked. And were not at least some of these practicing? And had they not invited me to join them? Yes, yes, but something was missing, I said. I was trying to explain the difference between ritual observance of the law and mystical experience when he bolted upright in his chair.

"Now I see! You want something *living*! Why didn't you say so? In that case," he said, "I'll take you to see the Pir-i-Kunduz. He's living in Bara in the Khyber Agency. He's the one for you."

The term *pir* means "old man" in Persian and is an honorific given to spiritual masters in Sufism. *Pir-i-Kunduz* meant this Sufi was from Kunduz, a province in the far north of Afghanistan. Pirs always had their names attached to a place name, perhaps the better for seekers to find them. Indeed, he was also called, more accurately, Pir-i Bara. As it turned out, the Khyber Agency was not far from Peshawar.

Despite its proximity, visiting the Khyber was not for the fainthearted. At that time, it was the most lawless and dangerous of Pakistan's seven tribal agencies and quite possibly one of the most lawless regions of the world. Few foreigners ventured into the Khyber or any of the other tribal agencies unless properly introduced. Tribal skirmishes, smuggling, kidnapping, heroin trading, and just plain xenophobia made the agencies inhospitable places even for Pakistanis. On a weekly basis the local papers carried articles of individuals who had been abducted from one of the tribal agencies for ransom or revenge. Those who were kidnapped usually disappeared without a trace.

On occasion, pressured by the US government, the Pakistani military conducted raids on suspected heroin houses, razing them to the ground with bulldozers. The tribes usually retaliated by kidnapping outsiders in the hope of discouraging the government from future threats to their territorial sovereignty. With their international complications, kidnapped foreigners were particularly vexing to the Pakistani government. Even Pakistanis from the settled areas—those under complete government control—avoided the agencies. In the face of these perils, the prospect of meeting the pir seemed as remote as Kunduz. But when I raised my concerns, the ever-confident Bacha assured me that if I went with him no harm would come to me. I had already come so far to meet a Sufi, I reasoned. It seemed worth the risk.

The following Saturday we hailed a taxi and headed for the Khyber Agency fifteen miles away. Outside town, the road wound through small villages and past brick kilns. The ground was scarred with deep crevices where the dirt had been excavated for brick making. When we slowed at a speed bump, an ear-shattering loudspeaker was blasting an angry religious sermon in Pashto, the local language. Bacha saw me wince.

"Fundamentalists," he sneered.

After thirty minutes on the road, we arrived at a sign clearly marking our arrival at the agency's border: "WARNING: FOREIGNERS ARE PROHIBITED BEYOND THIS POINT BY ORDER OF THE GOVERNMENT OF PAKISTAN." Despite the warning, the police paid no attention to me, perhaps because I was with Sayyid Bacha. Or perhaps at a glance I was mistaken for an Afghan, as I was wearing the traditional long shirt and baggy pants known as *shalwar kameez.* We hastily hopped into a Toyota pickup truck and made our way on a dusty road to the pir's hospice in the Khyber.

Although I had never visited a Sufi hospice or met a living shaikh, I thought I had a good idea of what I would find. I was about to see most of my preconceptions dissolve before my ethnocentric eyes. When we arrived in early afternoon, we were told that the pir was resting and would not be out until sunset prayer. In the intervening time, I sat in the shade of a veranda conversing with several of his disciples.

Among the pir's many visitors that day were a businessman from Karachi, two local merchants, two Afghan mujahiddin fighters, and some college students. In short, a cross section of modern Pakistani-Afghan society. In the course of an otherwise calm and thoughtful conversation about Sufism, a few would suddenly ejaculate, *"Ya'llah!"* (Oh, God!). The businessman's torso would suddenly jerk and twist as if a shiver had run up his spine. One of them saw my bewildered look and, attempting to reassure me, murmured, "Don't be scared. This is a laboratory . . . for human transformation."

Another peculiar thing I noticed was a pronounced beating of their hearts beneath their shirts. I wondered if this was some kind of learned behavior or a muscle spasm. The pupils of their eyes were dilated as if in trance, yet they were fully alert and articulate. Apart from these strange and bewildering phenomena, the men around me were, as far as I could discern, normal, rational, and perfectly sane.

Around five o'clock there was a sudden rushing about by everyone in the courtyard. I turned to see the pir entering. He was clad in a shimmering turquoise cloak and an immaculate white turban. Though he was of medium height, his piercing blue eyes and long hennaed beard gave him an imposing appearance. He walked about the courtyard greeting each of his disciples.

What happened next completely baffled me. I expected the disciples to start gathering for prayer quietly and without fanfare, like monks for vespers. Instead, as the pir approached, some of the men with whom I had conversed moments before suddenly began weeping, screaming, and shaking uncontrollably. One disciple shook the pir's hand and recoiled, holding his hand and screaming as if he had touched something hot. Another man fell to the ground at the sight of the shaikh, his body writhing violently in the dust at the shaikh's feet. Others stood back wailing and howling. Still others wept silently, in some way overcome at the sight of him. Unmoved by these apparent histrionics, the pir strolled imperiously about the courtyard, greeting everyone warmly and with perfect equanimity. When he saw me, he nodded but did not seem surprised to see a foreigner in the compound.

Shortly after, I followed the men to a raised concrete platform on the other side of the compound, near the entrance. The heat was sweltering, and even though we were outdoors a battery of fans turned overhead. We sat cross-legged on the platform. Some of the men were still shaking and trembling from their encounter with the pir. Just before prayer began, someone in the congregation noticed me and asked Bacha if I was Muslim. Then the stranger motioned for me to leave. Bacha insisted that I stay, but I was escorted back to my original place in the shade on the veranda until the prayer session ended.

I sat there for what must have been two hours, watching the arrival of the pir's many disciples. Dusk was falling and hundreds of mujahiddin were arriving from their battle positions in Afghanistan. I estimated about four hundred men in all. Automatic weapons were everywhere. Each time I stood to indicate my interest in joining the others, a disciple motioned to me with a lowering hand saying, "*Beshin. Beshin.*" (Sit. Sit.) Around eight o'clock, someone came to collect me, and I was led into what appeared to be the hospice library. Seated at one end of the room surrounded by disciples was another shaikh, Pir Habib ur-Rahman. Habib's sobriquet was *Pir-i-piran*, signifying that he was a master of other Sufi masters. He had flashing green eyes and a mischievous smile. I took an immediate liking to him.

I explained to him that I had studied Sufism and in fact held a master's degree in it, boasting that I considered myself something of an expert on the subject and had always wanted to visit a Sufi hospice. He seemed genuinely impressed by my assertions. So, too, were the disciples. We then discussed Sufi literature. After I quoted some Sufi poetry, one of the disciples shouted, "He is one of us!" As it was getting dark, I asked Pir-i-piran for his permission to leave, as is the custom among Afghans. I also told him that I would like to hitch a ride back to Peshawar if anyone was going that way.

"You can't go anywhere now," he said. "The roads are dangerous after dark. You might be killed or kidnapped. Even we don't travel after dark," he added, "and we *live* here!"

I had little choice but to spend the night there. I was given a bedroll and taken to a small room where some mujahiddin were already asleep on the floor. As I lay among a tangle of feet on the hard floor, I could not sleep. Strange sounds emanated from the mosque, sounds unlike anything I had ever heard. There were deep bellows and whoops, hissing, bloodcurdling screams, and even hysterical laughter. The sounds went on throughout the night, until dawn.

In the morning Pir-i-piran came in as we were being served black tea and sat at the head of the room. He and I resumed our conversation of the previous evening. At one point, I was quoting a verse from the thirteenth-century Afghan mystic poet Jalaladin Rumi's *Divan-i Shams-i Tabriz* when one of the disciples, a university student eager to join the discussion, leaned over my shoulder to interject something.

Habib looked over my right shoulder at him—it was just a look, and yet there was something in it, a kind of knowing, communicative look—and the young man was cut short in midsentence. He began to shake and stammer uncontrollably as if in a grand mal seizure. He fell backward on the floor, where his paroxysms continued. I turned around and looked askance at Habib. But his smiling countenance had turned to a scowl. He scoffed in Persian, "Sufism! What do you know about Sufism? All you know are books!" Gesturing with his hand toward the disciple now lying in peaceful afterglow on the floor, he added triumphantly, "*This* is Sufism!"

He was right. In terms of living Sufi practice, I had absolutely no knowledge or experience whatever. Habib's assertion carried all the more weight given his impressive knowledge of the texts and his historical antecedents. While my reading of Sufism indicated that these Sufis were encountering the *mysterium tremendum* that marks the spiritual encounter, I was nonetheless shocked by their dramatic, violent physical reactions, especially in the presence of the pirs.

What accounted for the violent nature of Sufi mystical experience and for some of the bizarre physical phenomena attendant to it, such as the beating heart? What role did the shaikh play in precipitating these energetic phenomena and by what means? Who were these pirs and what was the source of their teaching and methods?

Unfortunately, answers to these questions would have to wait some years. A few weeks after my visit to the pir, two US congressmen decided that the broader aim of my project, to develop alternative crops for Afghan poppy farmers, was tantamount, as one congressman put it, to "aiding drug dealers," and the project was abruptly terminated.

It would be several years before I would return.

Harith ibn Hisham asked the Messenger of Allah, may Allah bless him and grant him peace, "How does the revelation come to you?" and the Messenger of Allah, may Allah bless him and grant him peace, said, "Sometimes it comes to me like the ringing of a bell, and that is the hardest for me, and when it leaves me I remember what it has said. And sometimes the angel appears to me in the likeness of a man and talks to me and I remember what he says." 'A'isha added, "I saw it coming down on him on an intensely cold day, and when it had left him his forehead was dripping with sweat."

—Hadith

For each We have appointed a divine law and a traced-out way. Had Allah willed He could have made you one community.

—Qur'an 5:48

Chapter 1

Descent

The Naqshbandi order of Sufis, led by Pir Saif ur-Rahman, traces its origin, as do all Sufi orders, through an initiatic chain that reaches back to Islam's founder, the Prophet Muhammad.

The Prophet himself, however, never referred to himself as a Sufi, nor was his teaching explicitly mystical in outlook. In fact, Muhammad's life and the Qur'an were much more oriented to this world than the next. His overarching mission was to create moral order and social cohesion among the warring and polytheist tribes of the Arabian Peninsula. Esoteric matters, after all, speak only to the few.

The message that was revealed to Muhammad emerged from the long monotheistic tradition of the Middle East. Islam, Muhammad said, marked the culmination of a series of religious revelations among Semitic peoples, primarily through Abraham and then Moses, who conveyed the formal law encoded in the Ten Commandments, and Jesus, who encouraged spiritual union with God.

Early followers of Jesus saw no contradiction in both keeping the Judaic law and aspiring to the spiritual union described by the contemplative Christ. The two aspects of their belief formed, for them, an organic whole. Jesus himself had said, "Think not that I have come to destroy the law or the prophets: I came not to destroy, but to fulfill them."[1]

But religion tends to shape rigid identities. By the end of the first century, a gulf had widened between those committed to traditional Jewish practice and those committed to its Christian variant. Gradually, the two faiths separated. It subsequently fell to Muhammad to reunite the law—*shari'a*—with the spiritual path—*tariqa*—of mysticism into a single, organic religious system.

At first glance, Muhammad's life evinces far less of the loving mysticism of Jesus and far more of the righteous retribution of the Old Testament. He led his followers into numerous battles against his enemies on the Arabian Peninsula. He was also a businessman who was very much involved in the political and social problems of his time. In contrast to the image projected of the chaste Jesus, he had many wives and led a sensual life.

But there can be no doubt that the Prophet's life had a mystical dimension. Troubled by the immorality and corruption of sixth-century Mecca, he often sought solitude in a *ghar*, or cave, on Hira, a mountain near Mecca. There he would spend several nights at a time in solitary vigils, meditating and praying. It is an old practice, well established over the centuries by those seeking enlightenment. It was in this cave, at the age of forty, that Muhammad began to experience visions.

The year was 610. In what came to be called *Laylat al-Qadr* (the Night of Power), the angel Gabriel began to reveal to Muhammad the message that would eventually be gathered up from leaves and bits of paper and assembled into the Qur'an. The Night of Power also marked the descent of the divine spirit into Muhammad. Of that night the Qur'an says:

> The Night of Power is better than a thousand months.
> In it the angels descend, and the Spirit. (97:3–4)

The visions came on abruptly, often accompanied by violent shaking. Sometimes there would be a feeling of pain and a ringing in his ears. Even on the coldest days he would sweat, a sign that he was undergoing unusual experiences. The persistence of these visions over the next twenty-three years, and the inner changes they presumably induced, eventually convinced Muhammad of his prophetic mission.

Muhammad's cave vigils on Hira were, in fact, the beginning of a life marked by austerity and contemplation. His wife 'A'isha, commenting on his nightly meditative states, remarked that "when he slept, his eyes and heart did not sleep."[2] In many of the sayings attributed to him, Muhammad emphasized the importance of such night vigils and prayer.

In moments of mystical rapture Muhammad would sometimes utter cryptically, "I feel the breath of the beneficent from Qaran." Uways al-Qarani was a desert-dwelling mystic from southern Arabia and a contemporary of Muhammad. He and the Prophet never met, yet they appear to have enjoyed a kind of telepathic relationship that seems to have been common among later Sufis, including the Naqshbandis.

Legend has it that Muhammad was able to describe Uways al-Qarani as "a lowly man of middle height and hairy. On his left side there is a white spot, as large as a dirham, which is not from leprosy, and he has a similar spot on the palm of his hand."[3] After Muhammad's death, the first Caliph 'Umar went in search of Uways al-Qarani. In a village called Najd, residents told 'Umar that they knew a man of that name, "a madman who dwells in solitude and associates with no one. He does not eat what men eat, and he feels no joy or sorrow. When others smile, he weeps. And when others weep, he smiles."[4]

The caliph asked to be taken to Uways al-Qarani's place in the desert. When they arrived, Uways was praying. When he had finished, he turned to 'Umar and exclaimed, "The heart of the solitary is one free from thoughts of others." 'Umar then asked to see the white marks on Uways's body, which he displayed. How the Prophet had come to consort spiritually with Uways is a mystery.

Strangely for a man of peace, Uways died in 657 as a result of wounds he sustained while fighting in the battle of Siffin with Muhammad's nephew and son-in-law, 'Ali. But his name did not die with him. Centuries later, Naqshbandis who were initiated by dead spiritual preceptors would call themselves *Uwaysi*.

If the law-giving character of the Qur'an more closely resembles the Old Testament, then something of the New Testament may be found in the accounts of the actions and sayings of Muhammad collectively called *hadith*. The hadith include sayings of Muhammad, both about his own nature and about mysticism in general. Some of them allude to Muhammad as the first thing created by God, a luminous spiritual substance from which the world itself was fashioned. Of this Muhammad said, "The first thing that God created was my light which originated from His light and derived from the majesty of His greatness."[5]

Among the thousands of hadith Muslims deem reliable are special ones called *hadith qudsi*, or sacred hadith. Numbering about one hundred, these hadith present God speaking in the first person. Mystical in tone, many are reminiscent of the utterances of Jesus. For Muslim mystics, hadith such as the following provide a blueprint for those seeking to emulate the path of Muhammad:

> My servant draws near to me through nothing I love more than the religious duty I require of him. And my servant continues to draw near to me by supererogatory worship until I love him. When I love him I become the ear by which he hears, the eye by which he sees, the hand by which he grasps, and the foot by which he walks.[6]

Perhaps the most mystical event of Muhammad's religious career was a profound spiritual experience called the "Night Voyage" that occurred just before his historic migration from Mecca to Medina. One evening he was awakened by the angel Gabriel and led to a wondrous *buraq*, or white-winged ox. Mounting the ox, the Prophet rode to Jerusalem. There, from a large rock—the very rock where the Old Testament tells us Abraham was instructed to sacrifice Isaac—he ascended through the seven heavens to the divine presence. While most Muslims interpret the event literally, for Sufis it is the quintessential metaphor for the spiritual journey to God.

Similarly, Sufis maintain that the Qur'an is not always to be read in a literal sense but needs to be interpreted mystically in order to unlock its hidden knowledge. The idea of esoteric knowledge is found in a Qur'anic episode (18:60–82) recounting Moses's encounter with a mysterious figure, Khidr, "the green one." Moses and his cook were on a journey in search of the fountain of life. When the fish his servant was cooking came miraculously back to life, they realized they had found the spot. There Moses met Khidr, who, we are told, possessed special knowledge.

As Khidr prepared to take his leave, Moses tried to follow him, but Khidr did not allow him to come. Khidr said that Moses would not be able to understand him. But Moses persisted. Finally, Khidr relented, whereupon he performed a series of outrageous acts: damaging a boat, killing a child, and destroying a wall owned by miscreants.

When Moses protested the destructive nature of these acts, Khidr said he was accomplishing three hidden purposes: the fishermen's boat was about to be confiscated, the child would grow up to be a monster, and the wall was intended to hide a buried treasure from the townspeople. "That is the interpretation which you are unable to bear," he told Moses (Qur'an 18:82). Moses, the law-giving prophet, failed to comprehend the meaning of Khidr's actions because they can be known only to those endowed with knowledge of hidden things.

For Sufis, the story underscores the distinction within Islam between the legal, exoteric dimension represented by the clerics and the spiritual, esoteric one of the Sufis. Sufis say the Prophet passed along this secret knowledge only to his closest disciples, the Companions, of whom there were twelve. Referring to this arcane knowledge and the dangers posed by publicly sharing it, one of the Companions remarked, "The Prophet has poured into my heart two kinds of knowledge: one I have spread to the people and the other, if I were to share it, they would cut my throat!"[7]

The "two kinds of knowledge" eventually spawned a tension between their respective custodians—the clerics and the Sufis—that has prevailed throughout the history of Islam. Yet some clerics have also been Sufis, such as Pir Saif ur-Rahman. But since mysticism was not more explicitly defined in Muhammad's life and teachings, Sufis have been harassed and sometimes even killed by other Muslims as heretics, from the earliest times right down to Pir Saif ur-Rahman's own Naqshbandis.

Not long after Muhammad's death, in fact, disputes arose within the fledgling Islamic community as to the precise nature of his message. Some stressed the importance of the law and social norms; others sought to imitate the Prophet's austerity and contemplative nature. The latter were more concerned with inward personal experience, hoping in some measure to repeat in their own lives what Muhammad had experienced on Mt. Hira.

Stressing the inner meaning of the Qur'an and the behavior of the Prophet, they cultivated lives of simplicity and asceticism. They owned few possessions and were clad simply in cloaks of coarse wool (Arabic: *suf*) that was to give them their name. The cloak, or khirqa, symbolized the time when the Prophet enclosed himself, his son-in-law 'Ali, his daughter Fatima, and their two sons in his own mantle. These ascetics believed the true meaning of Islam lay in the direct experience of divine consciousness gained through acts of selflessness, austerity, and contemplation.

During the first two centuries of Islam, these Muslim ascetics often came into contact with Christian monks and hermits inhabiting remote areas of Syria. Some of these hermits were the remnants of Jesus's original community and were practicing what they believed was the authentic faith of their founder.[8] A close spiritual fellowship developed between the two, and Muslims learned from their Christian counterparts. While there has never been a monastic tradition in Islam as was common among Christians, the earliest Muslim ascetics arranged for cells to be built under their houses where they would periodically take retreat as they had seen Christians do. One Muslim ascetic, the renowned Ibrahim ibn Adham (d. 778), said he had acquired knowledge of God from a Christian hermit, Abba Simeon.

Despite such influences, Sufism would follow uniquely Islamic lines of development. Imitating the relationship between the Prophet and his twelve Companions, allegiance to a shaikh became indispensable for those wishing to travel the spiritual path. Young aspirants would travel far and wide seeking a well-known teacher, supporting himself through labor or alms. Usually, a newly arrived seeker had to perform three years of service before being bestowed with the woolen cloak signifying that he had been accepted as a disciple. The cloaks were usually dyed with indigo, the color symbolizing the mystic's sense of mourning and separation from the world. Later, Sufis would wear cloaks of a particular color to indicate their spiritual station. Cloaks of green, the color of Khidr—and the color worn by Pir Saif ur-Rahman—were considered the highest stage of a mystic.

The shaikh would sit in a corner encircled by his disciples, whom he would instruct. The shaikh considered the disciple to be "his son" and carefully shepherded his spiritual progress. The Iranian founder of one of the Sufi orders, Abu al-Najib al-Suhrawardi (d.1168), explained how a disciple should behave in order to profit from his master's company:

> When the sincere disciple enters under obedience of the master, keeping his company and learning the manners, a spiritual state flows from within the master to within the disciple, like one lamp lighting another. The speech of the master inspires the interior of the disciple, so that the master's words become the treasury of spiritual states. *The state is transferred from the master to disciple by keeping company* [my italics] and hearing speech.[9]

Even before the Sufis began describing themselves as such, a number of Muslim ascetics who laid a foundation for those who followed began to emerge.

Hasan al-Basri was among the first. He was born in Basra, the port city in the southern part of present-day Iraq, about ten years after the death of

Muhammad. Basri began life in comfortable surroundings that made it possible for him to become a jewel merchant. After reportedly experiencing a mystical conversion experience filled with visions, Basri condemned the possession of riches and preached self-transcendence and detachment from worldly things:

> Not he who dies and is at rest is dead,
> He only is dead who is dead while yet alive.[10]

By Hasan al-Basri's time, the wearing of wool had become fashionable among Muslim ascetics, prompting him to caution, "He who wears wool out of humility toward God increases the illumination of his insight and his heart, but he who wears it out of pride and arrogance will be thrust into hell with the devils!"[11]

Despite being forced into hiding for a time for publicly criticizing the repressive policies of a governor, Basri attracted large numbers of disciples during his life, which spanned more than eighty years.

One was a woman named Rabi'a al-'Adawi, who had been sold into slavery as a child after her parents had died. Set free in adulthood by her master, who was deeply moved by her piety, she withdrew to the mountains, where she became a hermit. A broken ewer, a torn reed mat, and a brick she used for a pillow were said to be her only belongings. She spent her time fasting, meditating, and writing poetry. In her poetry she attempted to convey the intense nature of the mystical experience in terms of a lover and the beloved, imagery that would become a permanent feature of Sufi expression:

> O Beloved of hearts, I have none like unto Thee,
> Therefore have pity this day on the sinner
> Who comes to Thee.
> O my Hope and my Rest and my Delight,
> The heart can love none other than Thee.[12]

Once in the streets of Baghdad, she was asked why she was carrying her ewer full of water in one hand and a lighted torch in the other. She replied, "I want to throw fire into Paradise and pour water into Hell, so that these two veils would disappear, and it becomes clear who worships God out of love, not out of fear of Hell or hope of Paradise."[13]

Evocative though they may have been, such effusive claims of love for and closeness to God were starting to be viewed with increasing suspicion by Muslim clerics. Since the Prophet's death, the clerics had reached a consensus that Muhammad's message stressed God's utter transcendence over man. So unique was God, the clerics contended, that an unbridgeable chasm lay between Him and man. Clerics, who viewed themselves as the rightful interpreters of the law, regarded Sufi claims of mystical union with God as blasphemous.

Sufis nonetheless continued to enjoy respect among those holding political power, in part because many Sufis were also scholars. Nevertheless, as the decades passed following the death of Muhammad, the clerics began conducting formal inquisitions into Sufis whose ecstatic utterances and strange behavior violated Islamic norms.

Sufis did little to help their cause. Some Sufis regarded themselves as elites who possessed a higher knowledge and a greater degree of self-control than other Muslims. Some also claimed an ability to perform miracles, *karamat*, which clerics considered a gift reserved for prophets alone. In the same way that some Jewish clerics had felt threatened by the charismatic Christ, so too were Muslim clerics beginning to be concerned by the reverence disciples paid to Sufi shaikhs. Fearing a shift away from the mosque as the place of instruction and a loss of their social prestige, clerics began to move against the Sufis.

The first salvo was fired in the early ninth century, nearly two hundred years after the death of Muhammad. Abu Sulaiman al-Darani (d. 830), an ascetic known for weeping while in worship, was expelled from Syria for claiming to have had a vision of angels.

Sufis responded by being less open in sharing their private experiences. Some began to bring their public teaching in line with official dogma to ward off official scrutiny. Abu al-Qasim al-Junayd (d. 910), a leading Sufi in Baghdad, a major center of Sufism, affirmed the primacy of the shariʿa in mystical life:

> If you begin by acquiring a knowledge of the Traditions and comprehending the fundamental principles of the faith and the Sunna, and then become an ascetic and devotee, you may hope to become an adept in the knowledge of Sufism . . . but if you begin with devotion and godliness and ecstasy, you will become preoccupied with them . . . and you will end up going astray because of your ignorance of the faith and the Sunna.[14]

As repression of Sufis loomed, however, Junayd developed an approach for disguising the essential ecstatic nature of the mystical encounter. He refined the art of using subtle allusion to disguise the radical truth of oneness with God. To restrain ecstatic Sufis, Junayd posited a state of sobriety he called *baqa'*, which was higher than the ecstasy brought on by *fana'*, or the ecstasy that accompanied loss of egoic consciousness. Junayd's distinction, however, may have been more politic than metaphysical, as evidenced by this admonishment by Junayd of the Sufi Shibli for divulging the secret of union with God:

> Be careful with the people. Always devise some means of camouflaging our words. . . . Here you come along and tear away the veil![15]

When Shibli cried out, "Oh, God!" when seized with mystical ecstasy in the streets of Baghdad, Junayd reproached him, "We [the Sufis] utter these words in grottos . . . now you have come and declare them in the marketplace." Shibli cleverly rejoined, "These are words proceeding from God to God, and Shibli is not there at all!"[16]

But there were those who even more brazenly proclaimed their spiritual ecstasies regardless of the social and political consequences. Ironically, the most audaciously ecstatic, Mansur al-Hallaj, had once been one of Junayd's own disciples. The drama of Hallaj bears an uncanny resemblance to the crucifixion of the mystical Jesus. The son of a wool carder, Hallaj was born around 858 in Persia. Educated in what is now Iraq, he became dissatisfied with formal Islam and began to wander in search of the inner meaning of the Qur'an. His peregrinations led him to Sahl al-Tustari (d. 896), the first Sufi to write a mystical interpretation of the Qur'an. Hallaj's next teacher became concerned when Hallaj claimed he was experiencing revelations similar to those of the Prophet.

Hallaj performed the hajj. In Mecca, he engaged in extreme ascetic practices, sitting in total silence while facing the mosque as well as fasting. He publicly proclaimed his search for God. Outraged, his teacher broke with him.

Hallaj returned to Baghdad but was becoming frustrated even with organized Sufism, especially the conservative school of Junayd. One day Hallaj knocked at the door of Junayd's house. "Who is there?" asked Junayd. Hallaj famously replied, "It is God!" (*ana al-haqq*!). His friends chastised him for recklessly divulging the secret of Sufism; his enemies accused him of heresy. Junayd chastised him for propagating an unsound religious principle and foretold a sad end for his former disciple.

Hallaj then left Baghdad. Traveling for five years, he eventually reached Khorasan in eastern Iran dressed in a soldier's uniform to avoid surveillance by military authorities. He undertook another hajj, this time accompanied by four hundred disciples. From Arabia, he next took a boat to India. His detractors said he was seeking to learn magic, especially the rope trick. Hallaj said he wanted "to call heathens to God." From Sindh, he followed trading caravans north through Afghanistan into Turkistan, where he continued to preach, to the chagrin of clerics, an ecstatic message of divine union.

In 905, he returned to Baghdad. He built a house and a miniature ka'aba on the left bank of the Tigris River. Under the suspicious eyes of clerics, he began to teach. Preaching his message of divine union, he maintained that the human personality was not shattered by the influx of divine consciousness, but was in fact deified:

> I am He whom I love, and He whom I love is I.
> We are two spirits dwelling in one body.
> If thou seeest me, thou seeest Him;
> And if thou seeest Him, thou seeest us both.[17]

He appealed to Muslims of all social ranks. In the suqs he was impassioned and charismatic: "As for me, look. There is no veil between Him and me!"[18] In the meetinghouse, he healed the sick and preached to the shaikhs of his exalted spiritual stature. In the mosque he claimed to be the eternal witness of the divine essence. He performed miracles, conjuring sweets and elaborate dishes. Clerics—even some Sufis—accused him of conspiring with jinn, malevolent spirits. Established Sunni and Shi'a clerics were concerned that Hallaj could incite a spiritual revival that would destabilize the social and political order.

By 910, both Junayd and Hallaj underwent an inquisition by the clerics of the Baghdad school of Sufis intended to prosecute those who held the possibility of union with God. Fearing a Sufi pogrom, Junayd and Shibli cast off their woolen cloaks. Eerily reminiscent of Judas, when interrogated at the trial Junayd said of the Christ-like Hallaj, "This man is an infidel. You must kill him." In a manner echoing Saint Peter, Junayd averted prosecution by claiming to be "simply a jurist." He subsequently retired to his house and refused to teach. "I cannot contrive my own destruction," he protested. He died quietly in Baghdad later that year.

Hallaj escaped to Sus with his brother-in-law. But two years later Junayd's dire prophecy of Hallaj's fate had begun to unfold. Implicated in an unsuccessful coup attempt against the Caliph Muqtadir, Hallaj was tried and sentenced to nine years in prison. While in prison, Hallaj won favor with the court by curing the caliph and the queen of a mysterious illness. His increasing influence in the court and continued miracle working—he revived a dead bird—moved his opponents to more drastic action.

His trial was reopened in 920. When asked what proved the existence of God, Hallaj replied, "The grace of God invested in pure believers as witnesses united with God." Shocked by this, clerics pressed the judge for a conviction. When a leading cleric signed an edict calling for capital punishment for Hallaj, his fate was sealed.

On March 26, 922, he was lashed a thousand times. Then he was taken out to be crucified. Weighed down with thirteen chains, Hallaj strutted as if were going to a picnic.

"Why do you walk so proudly," someone in the crowd shouted.

"Because I am on my way to the slaughterhouse," he replied.

Standing in the crowd was his Sufi friend, Shibli. As Hallaj passed, Shibli stepped out and threw a rose at Hallaj, who exclaimed, "O, the rose thrown by a friend hurts more than any stone!" He was then stoned by the crowd. His hands and feet were cut off and his eyes gouged out. Then his nose and ears were cut off. Hallaj continued to ask forgiveness for his tormenters. His last words were: "It is enough for the lover, that he should attain the One alone." Then, when almost nothing remained of Hallaj to extract, his tongue was cut out. At the evening prayer, he was decapitated. The next day his body was burned and his ashes scattered from a minaret into the Tigris River.

Shortly after Hallaj's death, Shibli was committed to a mental asylum to avoid persecution.[19]

The Naqshbandiyya are strange caravan leaders,
Who bring the caravan through hidden paths into the sanctuary
—Jami

Abu Bakr does not surpass you by virtue of much fasting or prayer,
but by virtue of a secret that took root in his heart.
—The Prophet Muhammad

Chapter 2

The Naqshbandis

Traveling in Syria's Jawlan Mountains in the late tenth century, the Arab geographer Muhammad al-Muqaddasi (d. 1000) came upon a community of men living there:

> I met Abu Ishaq al-Balluti with forty men, all wearing wool, who had a place for worship where they congregated. I found out that this man was a learned jurist of the school of Sufyan al-Thawri, and that their sustenance consisted of acorns, a fruit the size of dates, bitter, which are split, sweetened, ground up and then mixed with wild barley.[1]

By this time, half a century after Hallaj's death, Islamic mystics and their disciples were becoming amorphous groups in which individual Sufis could gather to collectively pursue their spiritual ambitions. Such groups persisted despite recurring attempts by clerics to suppress them and could be found throughout the Middle East and Asia. The group might have been the house of a shaikh, or a shaikh's shop linked to a particular craft guild such as textiles or metalwork. In other cases, the group consisted of little more than an itinerant shaikh and his circle of devotees wandering from town to town preaching, practicing, proselytizing, and dispensing grace. Such forms were generally temporary and usually dissolved with the demise of the shaikh.

Over time, however, some groups attracted private and official endowments that allowed them to become more permanent. In the eastern Islamic lands, these Sufi centers were called *khanaqah*, a Persian word meaning "hospice". Privately supported khanaqahs were small; those built with public endowments, on the other hand, could house several hundred disciples. Though rare, there were some khanaqahs exclusively for women as well.

Much like Saif ur-Rahman's khanaqah that I visited in the Khyber, these khanaqahs usually had a mosque, a religious school, a large kitchen, and guest quarters. The shaikh and his family lived in a house attached to the khanaqah. In addition to its main function as a place of spiritual retreat (although there is, strictly speaking, no monastic life in Islam), the khanaqah also served as a caravanserai for the many wandering Sufis, dervishes, and ecstatics (*madzub*), as well as for traveling Muslims who were not Sufis. Clad in nothing more than a woolen cloak and equipped with a staff and begging bowl, a spiritual wayfarer could generally find a khanaqah along the way to rest, practice, or benefit from the methods and grace of a particular teacher.

By the late twelfth century, khanaqahs were becoming increasingly popular and had begun to flourish. Visiting one such khanaqah in Damascus in 1183, the geographer and traveler Ibn Jubair (d. 1217) was struck as much by its prosperity as by the form of worship practiced there:

> They are ornamented palaces through all of which flow streams of water, presenting as delightful picture as anyone could wish for. The members of this type of Sufi organization are really the kings in these parts, since God has provided for them over and above the material things of life, freeing their minds from concern with the need to earn their living so that they can devote themselves to His service. . . . Their mode of conducting their forms of worship is peculiar. Their custom of assembling for impassioned musical recitals is delightful. Sometimes so enraptured do some of these absorbed ecstatics become when under the influence of a state that they can hardly be regarded as belonging to this world at all.[2]

Not all khanaqahs were legitimate, however. Unscrupulous men found that pretensions to mystic knowledge could be lucrative. Accusations of fraud soon became common. To ward against false teachers, earnest Sufis began to commit to writing the qualifications for a shaikh, the authentic practices of Sufism, and strictures for day-to-day life in the hospice. Sufis organized around a particular shaikh would, upon his passing, also form schools to preserve his name, particular spiritual methods, and rules of living, all of which furthered the evolution of Sufism as an institution within Islam.

Of growing importance in distinguishing the true Sufi from the charlatan was the *silsila*, the chain of teachers from whom the disciple acquired a particular teaching method, liturgical chant, and spiritual grace. Though partly a retrospective reconstruction, the silsila connected the disciple to a chain of preceptors or spiritual guides that reached back to the Prophet. Historically, such links are impossible to prove, at least beyond a certain point in time. But a silsila served to legitimize the various Sufi paths and to position each path's disciples within the context of a larger spiritual ancestry. In short, the silsila gave each path its pedigree.

By the thirteenth and fourteenth centuries, these paths had evolved into formal "orders," each with its own initiatic chain and founding patron saint. Why this happened is unclear. It may have been the growing emphasis on embracing a particular teacher or teaching style, or the insecurity created by the Mongol invasions that swept across central Asia, or the growing popularity of Sufism, or a combination of all of these.

The Naqshbandi order has its roots in an obscure school of mysticism, the Malamati, which appeared in the ninth century in Nishapur in what is now northeastern Iran. A thriving city at the heart of a fertile farming region, Nishapur had the resources to support scholars and mystics. The city became viewed as the home of the "eastern" school of Islamic mysticism—tending toward ecstatic expression—as contrasted with the more conservative center of Sufism in Baghdad led by Junayd.

One of the earliest references to the Malamati appears in the *Kitab al-Bad'wa al-Tarikh* (The Creation and the Chronicle), written around 966 by the historian Abu Nasr Mutahhar ibn Tahir al-Maqdisi. In it he writes,

> The Sufi groups: among them are the Hasaniyya, Malamatiyya, Suqiyya and the Madhuriyya. These are characterized by the lack of any consistent system or clear principles of faith. They make judgments according to their speculations and imagination, and they constantly change

> their opinions. Some of them believe in incarnationism, as I have heard one of them claim that His habitation is in the cheeks of the beardless youth. Some of them believe in promiscuity and neglect the religious law, and they do not heed those who blame them.[3]

The Malamati worked on constantly finding fault within themselves for the slightest deviation from the ways of God. They also cultivated a veil of anonymity around themselves. They are to be distinguished from the Qalandaris, who, by acting in socially unacceptable ways, deliberately sought out social criticism as a means to guard against pride and conceit brought about by advancement on the mystic path. The blame of the Malamati is that which was directed at oneself. Hence the ascription *malama*, the Arabic word for "to blame." Such utter reproachfulness toward the self was believed to hasten the mystic to perfect union with God.

Another teaching of the Malamati—one that appears more explicitly in the later Naqshbandi—was to disguise spiritual practice and spiritual states by living and working unobtrusively in the world. As one Sufi of the time described them,

> The Malamati is one whose veins are saturated with the nourishment of pure virtue, who is really sincere, who does not want anyone to become acquainted with his ecstatic states and experiences. Despised by men that they may lose themselves in God . . . the Malamati works for his living, absorbed in God *while engaged in affairs of this world* [my italics]. He does not parade his inward way, nor indulge in public dhikr gatherings.[4]

The Malamati do not appear to have been a specific group or school at that time. Rather, they were more of a movement or tendency within Sufism. One of the best known in the Malamati vein was the ecstatic Bayazid Bistami (d. 874), so associated because he broke with convention by speaking openly about his essential union with God.[5] With the exception of Hallaj, Bayazid's name appears more frequently in Sufi poetry than any other Sufi. Bayazid was the eastern school's equivalent of Hallaj:

an ecstatic who openly proclaimed that he had annihilated all trace of egoic consciousness in God.

Possessed of a strong ascetic bent, Bayazid said for twelve years he had been the "blacksmith of himself" until he had made of himself a pure mirror of the divine. When he had attained fana', which he regarded as the highest state, he proclaimed, "Glory be to me! How great is my majesty!"[6] The reaction of the clerics was predictably hostile, and for a time he was forced to hide. In the end, though, he was spared Hallaj's gruesome fate.

Bayazid was the first Sufi to describe his experience in terms of the Prophet's Night Journey. He testified that he had flown "beyond space three times thirty thousand years," where he found Bayazid on the divine throne. So deep was his immersion in the spirit that when someone came to see him, he said, "I myself am in search of Bayazid."[7]

His rhapsodic utterances were often paradoxes designed to convey the enigma of mystical experience:

> As soon as I attained to His Unity, I became a bird with a body of Oneness and wings of Everlastingness, and I continued flying in the air of Quality for ten years, until I reached an atmosphere a million times as large, and I flew on, until I found myself in the field of Eternity and I saw there the Tree of Oneness . . . and I looked and I knew that all this was a cheat.[8]

To avert the kind of legal scrutiny that had forced Bayazid into hiding—as well as having led to Hallaj's crucifixion—most Malamatis enjoined their followers to maintain privacy in mystical life. They eschewed the performance of miracles or engaging in ecstatic public displays while in mystical rapture. They also were careful to combine mystical practice—tariqa—with strict observance of the law—shari'a. In the eastern lands, the Malamatis seemed to have died out as a distinct movement, their true heirs in the region became the Naqshbandis. However, the Malamati exist to this day in Turkey and parts of the Balkans.[9]

The first real antecedents of the Naqshbandi emerged in the late eleventh century and were called the *khwajagan*, or masters. These Sufis not only shaped the Naqshbandi order in terms of doctrine and teaching style but are even today looked upon as exemplary models for spiritual development. A teacher who is generally acknowledged as the first in the Naqshbandi *silsila-i khwajagan,* or "chain of the masters," was Abu Ya'qub Yusuf Hamadhani (see fig. 2.1).

Once a popular preacher and religious scholar in Baghdad, Hamadhani abandoned these pursuits and took up an ascetic way of life. He traveled to the East, including Nishapur, where he studied under various Sufis, including the Malamati. Hamadhani's spiritual wandering would become a common practice of later Naqshbandi masters.

Eventually, he settled in Merv, a silk-route oasis city across the Kopetdag Mountains north of Nishapur in present-day Turkmenistan. He died there in 1140. He designated four *khalifas*, or successors, to carry on his teachings. Of these, the most important was Khwaja Ghujduwani.

Ghujduwani was born in a village near Bukhara, another major settlement on the silk route not far from Merv. While studying the Qur'an with a scholar in Bukhara, he experienced a calling to the spiritual path upon hearing the verse, "Call upon your Lord in supplication and hiddenness."[10] Ghujduwani was puzzled by this reference to hidden practices in Islam, believing them perceptible only to Satan. His teacher was equally puzzled and advised him to wait for a knowledgeable guide.

The guide who appeared was none other than Khidr, the mysterious and mythical man in green who had appeared to Moses, the Prophet, and later generations of Sufis. In this highly personal initiation, Khidr instructed Ghujduwani to submerge himself in water and recite (*dhikr*) the name of Allah silently in his heart. This practice of silent repetition of the name of Allah in the heart became a cornerstone of Naqshbandi practice. It was first given, Naqshbandis say, by the Prophet to his Companion and eventual successor, Abu Bakr, while the two were secluded in the cave at Mt. Hira.

Ghujduwani introduced most of the other mystic practices embraced by later Naqshbandis. For this reason, he is the order's true founder, or at least its cofounder.

His practices are embedded in eight precepts:

- *Yad kard* (remembrance, both oral and mental): repeating always the dhikr imparted to you, so that the aspirant may attain the beatific vision.
- *Baz gasht* (restraint): when engaging in the heart-repetition of the dhikr, interspersing it with such phrases as "My God, thou art my Goal and Thy satisfaction is my aim" to help keep one's thoughts from straying. Other masters have said that *baz gasht* means "return," that is, return to God by way of contrition.
- *Nigah dasht* (watchfulness): being watchful over wandering, passing, or evil thoughts when in contemplation.
- *Yad dasht* (recollection): concentrating upon the divine presence in a condition of foretaste of enlightenment and intuitively anticipating or perceiving the divine presence.
- *Hush dar dam* (awareness in breathing): inhaling and exhaling mindfully; every breath should hold the divine presence in awareness.
- *Safar dar watan* (journeying to one's homeland): making the inner journey of consciousness from blameworthy or human to praiseworthy or divine.
- *Nazar bar qadam* (watching over one's steps): maintaining vigilance during one's journey, whatever the type of country through which the spiritual traveler is passing, so that he does not let his gaze be distracted from the goal of his journey, the divine presence.
- *Khalwat dar anjuman* (solitude in a crowd): knowing always that the journey of the Sufi, though outwardly in the world, inwardly is with God.[11]

Ghujduwani taught his disciples to strictly follow the shari'a and to devote themselves to the study of prophetic tradition. Of particular importance was the injunction *khalwat dar anjuman*. Though this has several interpretations, it essentially enjoins Naqshbandis to be "in the world but not of it," a practice in which can be seen the Malamati injunction to shun public displays of spiritual ecstasies. Khalwat also enjoins Naqshbandis to engage with political leaders as a means of propagating the faith.

Some of Ghujduwani's precepts were idiosyncratic, such as his instructions to disciples to avoid associating with kings and noblemen and to reject government service—practices that were not always observed by

Figure 2.1 Spiritual Genealogy of the Early Naqshbandi *Tariqa.*

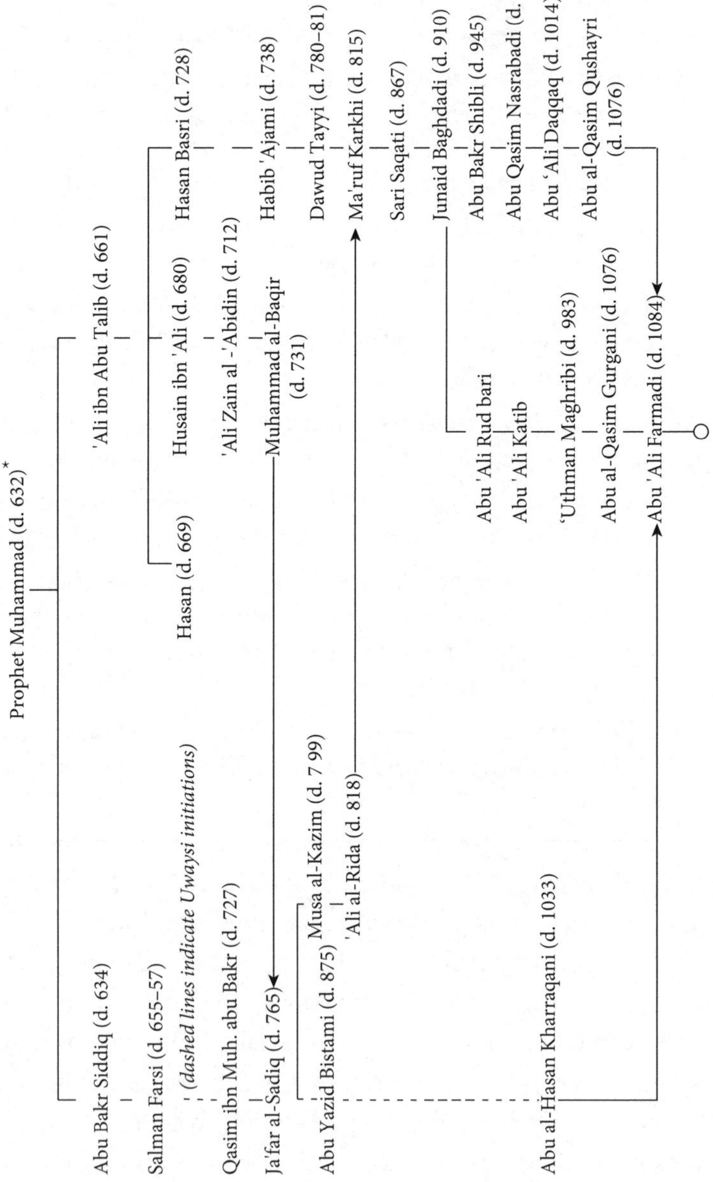

Muhammad al-Ghazali (d. 1111)

Abu Ya'qub Yusuf Hamadhani (d. 1140)
|
'Abd al-Khaliq Ghudjuwani (d. 1220)
|
'Arif Rewari (d. 1219)
|
Muhammad Anjir Faghnawi (d. 1317)
|
'Ali Azizan Ramatini (d. 1321)
|
Sayyid Amir Kulal (d. 1371)
|
Baha al-Din Naqshband (d. 1389) → Muh. Parsa (d. 1419)
|
'Alauddin 'Attar (d. 1400)
|
Ya'qub Charkhi (d. 1447)
|
Ubaidullah Ahrar (d. 1490)
|
Muhammad Zahid Wakhshi (d. 1529)
|
Darwish Muhammad (d. 1562)
|
Maulana Khwajagi Aminkinki (d. 1600)
|
Muhammad Baqi Billah (d. 1603)
|
Muhammad Baba Sammasi (d. 1354)
|
Ahmad Sirhindi (d. 1624)

Muh. Parsa (d. 1419)
|
other Naq. Lines

* Marijan Mole, "Autour du dare Mansour: l'apprentissage mystique de Najm al-Din Kobra," *Revue des Etudes Islamiques* (1958): 35–66.

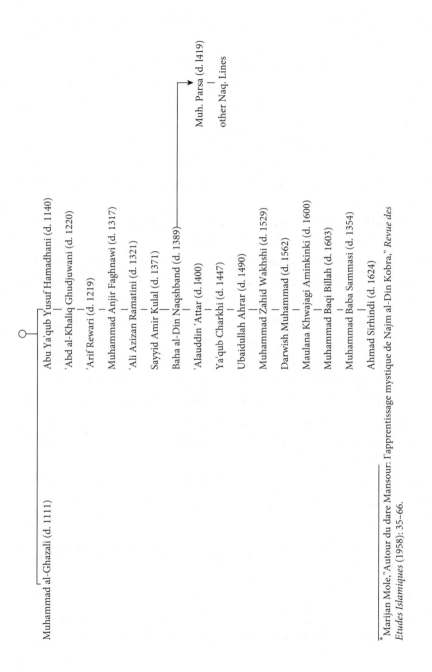

the later Naqshbandis. He also discouraged construction of, and dwelling in, khanaqahs.

The character of the Naqshbandi order remained in a state of development as the leadership passed through five successors after Ghujduwani. It would be fixed once and for all with the appearance of the eponymous Bahauddin Naqshband in 1318. Little is known of the specific details of his life, as he—in the spirit of the Malamati—forbade his followers to record anything of his deeds or sayings during his lifetime. A Tajik, he spent most of his life in his birthplace of Rewartun, a village near Bukhara where all of Ghujduwani's khalifas lived.

Bahauddin had come into contact with Naqshbandis in his infancy. According to Naqshbandi legend, a shaikh passing through Rewartun "smelled the scent of spirituality" rising from the ground and was moved to take him as a disciple. Bahauddin later studied with a Turkish dervish, Khalil, whom he had first encountered in a dream. When Khalil became sultan of Transoxiana, which included Bukhara and other major trading centers, Bahauddin served him for six years.

After the sultan's fall in 1347, Bahauddin became disillusioned with worldly affairs. Returning to his native village, he resumed spiritual practice. He intended, not to establish a formal organization, but rather to gather around himself like-minded mystics who sought to practice quietly and draw no attention to themselves. The only journeys he undertook were two to Mecca to perform the hajj.

Bahauddin added three additional principles of the Naqshbandi to the eight formulated by Ghujduwani:

- *Wuquf-i zamani* (temporal awareness): keeping account of how one is spending one's time, and, if rightly, giving thanks, or, if wrongly, asking for forgiveness according to the ranking of the deeds. This leads to insight into the divine presence.
- *Wuquf-i 'adadi* (numerical awareness): checking that the heart dhikr has been repeated the requisite number of times, taking into account one's wandering thoughts.

- *Wuquf-i qalbi* (heart awareness): forming a mental picture of one's heart with the name of God engraved on it so as to emphasize that the heart has no consciousness or goal other than God.

What moved Bahauddin to relinquish spiritual retreat is unclear. Perhaps it was the doctrine of khalwat dar anjuman. Whatever the motive, he established close ties with the ruling Timurids, the descendants of the Mongol conqueror, Timur, known in the West as Tamurlane. Bahauddin's successors continued this practice of political alignment, which accounted for the rapid expansion of Naqshbandis in central Asia.

With Bahauddin, the silsila-i khwajagan, as it had been known until then, was clearly established. It was also to take on a new name: the Naqshbandis. The term *naqshband* means in Persian to "fix" or "impress the sign." While various hagiographers suggest that Bahauddin may have been a weaver or metalworker at one time, spiritually the term *naqshband* refers to the fixing of the name of Allah within the heart. Once implanted, it creates the pronounced visible beating of the heart that I witnessed among the disciples at the Khyber khanaqah. A long line of spiritual masters would henceforth establish the Naqshbandis in Asia, providing a source of identity and inspiration for its adherents.

Bahauddin died in 1389. His mausoleum at Qasr-i Arifan, twelve kilometers from Bukhara, is today one of the most important pilgrimage centers in central Asia.

While Bahauddin gave the Naqshbandi order its distinguishing spiritual character, Khwaja Ahrar made it the dominant order in central Asia. Born in 1404, into a farming family, Ahrar spent his youth in Tashkent, then called Shash. He showed little interest in formal studies, preferring to spend time with local Sufis and to frequent saints' tombs.

Concerned about their son's future, his parents sent him to Samarkand in the hope of making him a respectable cleric. Ahrar proved to be a lackadaisical student, preferring instead to keep company with the disciples of Bahauddin and perform spiritual exercises. At twenty-two, he began a period of spiritual wandering. His first stop was Herat, where he lived for a time in various khanaqahs, impoverished but satisfied. (The Jami mosque where he used to practice is still used today by Naqshbandis there for their spiritual practices.) Four years later, he arrived in Qala Hissar, where he was initiated into the Naqshbandi order by a khalifa of Bahauddin.

At thirty, Ahrar returned to Tashkent and took control of his family's ancestral farm. He built a khanaqah and a mosque and began to attract followers high and low. Because it was believed pirs could influence worldly events, they were increasingly being enlisted in military campaigns to assure victory. Before marching against Samarkand in 1451, the Timurid prince Sultan Miranshah sought out Ahrar. Ahrar agreed to join him on the condition that the prince adhere to the shari'a and promote the welfare of his people. He accompanied the sultan on his campaign, providing spiritual and military counsel to the prince.

After the victory over Samarkand, Ahrar decided to settle there, continuing to advise the sultan. In return he received generous land grants. At one point, Ahrar's property was said to extend from Tashkent to Samarkand, a distance of nearly two hundred miles. Despite his wealth, he continued to live like the poorest dervish. Revenue from his farms went to an endowment for the indigent and the growing number of Naqshbandi khanaqahs and madrasas. Ahrar died in Samarkand in 1490. An intricately carved stele marks the great pir's final resting place.

Among Ahrar's disciples was the Emperor Babur, the founder of the Mughal Empire in India in the sixteenth century. The Mughals would rule a major portion of the Asian subcontinent for the next three centuries. Babur claimed that Ahrar, who had died ten years before, had appeared to him in a dream in which he correctly predicted Babur's victory over Samarkand in 1500. When Babur conquered Kabul and then India in 1526, he was accompanied by Ahrar's third son, Muhammad Amin. Soon after the Mughal conquest of India, Naqshbandis from central Asia began filing into the subcontinent, some assuming senior posts in Babur's administration. Naqshbandis also intermarried with the ruling family; Babur's daughter, for instance, was married to a Naqshbandi.

If Ahrar's successors implanted the seeds of Naqshbandi Sufism in Mughal India, then it was through the spiritual nourishment of Khwaja Baqi Billah that those seeds took root and flourished there. Baqi was born in Kabul in 1564, in a family related to Ahrar. Though he studied under an eminent cleric in Kabul, Baqi, like Ahrar, was less interested in formal studies and more inclined to spend time practicing devotional exercises with Sufis. Time and again in the hagiographies of Naqshbandis we find this tendency toward privileging itinerant Sufism over the formal law, if only for a time.

His spiritual yearning unquenched, Baqi went to Lahore in search of the perfect pir. There he had a failed love affair with a beautiful girl. This seems to have further dampened his already waning interest in worldly life. He began to pursue ascetic practices, idling aimlessly though the muddy streets of Lahore and frequenting graveyards and woods in search of ecstatics and holy men. His weak physical constitution, however, made him unsuited for the ascetic life. Yet he continued to wander in search of a spiritual master.

In Kashmir he finally met his long-sought master in Baba Wali, who initiated him into the Naqshbandi order. So impressed was Baba with his disciple's spiritual aptitude that he prophesied that Baqi would one day spread the order throughout the entire Asian subcontinent. Baqi then went to Samarkand, where he was warmly received by one of Ahrar's khalifas, who instructed him to return to India to propagate the teaching. He went back to Lahore, where he wrote mystical treatises and poetry, initiating only the most promising students. He resided there until his death in 1603.

Like other teachers in his line, Baqi embraced the unity of shari'a and tariqa. In keeping with Bayazid Bistami seven centuries earlier, he taught that fana' was the highest Sufi experience, one in which the ego was completely annihilated in God with no trace remaining of individuality. He articulated six duties of a Naqshbandi in the journey to God: repentance or dissociation from sin, renunciation of worldly desire, trust in God, austerity in food and dress, seclusion, and patience in achieving mystical illumination.

As influential as Baqi was, his contribution—and one might say even that of all previous teachers since Bahauddin Naqshband himself—would be eclipsed by one of Baqi's disciples, Ahmad al-Sirhindi. Sirhindi's life would coincide with one of the greatest crises in Islam since the Prophet's flight to Medina in 622.

Sirhindi was born on May 26, 1564, in the Punjab. Sirhindi's father, himself a Sufi, directed his early religious education, arranging for his son's initiation in two of the other major Sufi orders of the region, the Chishti and the Qadiri. Having exhibited signs of outstanding literary potential, Sirhindi was sent to Agra, where he studied the religious sciences with eminent scholars of his day.

A few years later, he returned to Sirhind and taught the mystical path to a few of his father's friends, evidence of his spiritual precocity. Restlessness overcame him and upon the death of his ailing father in 1599, he set out for Mecca. On the way he stopped at the khanaqah of Khwaja Baqi Billah in Lahore. So affected was he by Baqi's spiritual power (*baraka*) that he decided to take initiation from him in the Naqshbandi order.

Baqi described his new disciple as "a lamp to brighten the whole universe."[12] It is said that on Sirhindi's first day as a Naqshbandi his repetition of the divine name transported him into a state of ecstasy. After two days of such practice, he appears to have had a glimpse of fana'. In subsequent sessions, he would burst into tears followed by a trance-like state in which he was oblivious to the phenomenal world. Many times he would lie in such a state the entire night.

Within three months, he had attained the state of fana', or nonduality, an accomplishment that took even great shaikhs years to achieve. In his later career, Sirhindi claimed to have reached a state higher than Abu Bakr, a bold assertion that led to his imprisonment for a time. Upon Baqi's death, Sirhindi became shaikh of the lineage, though not without objection from two other pirs, who eventually relinquished their claims.

Possessed of the rare combination of exalted spiritual stature and exceptional literary and intellectual skills, Sirhindi seemed destined for the historical role that he was about to play.

In the early seventeenth century, Muslim adoption of popular Hindu practices was profoundly changing Indian Islam. The Mughal emperor

Akbar, universalist in his approach to religion, did not recognize the Prophet as the sole exemplar for Muslims, preferring to draw eclectically from both Hinduism and Islam. In the ecumenical environment endorsed by the royal court, individual Muslims began diluting Sufism by transforming a reasonable reverence for the shaikh into the extreme devotional worship of the holy man (*bhakti*) practiced in Hinduism.

Enacting the Naqshbandi principle of khalwat dar anjuman, Sirhindi undertook a powerful intellectual and spiritual revival movement to restore Sunni mystical Islam. The 536 letters that he is known to have written to the members of the royal court, influential individuals, and disciples comprise the canon of his revival teachings.[13] In writing them, Sirhindi drew from his own spiritual experiences, maintaining that the true mystic path entails strict adherence to Islamic law and the sunna, the exemplary behavior of the Prophet.[14]

According to Sirhindi, these norms were encoded in the Qur'an, hadith, and other major components of the Sunni tradition: law, theology, philosophy, and especially mysticism. Shari'a and tariqa formed aspects of an organic whole, which represented the original synthesis of Middle Eastern Abrahamic religions that the Prophet Muhammad had established. Like his Naqshbandi ancestors, however, Sirhindi clearly valued the mystical aspect of Islam above its outward or formal one.

Sirhindi's efforts to reaffirm the primacy of the Qur'an and the sunna in Sufi doctrine and practice were successful in cleansing Islam of Hindu influence.[15] For reversing a cycle of spiritual decline that had been thought to last a thousand years, he earned the exalted title *Mujaddid 'Alf al-Thani*, or "Renewer of the Second Millennium."

In the eyes of Naqshbandis, Sirhindi assumes the stature of near prophethood. Although, strictly speaking, Sirhindi cannot be a prophet, "prophetic perfections" were bestowed on him, for Sirhindi had successfully reunited shari'a and tariqa and affirmed the original message of Muhammad. In so doing he staved off the absorption of Islam by Hinduism in the Indian subcontinent. So important is Sirhindi to the thought and practice of the Naqshbandi order today that it would not be an exaggeration to say that he occupies a place in it second only to the Prophet himself. Henceforth, the order would be called the Naqshbandi/Mujaddidi, or often simply the Mujaddidi.

Sirhindi's practice of dispatching khalifas back to their native regions to carry on missionary work led to the implantation of the Naqshbandi/Mujaddidi teaching in Afghanistan (see fig. 2.2). Fourteen of the twenty khalifas he designated were from Afghanistan and central Asia. Three of his leading

Shaikh Ahmad Sirhindi, *Mujaddid 'Alf al-Thani* (d. 1642), Sirhind

Khwaja Muhammad Ma'sum, *Zia al-Khaliqun* (d. 1668), Sirhind

Khwaja Muhammad Sebgatullah, *Qayyum-i Zaman* (d. 1708–9), Sirhind

Khwaja Muhammad Ismael, *Imam al-'Arifin,* d. Sirhind

Haji Ghulam Muhammad Ma'sum-i Thani, *Qutb al-Aqtab,* d. Sirhind

Hazrat Shah Ghulam Muhammad (d. 1799), Peshawar

Haji Saifullah, *Qayyum-i Jahan* (d. 1833), Yemen

Silsila of Mujaddidi family in Afghanistan	**Silsila of Pir Saif ur-Rahman**
Shah Abdul Baqi, d. Kabul	Muh. Zia al-Haq, *Ishan Shahid* (d. 1835), Mazar-i Sharif
Khwaja Ghulam Siddiq, d. Kabul	
Shah Ghulam *Qayyum* Jan Agha	Mia Ji Sahib (d. 1896), Laghman
Fazl Muhammad al-Mujaddidi *Shams al-Mashaykh* (d. 1923)	Shams al-Haq Kohistani (d. 1930), Gulbahar
Fazl 'Umar al-Mujaddidi *Nur al-Mashaykh* (d. 1956)	Maulana Shah Rasul Taloqani (d. 1962–63), Bihark
Muhammad Ibrahim Mujaddidi** *Zia al-Mashaykh* (executed 1979) Kabul	Muhammad Hashim Samangani (d.1971), Pir-i Sabeq, Pakistan
	Akhundzada Saif ur-Rahman (d. 2010), Lahore, Pakistan
	Maulana Said Haidri

** Indicates last initiating shaikh in the immediate family line.

Figure 2.2 Spiritual Genealogy of the Naqshbandi/Mujaddidi in Afghanistan.

Afghan shaikhs were Maulana Ahmad, Shaikh Yusuf, and Shaikh Hassan, all of whom had originally come from Baraki, south of Kabul. After taking initiation with Sirhindi, they returned to their native towns and villages to proselytize Sunni mystical Islam. Shaikh Hassan was particularly active in eradicating religious innovation in the Kabul-Qandahar region in the early 1600s. Other khalifas settled in virtually all the major towns and cities of Afghanistan: Balkh, Kabul, Badakhshan, Kohistan, Laghman, Ghorband, and Logar.

Sirhindi's third son and successor, Ghulam Muhammad Ma'sum, designated a veritable spiritual army of seven thousand khalifas. Many of these khalifas were from Afghanistan and, after receiving the *ijaza*, or teaching certificate, returned home to conduct Sufi missionary work. The order's strict observation of the shari'a and the absence of a major institutional center of Islamic learning in Afghanistan helped to mitigate the usual opposition from clerics.

The rapid spread of the Mujaddidis is also attributable to the renewed spiritual vitality of the order, one of Sirhindi's most important and enduring legacies. In time, the Mujaddidi supplanted rival Naqshbandi branches and became the most widespread and influential order in central Asia.

Sirhindi's direct descendants eventually established close ties to the Pashtun king, Ahmad Shah Abdali, who founded the Afghan state in 1747. When the king's son and successor, Timur, moved the capital from Qandahar to Kabul, he granted land and a residence in the Shur Bazaar district of the city to Sirhindi's family. There the Mujaddidis set up a khanaqah and madrasa. Henceforth, its pir would be known as the "*hazrat* [lord] of Shur Bazaar." *Hazrat* is a title given to the head of the lineal descendants of Sirhindi in Afghanistan.

Despite the family's close proximity to the royal court, the Mujaddidis played little direct role in Afghan political life in the nineteenth century, content to remain apart from courtly affairs so long as the integrity of Islam was not threatened. The hazrats devoted themselves exclusively to the activities of pirhood: teaching, preaching, and transmitting spiritual grace.

Since their days as solitary ascetics, Sufis had risen to prominence in central Asia principally through the Naqshbandi order. They played roles in spiritual as well as temporal spheres, advising kings and amirs, preaching, educating the young, dispensing grace, and looking after the welfare of the poor. Having established an extensive network of khanaqahs and madrasas throughout the region, they supervised the religious and spiritual education of tens of thousands of Muslims. To be sure there were setbacks, occasioned by political upheavals or leadership disputes among Naqshbandis themselves. Notwithstanding, Naqshbandis had become an integral part of central Asian society, influential with political leaders and peasants alike. In Afghanistan, in particular, Naqshbandis had made themselves valuable as religious legitimizers of a state at once tribal and Islamic.

The preeminence Naqshbandis enjoyed in Afghan politics and the relative social stability that allowed them to practice unfettered continued right up to the end of the nineteenth century. Major threats to Afghan society that did arise, such as the Russian and British advances, were external and only served to unite Afghans against them. That Afghanistan had been able to resist foreign domination, even foreign influence, was due largely to its geographic isolation and rugged, inaccessible terrain. Indeed, so remote was this country of mountain and desert that, at the end of the nineteenth century, Afghanistan was still one of the most isolated regions of the Muslim world, nearly completely cut off from the processes of modernization.

By 1920, however, the modern world was lurking at Afghanistan's doorstep in the form of Afghanistan's longtime nemesis the British, in India. Afghan amir Amanullah was deeply wary of the British. He had reason to be. In 1839, the British had invaded Afghanistan and replaced the king with a more malleable leader. Dubbed the First Anglo-Afghan War, the invasion (1839–1842) ended catastrophically for the British, when four years later the Afghans revolted, wiping out nearly the entire departing British army. Only a handful of survivors made it back to India through the Khyber Pass. The British invaded again in 1878 in response to a Russian advance in the north. This time they obtained numerous concessions from Afghanistan by forcing the amir to sign the Treaty of Gandamak. Once again, however, the British suffered disastrous losses at the hands of the Afghans before withdrawing in 1881.

Over the next several decades, the British and the Russians vied for influence in and control of Afghanistan. Though Afghan leaders tried to play one power against the other, they saw their territory gradually eaten away by the colonial powers. The Russians seized Turkistan in the north; the British moved into the tribal areas, including the Khyber, in the east. Uninterested in outright colonization of the tribal regions, the British did not disarm the tribes. Extending their sphere of influence into Pashtun areas was an aspect of Britain's so-called forward policy of creating a bulwark against periodic tribal incursions in British India, and more important, a feared Russian invasion.

The policy was unsuccessful, however, as tribal attacks and banditry continued. Eventually, the British were able to convince the king to negotiate a border between British India and Afghanistan. It was called the Durand Line, after the Indian foreign secretary Sir Mortimer Durand, who negotiated the agreement. Although negotiations were peaceful, the commission charged with fixing the line sometimes came under attack by the tribes, who were angry at having foreigners on their land. At other times, boundary commissioners treated their assignment with imperial disdain. When a village that straddled the line could not make up its mind on which side of the line it wanted to fall, the commissioners would go off quail hunting, telling villagers to have made up their minds by the time they returned. The boundary effectively split the Pashtun tribes in half. The Afghan amir Abdur Rahman, who signed the Durand agreement, never meant for the line to be permanent, and to this day the Afghan government does not recognize its legality.

In 1919, a young king named Amanullah came to power and launched the Third Anglo-Afghan War in a bid to regain the tribal regions. Neither side had much stomach for bloodshed, however, and within a month the Treaty of Rawalpindi (1919) was signed. The treaty returned control of Afghan foreign affairs, a portfolio that the British had seized during the First Anglo-Afghan War, to Kabul. Immediately, the Afghans sent a mission to Moscow to explain their new independent policy in foreign affairs. Thus began the ill-fated Soviet-Afghan relationship that would culminate in a devastating war a half century later.

The treaty with the British and the embassy to Moscow did nothing to resolve the amir's apprehension. After all, most Islamic countries of Africa and Asia had been overtaken during the preceding century, as one country after another succumbed to European colonial expansion. By the early 1920s, the amir was hemmed in on the north by Russians and on the east and south by the British. If nothing were done to stop them, further attempts at conquest seemed inevitable. So to counter the British, Amanullah decided to undertake a program of modern reforms aimed at strengthening the state along Western lines. From the very beginning, the driving force behind modernization in Afghanistan had been the state itself, under pressure from competing outside powers.

Amanullah's reform policies had been heavily influenced by his father-in-law, Muhammad Tarzi. Tarzi's family had been exiled from Afghanistan when he was sixteen years old. He had spent his formative years traveling in Egypt, Syria, France, and Turkey. In Damascus, he came into contact with Turkish intellectuals who had impressed him with the need for Islamic countries to modernize in order to counter European power and influence, a tactic the Ottomans had already adopted in the nineteenth century. When his father died in 1903, Tarzi returned to Kabul. By now a persuasive Afghan nationalist, he succeeded in winning over Amanullah's father, Amir Habibullah, to his reformist ideas.

Unlike Habibullah, whose idea of reform was more a fascination with Western gadgetry, modernization for Amanullah was an ideology. He sought to bring about a complete social revolution in Afghan society. To meet the state's needs for a new cadre of bureaucrats, for example, the amir created madrasas to teach secular subjects, to the detriment—though not the complete elimination—of religious studies. He also banned Sufi pirs and their disciples from the army and attempted to replace the shari'a with a new secular legal code. He emancipated women, forced Afghans in Kabul to wear Western clothing, and denied clerics the right to attend the conservative Deoband seminary in India.[16] Both the nature of these reforms and the alarming speed with which Amanullah enacted them were symbolized in a single dramatic event. At a soccer match in the Kabul stadium,

Queen Soraya, Tarzi's daughter, shocked Afghans by publicly tearing off her veil.

Clearly, the state's modernizing reforms posed a threat to the established social and religious order. For once clerics and Sufis were in perfect unison in their opposition to the reforms. Both regarded reforms not as a foil to imperialism but, in fact, a capitulation to it. Modernization, they believed, inevitably led to profound changes in the social order, changes that undermined the Islamic concept of life—as well as their own religious authority. Clerics and Naqshbandis believed the only true defense against the West was to return to traditional Islam. They maintained that it was by having strayed from such fundamentals in the first place that Afghan society now found itself in such a feeble state.

These religious sentiments came to a head in 1925 when a Naqshbandi, Pir-i Lang, led a revolt against Amanullah in the eastern mountain region of Khost. The pir did not have the backing of the tribes, and in several months the uprising was crushed. The pir was brought to Kabul and summarily executed.

The revolt prompted Amanullah to take preemptive action against Naqshbandis. In an unprecedented breach of the longstanding ties between Naqshbandis and the court, Amanullah arrested Fazl Muhammad, the reigning hazrat of Shor Bazaar in Kabul (the seat of the Mujaddidi family), and other religious leaders on charges of treason. Fazl had once enjoyed close personal relations with the king. He had presided over the king's coronation ceremony, as had previous hazrats. Fazl and his younger brother, Nur, had also enlisted tribal support for the amir's jihad against the British in 1919. In return for their political support, Amanullah had given the family several thousand acres of land in the Koh-i Daman region north of Kabul. Amanullah's actions marked an unprecedented rift in the close ties between the court and Naqshbandis dating to the eighteenth century, when the king, Ahmad Shah Durrani, had invited them to set up a madrasa and khanaqah there. In 1926, Amanullah further distanced himself from the Naqshbandis, changing his title from the spiritual *amir* to the more secular Persian title of *padishah*, or "great king."

Chapter 2

By 1928 the king's actions were becoming widely unpopular. He was publicly accused with having "turned against Allah and Islam." Religious and tribal discontent came to a head in Pir Saif ur-Rahman's native province of Nangrahar. With tensions running high, in November of that year the Shinwari Pashtun revolted against government interference in their *badragi*, or highway toll system along the road to the Khyber Pass. They burned down Amanullah's winter palace and the British consulate in Jalalabad. The revolt quickly spread. As the Shinwari moved toward Kabul, other religious and tribal leaders joined in, rallying around a Persian-speaking Tajik, Bacha-i Saqqao, whose name means "Son of a Water-carrier."

Bacha had been something of a Robin Hood in his native Kapisa Province north and east of Kabul. He was notorious for robbing highway caravans and distributing the booty to the poor. He had unsuccessfully attempted to overthrow Amanullah in November of 1928. Two months later, with both the Shinwari and the clerics behind him, he seized the throne. His success was more than simply a Tajik triumph over longstanding Pashtun control of Afghanistan; it reflected the underlying power of clerics and Sufi brotherhoods within Afghan society to assert their vision of how Afghanistan should be ruled.

Indeed, when Bacha seized the throne, his father's pir, Shams ul-Haq Kohistani Mujaddidi, performed the coronation ceremony with the customary tying of a cloth belt—the *kamarband*—around Bacha's waist. Bacha may himself have been a disciple of Shams ul-Haq. Shams gave him the title *Khadm-i Din-i Rasullah*, "servant of the religion of the Prophet." Bacha reverted to the religious title of *amir*, rather than *king*. Once in power, Bacha began to reverse Amanullah's reforms, especially those involving secular education and the status of women, who were henceforth required to wear the veil.

For his part, Shams ul-Haq was a direct descendant of Sirhindi and a pir from a rural branch of the family. (He was also the preceptor of Saif ur-Rahman's first teacher, Shah Rasul Taloqani.) Like many Naqshbandi pirs in the north, Shams had an aversion to contact with the government and other forms of *modern* political activity. He was antagonistic toward

Amanullah's government because of its antireligious policies, but, apart from his investiture of Bacha, he did not actively oppose it. As a singular act, Shams's sanctioning of Bacha as amir is emblematic of his lineage's attitude toward the emerging modern secular state: only when the existence of Islam is in jeopardy does one actively oppose the state. Otherwise, the shaikhs of Shams's lineage have consistently followed a policy of political neutrality while continuing to extract favors from the state in the form of land grants, tax exemptions, and the like.

From the perspective of religious leaders, the power of the tribes had been harnessed to reverse Amanullah's modern reforms and bring about restoration of the shari'a. In Naqshbandi eyes, Bacha's enthronement represented the perfect realization—if only momentary—of Islam's triumph over Western influence.

Bacha's victory, however, would be short-lived. Despite recognition by a Mujaddidi shaikh, Bacha was a Tajik and therefore unacceptable to the numerically dominant Pashtun tribe who had ruled Afghanistan since its inception. Bacha did attempt to win over the Pashtuns by courting Nur, the younger brother of the hazrat. Nur, however, who remained in Lahore during the entire period of unrest, was neutral toward Bacha, probably biding his time until he could identify a more durable successor to Amanullah. When Bacha began to imprison some of the Mujaddidi leaders over differences with them, Shams ul-Haq and the acting hazrat withdrew their support, precipitating Bacha's downfall.

Before even nine months had passed, Bacha was assassinated and replaced by King Nadir Khan (r. 1929–1933), a Pashtun. Nadir Khan abolished most of Amanullah's reforms, and the more conservative religious elements in the country, as well as Naqshbandi shaikhs, were mollified. For decades after, no leader would attempt to enact reforms that would threaten the role of Islam—or tribal power—in Afghan society.

Pir Saif ur-Rahman was born in 1928, on the eve of these momentous events. The conflict between Islam and a secularizing state that had come to a head under Amanullah and subsided for a time would eventually resurface and shape the long and difficult trajectory of his life.

I was in my mother's womb during the reign of Amanullah.

—Pir Saif ur-Rahman

Whomsoever God desires to guide,
He expands his breast to Islam.

—Qur'an 6:125

Chapter 3

The Making of a Saint

Saif ur-Rahman was born in the village of Baba Kilai in Nangrahar Province in 1928. Baba Kilai was little more than a huddle of mud-brick huts on the Papin River. In spring and summer, snowmelt from the Sulaiman Mountains in the south provided abundant water, making the Kot Valley around Baba Kilai an important producer of rice, wheat, and fruits. A gravel road allowed farm produce to be taken fifteen miles north to markets in the provincial capital of Jalalabad.

Little is known about the family's origins or Saif ur-Rahman's father, Qari Sarfaraz Khan.

The Akhundzada family belonged to the Musa Khel clan of the Baezai section of the Mohmand tribe of the Pashtun. The Musa Khel have long been successful wood traders, harvesting the trees on the northern slopes of the Sulaiman range. The Mohmand around Kot were neither of the hill Mohmand who inhabit the Mitai and Suran valleys north of the Kabul River, nor of the settled Mohmand of the southwest plain of Peshawar District. Rather, they formed a tiny enclave within the Shinwari tribe. Mohmand oral history has it that they originally settled in Kot during the reign of Sultan Mahmud of Ghazni in the eleventh century. Tirahis, who themselves had migrated there from the Khyber area south of the Sulaiman Range, offered the hill Mohmand land in Kot in return for protection against raiding by Shinwaris. A Pashtun custom still practiced today, obtaining tribal protection in return for payment is called *lokhai*. Over time the two tribes intermarried, and today many of the subdistricts are comprised of a mix of

Shinwari and Mohmand. Nonetheless, disputes between clans of the two tribes—usually over land—persist to this day.

A small landholder, Qari owned several acres of hilly, stony land on the Sulaiman slopes. From this, he probably eked out a modest living from farming and lumbering. As a khan, or tribal notable, he occupied a seat on the village tribal council, or *jirga*, indicating that he played an integral part in tribal affairs. One can only wonder what role he played, if any, in the uprising against Amanullah that broke out in his province.

His more distinguished social position was that of *akhund*, or religious scholar. In Afghanistan the term denotes not just a single individual but a family descended from several generations of religious scholars. For this reason, *akhundan* are highly revered. As a scholar, Qari's knowledge of Islam would have been more extensive than that of the local mullah. He could recite the entire Qur'an according to prescribed rules, hence the title *qari*. He also possessed extensive knowledge of hadith, jurisprudence, and Qur'anic interpretation. As a religious specialist, he led the prayer customarily recited before the village jirga met to discuss tribal issues. His religious position allowed him to transcend tribal affairs, at times placing him above or outside tribal conflicts.

He was also a Sufi. The entire region along the northern Sulaiman slopes seems to have been a stronghold of Sufism at the time. Qari was a khalifa of Haji Sahib Pachir, a prominent pir in the Qadiri order, the dominant order in the Pashtun tribal area.[1]

Haji Pachir himself was a disciple of a khalifa of the Hadda-i Sahib, who had become the most famous Afghan pir in the mid-1800s because of his reputation for karamat, or miracles.[2] Opposing the reforms of Amir Abdur Rahman, who came to power in 1880, Hadda refused government attempts to co-opt him with offers of a stipend. Eventually his conflict with the government forced Hadda and his disciples to flee across the border to the tribal area in present-day Pakistan, a journey that Saif ur-Rahman himself would make a century later . . . and for similar reasons.[3]

Haji Pachir is remembered as a colorful, outgoing figure who rode about town on a donkey. He lectured in Islamic sciences at the Najmuddin

Madrasa in Jalalabad, which had been established by King Amanullah. When Pakistani fundamentalists began to proselytize in Nangrahar in the 1950s, Pachir spearheaded the opposition to them. He would travel fifteen miles on his donkey to Jalalabad to debate them in the main mosque, his religious books strapped comically in great heaps on his donkey's back.[4]

Growing up in a prominent religious and tribal family, Saif ur-Rahman and his four brothers, all older than he, inevitably embarked on religious careers. As scions of an akhund family, Saif ur-Rahman and his brothers were carrying on a family tradition. It was a career to which his father—and most likely his father's father—had dedicated his life. A religious career represented a sense of moral responsibility, a deeply felt social imperative to embody and transmit the values and institutions of Sunni Islam. From the beginning of the twentieth century onward, this mission would be undermined increasingly by government reforms and outright foreign interference.

When Saif was seven years old, his father began to instruct him in the Qur'an and the life of the Prophet. One can imagine the two seated outside the small adobe house, the son seated cross-legged on a crimson Turkmen carpet, listening intently to his father's instruction as children still do today. Years later, Saif would recall fondly how his father was so devout that he was often moved to tears when recounting the events of the Prophet's life.

From his earliest days, Saif ur-Rahman was drawn to the mystical aspects of Islam. As part of his education, his father brought him regularly to local mosques, where Saif particularly enjoyed the *na'at khwani*, or melodious chanting of praise for the Prophet. One day, at one of these recitals, he was introduced to a well-known Pakistani Naqshbandi shaikh, Haji Muhammad Amin.[5] Amin placed a small amount of his saliva in the young boy's mouth, prompting Saif to fall into a state of ecstasy. Saif also experienced childhood visions in which he saw heaven and hell, jinn, and other invisible creatures. Believing him to be disturbed, Qari instructed his son to ignore these experiences in the hope they would go away.

Chapter 3

When Saif was about ten years old, his father died. It was one in a series of painful losses and sudden upheavals in his life. Just a few years before, his mother had passed away. With no one to look after him, relatives sent him off to Peshawar to continue his education. He studied at several schools in and around the city, notably at Tahkal-i Payan, a religious school that had been established in the late nineteenth century to counter the proliferation of British missionary schools in the region.[6]

As they still do today, religious schools provided room and board at no charge to the student. With little in the way of endowments, these schools rely on donations and annual tithing to cover their operating expenses. Not surprisingly, living conditions are spartan and the quality of food poor.

At that time, a student was required to read several Persian texts before undertaking study of the more difficult Qur'an and hadith. Among the Persian works were Nizami Ganjavi's *Panj Ganj* (Five Treasures), a long narrative poem of five epics, his *Sikandar Nama*, a mythical account of Alexander the Great, and works by the Persian mystic poet Sa'di entitled *Bustan* and *Gulistan*, which contain imaginative tales containing morals.

After mastering these, a student would move on to the Qur'an and some basic religious subjects. Typically, a student would move from one school to another to work with a teacher deemed strong in a particular subject: one for the Qur'an, another for hadith, and so on. This would explain Saif's frequent movement from school to school, each with its own field of specialization. The itinerant nature of religious education in the region was not unlike the life that awaited a Sufi teacher.

Upon completion of primary school at the age of twelve, Saif moved on to higher studies. Ambitious or gifted students usually went to the renowned Deoband seminary in India. After partition of India in 1947, however, it became more convenient for Afghans to study in one of the local Deoband schools in the NWFP of Pakistan. These schools had been established in a chain along the tribal frontier by Deoband missionaries in the late nineteenth and twentieth centuries. At the Deoband madrasa in Charsadda District, Saif studied Arabic, logic, hadith, and jurisprudence.[7]

Alternatively, Saif could have returned to Afghanistan to attend the state-run Najmuddin Madrasa in Jalalabad. By the late 1940s, there was a state madrasa in virtually every province in the country. King Amanullah had designed their curricula after the modernist College of Aligarh in India, which itself had been modeled along lines of the French lycée. The curricula in these state schools were more secular and placed greater emphasis on subjects such as math and physics than on religion. Moreover, state schools employed modern methods such as lectures, classes in several subjects simultaneously, and standardized curricula, whereas in private schools the student proceeded individually with one subject at a time.

Students who graduated from a state school were guaranteed a job in the state's burgeoning bureaucracy, whereas those from traditional schools had to pass entrance exams to gain employment. That Saif ur-Rahman did not return to his native province to attend Najmuddin Madrasa reflects his rejection of secular education and, by extension, the secular state. It underscores the importance he placed on traditional religious teachings over and above the guarantee of a government job that others in his circumstances would have welcomed.

Charsadda, where Saif went to study, had once been the capital of the legendary Buddhist Gandhara Kingdom. Under Islam, Charsadda continues to be a major center of religious learning. In the 1940s, a number of prominent clerics taught there; the most eminent was Saif ur-Rahman's own teacher, Muhammad Sandani, a Pakistani Pashtun.[8] Sandani was regarded as an expert in all of the religious sciences and was particularly renowned for his knowledge of jurisprudence and hadith. In the 1970s, for example, he was summoned to Islamabad to brief the Pakistani Supreme Court on his interpretation of the laws on property disputes.

In the late 1940s, students at the school had to sleep in the mosque, which served as both classroom and living quarters for some sixty to eighty students. With little family support, students relied on the generosity of villagers to support their studies. For this reason, the madrasa generally did not accept more students than the village could reasonably support. Each night, students would take turns going from door to door canvassing for food, clothing, and other items of necessity.[9]

Sandani taught in the Deoband tradition, there having been almost no other schools in the NWFP at the time, though that would soon change. The school curriculum consisted of 106 books on theology, hadith, Qur'anic interpretation, jurisprudence, literature, Arabic philosophy, medieval geometry, astronomy, Greek medicine, and logic. A student of Sandani typically required ten to twelve years to obtain a certificate authorizing him to teach.

In 1946, upon completion of formal studies, Saif joined the Afghan army to fulfill a two-year obligation.[10] He was assigned as a private to the district of Chowki in Kunar Province. His service there seems to have been uneventful, consisting of the usual routines of a soldier's life. A former member of his regiment described him as quiet soldier who did not distinguish himself in any way from his compatriots. When his military service was fulfilled, he went north to Kunduz Province to join his older brothers, who had moved there from Baba Kilai, possibly after the death of their father.

Saif ur-Rahman and his brothers may well have been attracted to Kunduz so that they could start a madrasa and mosque in an area unencumbered by the tribal skirmishes that traditionally plagued the eastern border area. With its rapid influx of Pashtuns, northern Kunduz was a promising place, as the new immigrants needed places to worship and schools to educate their children.

Also, like the tribal belt where Saif ur-Rahman had been born, the north was another fertile region for those interested in Sufism, with the Naqshbandi order being dominant there. Sufism was so strong in the north that, in some cases, residents of an entire village were disciples of a particular shaikh. Unlike the eastern tribal belt, where Qadiri pirs were often intimately linked to the tribes, northern pirs played little role in tribal affairs. They shunned relations with the state and sought to live beyond the reach of an increasingly meddlesome and modernizing government in Kabul.

Kunduz Province was inhabited chiefly by Tajiks and Uzbeks. However, in the late nineteenth century, the Afghan king Amir Abdur Rahman forcibly resettled several thousand Pashtuns there as a bulwark against the ever-dreaded Russian advances. Pashtuns were given land at the expense of other ethnic groups already there. Cut off as it was from the rest of Afghanistan by the towering Hindu Kush Mountains and possessed of fertile soil, Kunduz was an attractive candidate for Russian annexation. Already Russian settlers in large numbers had begun appearing just north of the Afghan border in places like Merv and the Sarakhs Oasis in what is now Turkmenistan. A few years later, Amir Abdur Rahman encouraged more Pashtuns to take up migration voluntarily to spur economic development of the region. The government offered financial incentives such as tax relief and land to those willing to relocate as part of a wider effort to Pashtunize the country. To Pashtuns seeking greater opportunities outside the relatively high population density in their tribal belt, Kunduz was thus an attractive alternative. By 1907, several thousand Pashtun families were living in Kunduz.

At first, Pashtuns settled in villages apart from their Uzbek and Tajik neighbors. In time, however, the scarcity of Pashtun women led the men to marry their ethnic neighbors. (Pashtuns, however, seldom reciprocated by allowing their own women to marry non-Pashtun men.) Later, Amir Abdur Rahman's governors moved these mixed families from their territorial base, further attenuating the tribal system. Despite this, Pashtuns quickly rose to prominence in the region, serving as *maliks*, or heads of intertribal councils.

In the 1920s, a wave of entrepreneurial activity further boosted the development of the area. The lowlands along the Amu Darya River had long been little more than malarial swamps. One of the country's leading entrepreneurs, Abdul 'Aziz Londoni, whose ancestors were Kashmiri, purchased a thousand acres of swampland, drained the swamps and began raising cotton for sale to the Russians. Later, 'Aziz established a cotton company there, Spin Zar, which was nationalized in 1953.

Chapter 3

Initially, Saif ur-Rahman's brothers may have worked as sharecroppers while waiting for title to their land. Saif moved around the province several times between 1948 and 1953, suggesting that he, too, may have been working as a sharecropper. In his spare time, he frequented the tombs of holy men. After six months at an unnamed location in Kunduz Province, he went briefly to the nearby Qataghan Province (now defunct) and then Ludin in the northern part of Kunduz, where he stayed for three years. By this time, he had taken the first of his four wives.

In 1953, Saif and two of his brothers obtained enough government land to start a small farm on the Amu Darya River in the village of Nahr-i Jadid, in the Dasht-i Archi subdistrict of Kunduz Province. There they set up a mosque and a madrasa, and Saif began teaching and counseling. Soon a cluster of houses formed, which they named *Sra-Mata*, Pashto for "red earth." His congregation was called *al-qawm*, "the folk," one of the many terms that Sufis use to describe themselves.[11]

It was not until 1960 in Dasht-i Archi that Saif ur-Rahman met his first Sufi pir, Maulana Sahib Rasul Taloqani. Taloqani was originally from Kohistan, a Persian-speaking region in northern Afghanistan with few Pashtuns.[12] Religious leaders, most of whom were Naqshbandi, including the Mujaddidi family, enjoyed immense prestige there and had thousands of disciples. After completing his formal education there, Taloqani began Sufi study and over time was bestowed with the khalifate in three orders, the Suhwarardi, the Qadiri, and the Chishti.[13] In Afghanistan, a Sufi teacher typically will master two or more orders. Naqshbandis usually undertake study of the other orders once the basics of their own order are mastered. The intent is to benefit from both the different spiritual practices used and the grace, or baraka, inherent in each order. Taloqani was later initiated into the Naqshbandi path by Shams ul-Haq Kohistani Mujaddidi, the shaikh who had performed the historic cornonation ceremony for Bacha-i Saqqao in 1929.

When Shams first encountered Taloqani, he noticed that his disciple's spiritual work was incomplete. To hasten his development, Shams would make Taloqani walk while Shams rode his horse and dispensed baraka to his disciple. Before he died, Shams conferred Taloqani with the exalted rank of *qutb al-irshad*, "pole of the masters." According to Sirhindi, this title designates the highest living Sufi master of his time, who appears once every few centuries.[14]

It was not surprising then, when Shams selected Taloqani as his successor. Yet Taloqani's appointment marked the first time that the head of the Mujaddidi order was *not* a direct descendant of Sirhindi and thus not in the bloodline of the hazrat of Shur Bazaar in Kabul. This provoked a leadership dispute, which was settled in Taloqani's favor by the reigning hazrat, Nur Mujaddidi, the leading Naqshbandi shaikh in Afghanistan and a direct descendant of Sirhindi. Nur was also minister of justice. The affair underscored the close ties that then still existed between the hazrat of Shur Bazaar and this nonlineal northern branch of the Mujaddidi. Within a generation, however, these ties would be severed as a result of differences over the preferred means of countering the growing influence of the state.

After Shams's death, Taloqani became so popular a shaikh that the local inhabitants would applaud him as he passed through the streets. Nonetheless, shortly after the leadership dispute, Taloqani moved to the village of Bihark in the Taloqan district of Takhar province. Nur may have offered him a khanaqah there to run. In Bihark, Taloqani made a major literary contribution to the Naqshbandi order by formulating a more complete set of Contemplations to accompany those originally set down by Sirhindi.

It was on one of his periodic trips to nearby Dasht-i Archi to visit his disciples in 1960 that Taloqani first met Saif ur-Rahman. During this encounter, Taloqani saw a light (*nur*) in Saif's forehead, taken as a sign of his spiritual precocity. That same year, at the age of thirty-two, Saif took *bay'a*, the Naqshbandi oath of allegiance. Saif ur-Rahman credits Taloqani with activating his heart dhikr. Saif's spiritual tutelage under Taloqani would be all too brief, however. Within two years, Taloqani became gravely ill. Before his death in 1963, he sent word to his disciples that he had designated Maulana Hashim Samangani as his successor, the *sajjada nishin*, or "master of the prayer rug."[15]

Chapter 3

A Turkmen from Ghaznigak village in neighboring Samangan Province, Maulana Hashim would become Saif ur-Rahman's main mystic preceptor. Known to his disciples as Maulawi Bozorg (Great Master), Hashim was revered as a religious scholar and a Sufi. He began his studies in the legal sciences at the late age of twenty-five, finishing in fourteen months. By then, he could recite the Qur'an from memory in the astonishingly short time of five hours. He often took leave from his studies to visit the tombs of holy men, especially that of Akhundzada Sahib-i Tagab, the teacher of Taloqani. While visiting Tagab's tomb, Hashim is said to have had a vision in which the deceased pir imparted a vast body of esoteric knowledge to him.

Maulana Hashim was an outgoing person who loved to wear colorful clothes. His turban, for example, was striped green and black, not the traditional white worn by Naqshbandis. A spiritually intense nature prompted him once to extend his observation of the fasting month of Ramadan for five years in order to hasten his development. He also authored several Sufi manuals. His baraka was said to have been so powerful as to calm wild animals. He freely dispensed his baraka to his disciples. Because of a debilitating disease, he withdrew in his final years, limiting access only to those who could profit spiritually from being in his physical company.

Saif went on to complete his mystical education with Hashim, whom Taloqani praised as a pir whose heights few would attain in the centuries to come. When Hashim first met Saif, he noticed that the younger man was wearing a cloak to hide the visible beating of his heart, characteristic of the Naqshbandi dhikr. When asked the reason for his secrecy, Saif said it was so as not to arouse the criticism of mullahs and clerics who believed the phenomenon to be witchcraft. Citing a verse from the Qur'an, which enjoins Muslims to "show the gifts of God to the people," Hashim instructed Saif to remove the robe and never again to conceal his heart dhikr.

Under Hashim's tutelage, Saif ur-Rahman's spiritual development progressed rapidly. Hashim initiated him in the other major orders: the Suhrawardi, the Chishti, and the Qadiri. After sitting only twenty times in spiritual company with his pir, Saif was bestowed with the khalifate in all four orders.

Saif subsequently requested permission to go to Nangrahar for additional training in the Qadiri order with Haji Pachir, his father's pir. In central Asia, the Naqshbandi and Qadiri orders are very closely linked because of their strict adherence to the shari'a and their emphasis on sobriety in mystical experience. In addition, Qadiris believe that Bahauddin Naqshband was aided in his own spiritual development by 'Abd al-Qadir al-Jilani (d.1166), the founder of the Qadiri order.

Saif was warmly welcomed home by Haji Pachir, who quickly perceived that Saif had advanced in wisdom and knowledge since they had last met. In their first sitting, Haji Pachir gave Saif all nine of the Qadiri contemplative practices and invested him in the order. Haji Pachir also designated him to act on his behalf as pir.

When Saif returned to Dasht-i Archi, he resumed his education with Hashim, this time studying the Chishti path. Although they were living more than a hundred miles apart, Saif frequently traveled to Hashim's house in Aibek village in Samangan Province. When Hashim traveled, he would visit Saif in Dasht-i Archi. As pir of a Mujaddidi silsila, Hashim eventually decided to open a khanaqah, not in Aibek, but in a village in Kunduz Province, Zar Kharid, presumably so that he could be closer to Saif. Perhaps Hashim had already identified him as his successor.

At about this time, Saif had fallen into financial straits, possibly because of a poor harvest. He was still a farmer and depended on agriculture to feed his family. His brothers may also have been in debt. To make ends meet, he began skipping visits to the khanaqah in order to work. His absence quickly met with Hashim's disapproval. To free his student to come to the khanaqah, Hashim paid the family's bills. Even though Saif worked as an imam in the village mosque, Hashim forbade him from receiving emoluments for his work. Eventually, Saif had to sell some of his ancestral land in Baba Kilai to pay his debts.[16] As Saif's troubles mounted, Hashim remarked that he would not always be around to create such difficulties conducive to his disciple's spiritual development. Not long after this, Hashim contracted a debilitating illness, possibly tuberculosis, which left him too weak to perform his duties. In 1966, Hashim asked Saif to move into his khanaqah with him. Saif acquiesced.

Saif was not in Zar Kharid very long when a serious problem arose between him and his brothers, who were also Hashim's disciples. The issue concerned his brothers' involvement in politics. As elsewhere in the world, Afghanistan in the 1960s was undergoing a period of heightened political activity. There were violent debates in parliament and on the campus of Kabul University over issues ranging from the liberalization of the monarchy and the independence of Pashtunistan to the American involvement in Vietnam. While many religious leaders remained aloof from these and other political and social issues, some clerics, especially the Islamists, were very much at the forefront of these debates.

Like most Naqshbandis in the north of the country, Saif shunned modern forms of political activity—even contact with government officials. So angered was Saif at his brothers' behavior that in 1969 he left Zar Kharid for Pakistan and other parts of Afghanistan. His first stop was the village of Pir-i Sabeq in the NWFP. There he consulted with a Naqshbandi pir, Abdul Salaam, who had probably also been a disciple of Maulana Hashim. Then he traveled to eastern Afghanistan, possibly to seek counsel from his first teacher, Haji Pachir.

Saif may have been thinking of returning to his native village to teach. While in eastern Afghanistan, Saif received a message from Hashim asking him to return to run the Zar Kharid khanaqah so that Hashim could seek treatment for his illness in Kabul. Saif staunchly refused, complaining that his older brothers had "met with high ranking officials of the government, so propagation of the teaching is impossible."[17] To mollify his pir, Saif offered instead to go to other major cities such as Jalalabad or Mazar-i Sharif or to rural Faryab Province to teach. Hashim rejected these suggestions and the stalemate continued.

Finally, Hashim offered to mediate the conflict between Saif and his brothers. During the meeting, Hashim chided the brothers, saying,

> Don't know him [Saif] by his name. Rather, look at him as you look at me. Your brother has attained a high degree, and darkness retreats from him wherever he goes. If you respect your brother, you will be respected, and if you treat him with disrespect, you will be defamed in the other world.[18]

At the conclusion of the meeting, Hashim instructed the brothers, all of whom were older, to obtain Saif's approval before talking at official assemblies or public gatherings.

Hashim's mediation was partly successful. Saif returned to Kunduz, though not to the khanaqah in Zar Kharid. Perhaps because two of his brothers were still in Zar Kharid, Saif went to Dasht-i Archi instead. His decision to settle there occasioned the following letter from Hashim in March of 1971:

> My Dear Brother,
> You are in the chain of my perfection and honesty, Akhundzada Sahib. Give my loving regards to Bachalala [Saif's other brother] and all of your relatives. Praise to God, for now I wear the cloak of health. But the distance from you is very sorrowful, and I don't know the reason for it. So cry when you read this letter, because I cried very much when I wrote it.[19]

So intimate were the master and his khalifa that Hashim wanted to go and live in Dasht-i Archi in order to be closer to Saif. So when Hashim's health began to deteriorate again, he moved into Saif's house in Dasht-i Archi—despite jealous protests from his disciples—and made Saif ur-Rahman his sajjada nishin.

If there was any doubt in Hashim's mind regarding whom among his many khalifas to designate, it was dispelled by a number of instructive visions both he and some of his disciples experienced at the time. The first occurred one evening after Friday prayer. Hashim saw Bahauddin Naqshband standing next to Saif and interpreted this as a sign that Saif was to be his successor. (Saif also saw Bahauddin, but did not know who he was.) Shortly after this vision, Saif and his sons were sitting in the presence of Hashim when the eldest, Muhammad Haideri, who regularly experienced visions, had one involving his father. Hashim asked him to describe what he saw. (Sirhindi wrote that a disciple is obliged to share visionary experiences with his pir.)

Muhammad Haideri said that in the house he saw a box, which was divided into two compartments. In the right one was a note that read, "Saif ur-Rahman, son of Qari Sarfaraz Khan, *al-mashrab* [spiritual character]." On the left side of the box the note read, "Maulana Hashim Samangani, al-mashrab." Interpreting the note, Hashim said the left side represented his own spiritual nature as that of Moses, or Hebraic mashrab, indicating anger and righteousness. Complimenting this on the right side was "Muhammadan mashrab," signifying that Saif was gentle and compassionate.

Not long after this, in the manner of transmission from the Prophet's time down through the long line of Naqshbandi shaikhs, Maulana Hashim conferred Saif with the khalifate. Transferring his spiritual power to Saif, Hashim said, "What I have in my body, I transfer to the body of Akhundzada in the manner that has been observed since the first khalifa of our line." [20]

Hashim then embarked for Noushera in Pakistan's NWFP to seek further treatment. He stayed at the khanaqah of Abdul Salaam in Pir-i Sabeq twelve miles south. His condition had progressed beyond remission, however, and he died before the year was out. He was forty years old.

When informed of his pir's death, Saif and the other disciples went to Hashim's simple grave in Pir-i Sabeq and built a shrine (*ziyarat*) in his honor. A large, green-domed structure with a small mosque and garden, the shrine sits prominently in the middle of the village cemetery. Many of Saif's disciples testify as to the powerful spiritual power or baraka at the tomb site. One khalifa, a scholar at a prestigious Pakistani research center, claimed that when he approached Hashim's shrine, the baraka "came rushing into my heart like a great wave."

Although Maulana Hashim had named Saif to succeed him in the Naqshbandi order, he had not given him formal permission to teach the Chishti path. Typically, in the Mujaddidi line, the shaikh bestows the khalifate with a signed, one-page document (*ijaza nama*) that serves as both formal authorization and recognition of the khalifa's spiritual attainment. To obtain permission, Saif traveled to Hashim's shrine in Pir-i Sabeq. Hashim himself had to do this when his own pir died, which perhaps explains why he had not given Saif an ijaza.

As he knelt at the foot of his master's grave, Saif beheld a vision of Hashim. But instead of giving his assent, Hashim instructed him to go to the shrine of his own pir, Maulana Taloqani. Saif then journeyed some five hundred miles to Taloqani's shrine in Bihark. When he arrived, he saw Taloqani in a vision, standing near his tomb and smiling broadly. Saif interpreted this as the approval he had come so far to seek.

Saif claimed to have received at the same time direct spiritual initiation from Haji Pachir, his father's teacher, who gave him permission to teach the Qadiri path. Initiations by deceased saints is a teaching of the *tariqa Uwaysi*, named after Uways al-Qarani. The name *Uways* means "wolf," which may symbolize the solitary nature of these spiritual encounters.[21]

As head of the Naqshbandi order, Saif quickly set about to organize and expand it. His success in this attests as much to his organizational skill as to his extraordinary spiritual power. As word of his baraka spread, Afghans from most of the country's provinces started coming to the hospice in Dasht-i Archi to take initiation with him.

The "Pir-i Kunduz," as he came to be known, even attracted Shi'a Hazaras, Persian-speaking Tajiks from Tajikistan, and Turkish-speaking Uzbeks from Uzbekistan. He also won away many disciples of a leading Qadiri shaikh in Mazar-i Sharif, Lal Bacha. Saif's disciples came from the entire spectrum of society: teachers, government officials, military officers, artisans, and peasants.

Some individuals became khalifas after only one meeting with Saif ur-Rahman. Still others came to the khanaqah intending to discredit Saif but ended up becoming his disciples. Reminiscent of Sirhindi's revival, these initiates returned to their native villages and countries to conduct missionary activities on behalf of their pir.

Miracles were attributed to Saif during this period. On one occasion a disciple had written a paean to Saif, which he planned to recite for him in the mosque after the noon prayer. He told no one of his poem or of his intention to recite it for the pir. When the time came, however, the disciple became nervous and decided against it. Saif turned to the shy devotee and asked, "Why don't you recite that poem you wrote for me?"

It was during this period that Saif had a dream-vision confirming his spiritual stature as that of a *wali* (saint). The term *wali* derives from the Arabic root *w-l-y*, meaning "to be close to." In the context of Sufis, it refers to those who are close to God. The Qur'anic verse commonly referred to is, "No fear shall come upon the friends of Allah, neither shall they grieve" (10:62). The dream occurred one Friday, after evening prayer. Returning to his house, Saif performed the supererogatory prayers one thousand times and went to sleep. Then he had the following dream:

> [Saif] was standing in an open field next to a close friend. The two of them were facing west [the direction of Mecca] and noticed a stream flowing from that direction. A small bridge spanned the stream. On the far side of the bridge was a large river. His friend remarked, "I have never seen a flood." No sooner had he said this than the river surged and a great wave rushed at them. Some of the local landowners soon appeared, concerned that the flood would sweep away their livestock. One of the landowners started to approach them angrily. Saif turned to his friend and said, "It's all due to you, because you thought about the flood and created it." Leaving the scene, Saif came upon a large crowd. All of the Prophets were in the crowd. Abraham, the first Prophet, was speaking softly and his face was gentle and white. Moses by contrast was angry and his face was red. Muhammad was also in the crowd, but Saif could not see him.

> Then a voice addressed Saif: "There's a wali here whom you cannot see." With this, Saif shook hands with Moses and Abraham [probably the ritual Sufi handshake, a common leitmotif in such dreams], who received him warmly. Saif then walked around Abraham in a circle. Abraham said, "Let us leave this world." Standing under the roof were two persons responsible for the destruction of the world. But before they began their work of destruction, Abraham instructed Saif to remove from the wall all of the names of Allah so that they would not be destroyed. As the destruction began, Saif became worried that Abraham would become angry with him because some of the divine names were still affixed to the walls of his bedroom. Then he awoke.[22]

Saif's circumambulation of Abraham symbolized the circling of the Ka'aba, which is variously said to have been built or repaired by Abraham.[23] In the dream-vision, the Ka'aba signified the mystical experience of contact with God. So, too, do visions of the Prophet Muhammad and the saints.

In another of Saif's dreams, he saw himself appear in the sky as the sun and 'Abd al-Qadir al-Jilani as the moon reflecting Saif's illuminating presence.

One Sufi scholar has noted that such dream-visions constitute a "rhetoric of sainthood" in which grandiose claims and other forms of hyperbole are encouraged as a means of communicating one's direct contact with God.[24] Not all was spiritual glorification in Saif's dream, however. His inability in these dreams to see the Prophet Muhammad, who symbolizes the highest state of spiritual development, indicated his spiritual journey was unfinished. Mystic dreams of the Prophet Muhammad are essentially symbolic events signaling God's favor.

If inwardly Saif's spiritual life was deepening, outwardly he was becoming concerned over the growing political turmoil in Afghanistan. In July 1973, Muhammad Daoud Khan overthrew the monarchy of his cousin, King Zahir Shah, who had ruled since 1933. The bloodless coup had been carried out by a faction of the Communist Party known as Parcham.

Chapter 3

The Communist Party in Afghanistan had been founded in January 1965. Two years later, differences over strategy led to a split into the *Parcham* (Flag) and *Khalq* (People's) factions. The Parcham based its strategy on control of the state apparatus, while the Khalq sought to instigate mass uprisings. Although the average Afghan did not view Daoud as a Communist himself, both Islamists and clerics were becoming increasingly concerned over the degree to which Communists were being given positions in his government. Communists began taking to the streets to muster support for issues ranging from a free Pashtunistan to denunciation of Daoud's regime.

On February 22, 1974, Communists turned out in the Dasht-i Archi bazaar to demonstrate. Alarmed by this, Saif and several clerics led a group of armed disciples the next day to break up the demonstration. Precisely what enraged Saif is unclear, though given his strong sense of history he probably had not forgotten how Naqshbandis in the Soviet Central Asian Republics had fared under Communism.

For two tense days, Saif and his armed disciples marched in the bazaar, garnering the support of merchants and patrons alike. Although such armed demonstrations were illegal, the Kunduz District head, Muhammad Hassan, was sympathetic toward Saif and his disciples and did not intervene.

On the morning of the second day, the governor of Kunduz phoned Hassan and ordered him to remove Saif and his disciples from the bazaar. Hassan went down to the bazaar and apologetically asked Saif to leave, explaining that their actions were becoming an embarrassment to the government. But Saif and his followers were defiant and continued to march well into the evening. By this time, the Communists, realizing they were outnumbered and losing support in the bazaar, had begun retreating to their homes. Fearing reprisal, some fled to Takhar Province.

Satisfied that they had driven the Communists from the bazaar for good, Saif and his disciples stood down. His leadership of the counterdemonstrations was quite possibly the only time he ever engaged in this type of political action.

In early 1978, at the age of fifty, Saif performed the hajj for the first time. In Mecca, he made the acquaintance of an Afghan Naqshbandi shaikh from Balkh, Muhammad Muqim Shah. On his return, he visited Muqim while on a lesser pilgrimage to the shrine of Hazrat 'Ali in Mazar-i Sharif. After stopping off to visit with his disciples at the Zar Kharid khanaqah, he returned to Dasht-i Archi. He would not stay there for very long, however. In April 1978, Nur Muhammad Taraki brought the Communists to power in a coup. The coup would usher in a period of turmoil that today, more than thirty years later, shows no sign of abating.

Taraki spent the first few months of his rule purging his Marxist rivals from the government. In late summer 1978, he then proceeded to undertake three types of reforms: land tenure, education, and public administration. The reforms to public administration were intended to strengthen the state apparatus.

History was repeating itself in Afghanistan. The reforms proved unpopular with all sectors of the population and once again widespread uprisings ensued. According to one account,

> Those who led the first revolts were religious leaders, people of influence such as village headmen, or other individuals who were usually elderly. The revolt usually took the form of a mass uprising preceded by preaching and followed by an attack on the government post of the principal town of the district, using small arms. The post was usually captured with heavy causalities on both sides. The communist militants were executed, noncommunist soldiers and officials allowed to go. Then the revolt would spread to the whole area in which there was tribal solidarity.[25]

Clearly, King Amanullah's experience in challenging the established social order fifty years earlier was still fresh in the collective mind. Seemingly oblivious to the lessons of history, Taraki persisted, viewing the religious establishment as his major obstacle to implementing the reforms. And among all the religious groups, the Sufi orders were considered the government's arch enemy. Taraki was also cognizant of the Soviet experience in neighboring central Asia. Faced with Communist repression there, the Sufi orders, mostly Naqshbandi, had gone underground, from where they waged a highly effective resistance. Sufis in the USSR had also been less amenable to co-optation than were the clerics.

Doubtless for all of these reasons, in the fall of 1978, the government launched a preemptive campaign of systematic repression and outright extermination of Sufis. Taraki's government targeted both political and nonpolitical orders. Seventy-nine Mujaddidi males were arrested and thrown into Kabul's notorious Pul-i Charkhi prison. In January 1979, they were all executed, including the hazrat of Shur Bazaar, Muhammad Ibrahim. One of the Mujaddidis described to me how one morning, he was preparing to head off to his job at the Ministry of Agriculture when agents of the dreaded secret service, Khadamat-i Ittela'at-i Dawlati (KhAD), stormed into his house and took him away. He was summarily thrown into Pul-i Charki and tortured. Three months later he was released. By then, most of his male relatives were dead.

The full tragic story of this pogrom of Sufis in Afghanistan has yet to be told. In the north, the government bombed villages where the Naqshbandi orders were strong. One Naqshbandi disciple recounted to me that in Badakhshan Province, he had witnessed several dozen pirs and their disciples bound and thrown into the Kokcha River, where they drowned. In other regions, Sufi shaikhs and other potential opposition leaders were led away in large numbers by "security groups" from the provincial capitals, never to be heard from again. In all, it is estimated that fifty to one hundred thousand individuals, among them many Sufis, disappeared in this way.

That so many pirs allowed themselves to be taken in this manner indicated that they were not anticipating arrest; they were not engaged in antigovernment activities at the time. Those who were not imprisoned or killed fled to Iran, Pakistan, and other Islamic counties and never returned.

Initially, Saif did not oppose the Taraki regime, though he and his disciples knew they were under close government surveillance. Nor did other religious leaders from Kunduz west to Shibergan take part in the fighting that had broken out in other parts of Afghanistan. The precise reasons for Saif's inaction are not known. Given his disdain for politics, he was possibly reluctant to get involved in dissident activities. He may have felt that as long as he could teach unfettered, he would not actively oppose the government.

Indeed, when he was later singled out by critics for having stayed in Afghanistan under Taraki, Saif defended doing so on the grounds that he had been mollified by Taraki's statement, "Those who prayed two prayers previously, may now pray twenty." Saif said, "So I was not prohibited from worshipping."[26]

In time, however, the government abandoned its laissez-faire policy toward the remaining Sufis. In early August 1978, Saif received a tip from a government official that his arrest was imminent. The next night, under cover of darkness, he and his family fled overland through the Khyber Pass to Pakistan's NWFP.

He would never again live in his homeland.

In fleeing his homeland, Saif reenacted *hijra*, the flight of the Prophet from Mecca to Medina. To flee a Muslim land occupied by infidels without fighting, while not actually recommended by the Qur'an, is at least permitted:

> Those who believed and left their homes and strove for the cause of Allah. These are the believers in truth. We were oppressed in the land. (8:74)
> Then the Angels will say: "Was not Allah's earth spacious that ye could have migrated therein?" (4:97)

At the same time, the pir declared jihad against the Communist government in Kabul, much as the Prophet Muhammad had done when he return to Mecca after having been banished. Saif's declaration of jihad was an expression of his broader social role. It was now incumbent on him, as imam of the community, to defend Islam against infidel aggression.

Chapter 3

By the spring of 1979, the rebellion had spread to all parts of the country, prompting Soviet intervention in December of that year. The response of the Sufi orders to the invasion was swift, as pirs hitherto quiescent now rushed to declare jihad against the Soviets. Because of its numbers and geographical diffusion, the Naqshbandi order became the most active order in the resistance. Naqshbandis from Kabul to Mazar-i Sharif acknowledged the leadership of the Mujaddidi family and adhered to reigning Hazrat Sebghatullah's Mujaddidi's resistance party, the National Front for the Salvation of Afghanistan. From the northwestern city of Maimana eastward, Naqshbandis—tens of thousands of them—followed Pir Saif ur-Rahman.[27]

During the nineteenth century, in an effort to legitimize their efforts to subjugate the populace, the British dubbed Sufis who opposed them "mad mullahs." As a reporter for the *London Daily Telegraph*, the young Winston Churchill had referred to the saintly Qadiri Sufi, the Akhund of Swat, as "a mad fakir" for his tenacious opposition to the British.

In a similarly self-serving manner during the war against the Soviets, Western governments and the media referred to the Islamic mujahiddin as "freedom fighters." But it was not in Western terms of individual democratic freedoms that Sufis and other Muslims fought. The concept of jihad must be understood in Islamic terms. Jihad is an armed defense of Islam against the imposition of what is perceived to be a corrupt, alien, or immoral system. The quest for freedom may be the mujahid's motive, but it is the freedom to obey God and direct others to obey God.

The hierarchical structure of the Sufi orders made them highly adaptable to the exigencies of resistance warfare. In general, pirs, especially those who were elderly, fled the country, leaving their disciples to fight, as did Saif. In such circumstances, the pir delegated his military authority to one of his older khalifas, some of whom had been senior military officers under the former king. One of Saif's disciples, who had served as a general in a king's army, became a mujahiddin leader.

Although each pir commanded the allegiance of several hundred or thousands of disciples, the wider Naqshbandi identity provided an overarching framework for resistance activities. The obedience underlying the khalifa-disciple relationship carried over easily into a political-military one. Close fraternal ties between disciples tended to make the orders resistant to penetration by outsiders as well.

With the resistance under way, it became necessary for religious leaders to join one of the dozens of political parties springing up in Peshawar in order to obtain foreign aid and weapons. Saif ur-Rahman joined the Harakat-i Inqilab-i Islami (HII; Movement for the Islamic Revolution). It was led by one of his disciples, Muhammad Nabi Muhammadi. The HII was *the* clerical party of the resistance, consisting mostly of Pashtun clerics who had been educated in private madrasas as had Saif ur-Rahman.

The HII lacked a rigid structure or ideology, tending to view itself as a clerical association. It favored a return to shari'a but without desiring an Islamic republic as did the Islamists. It thus viewed the former monarchy as compatible with Islam chiefly because of the monarchy's historical laissez-faire policy toward Islam. The HII was strong in the north, where it employed madrasa networks in the guerrilla campaign. Despite these strengths, the mujahiddin were outnumbered and outgunned. The Soviets had put more than 100,000 troops in Afghanistan. By comparison, there were only 30,000 full-time and 120,000 part-time mujahidin, often equipped with little more than a replica of a British Lee-Enfield rifle.

Saif assigned his brother Fazalul Rahman the task of organizing and recruiting disciples in Afghanistan for the HII. For the next several months, Fazalul and a cleric, Maulawi Abdul Hai Zafarani Sahib, the regional HII director, secretly shuttled between Peshawar and the eight northern provinces to recruit members and distribute membership cards. In the autumn of 1980, sixty-four of Saif's disciples, including his khalifa in Mazar-i Sharif, Juma Gul, were staying at the Hotel Babur in Qala-i Zal, Baghlan Province.[28] Government forces stormed the hotel and arrested the entire cohort of Naqshbandis.

They were never heard from again.

Another major figure who disappeared at that time was Rahmatullah Taloqani, the khalifa of Takhar Province. Several more of Saif's khalifas in Mazar-i Sharif would soon disappear, including his brother Fazalul. A list of some of Saif's other khalifas who disappeared at that time shows the geographic extent of his following, as well as of the government purge against Naqshbandis: Malawi Abdul Ghaffur, Faryab; Muhammad Amin, Laghman; Malawi Abdul Khaliq, Kunduz; Mullah Sayyid Habib, Nangrahar; and Malawi Khan Gul, Qandahar.

For the first three years of the war, the HII was the leading resistance party. But by 1983, it had begun to unravel over petty squabbling. Clerics in the HII, especially Tajiks, were complaining that the bulk of weapons that the HII was obtaining on credit were going to Pashtuns, and many of the weapons were being sold on the black market. Even one of Saif ur-Rahman's sons, Muhammad Hamid, was involved in this illicit activity, to his father's great shame.[29] Subsequently, Tajiks in the HII began to defect to the leading Islamist party, the Jami'at-i Islami (JI).

Another problem was the party's loose organization. What had initially been HII's chief appeal in time proved to be its chief liability: the lack of strong leadership or a clear organizational structure. These weaknesses made it possible for Maoists and KhAD intelligence agents to infiltrate the party. A Naqshbandi Maoist sympathizer, Ghulam Mahiddin, "the pir of Obe," succeeded in creating a dissident movement within the HII known as the Jami'at-i 'Ulama (JU). The JU soon became the rallying point for other Maoists, which increased disputes with other parties. Eventually these disputes became so acute that one of the Maoists betrayed the leaders of the JU to the government, prompting the HII's demise.

With the HII gone, Saif and several other Naqshbandi shaikhs joined the Jami'at-i Islami. The JI had become the ascendant party because it lay at the confluence of the three religious groups in Afghanistan: the clerics, the Sufis, and the Islamists. Nevertheless, because most of its members were Tajiks from the north, the JI never achieved wide acceptance among the Pashtun tribes.

When Saif fled Afghanistan, he first went to stay at Pir Abdul Salaam's khanaqah in Pir-i Sabeq, near the shrine of his teacher Hashim. There, Saif continued to teach, attracting not only his Afghan disciples but an increasing number of Pakistanis as well. In fact, his baraka was so powerful that Abdul Salaam soon became jealous, claiming that the dramatic physical reactions of the disciples in the presence of the two pirs, such as shaking of the limbs and verbal ejaculations, were due not to Saif ur-Rahman but to himself.

After eighteen months, relations between the two became so strained that Saif was forced to leave. In 1980, he accepted an invitation to become the imam of the Del Aram mosque in Noushera, twenty kilometers north of Pir-i Sabeq.

Before taking up his position, he made a pilgrimage to India, to the shrine of Ahmad Sirhindi. Perhaps he had gone to seek inspiration, as it was a time of great trials for him. He had already lost a brother and hundreds, perhaps thousands, of disciples. His disciples continued to perish in the war or be dismembered by some of the millions of land mines the Soviets had planted in Afghanistan. "These were my moral offspring," he later lamented. "How much I have suffered for their martyrdom, for the loss of the Harakat-i Inqilab, broken into pieces, and all the disunity among the mujahiddin."[30] With his country overrun by Communists, he was without a permanent home or place to teach. Even his baraka was becoming a problem for him.

In Noushera, Saif once again experienced difficulties stemming from his baraka. This time, tribal elders had become upset with the behavior of his disciples in the mosque during the dhikr ceremony. Complaints mounted that running, shouting, and laughing in the mosque were blasphemous behaviors. Living in the conservative towns of the NWFP was proving to be an ongoing problem for the mystic.

Saif seemed to have nowhere to go until three of his disciples from the Afridi tribe—Sultan Muhammad Khan, Haji Mir Asghar, and the latter's nephew, Haji Muhammad Yusuf—offered him a house and thirty acres of land on which he could start his own khanaqah. Saif would call it "Murshid Abad" (abode of the master). An entirely safe retreat it would not be, for Murshid Abad was in the heart of the forbidding Khyber Agency.

There is a strange fascination in living among the Pashtuns.
—Sir Olaf Caroe

They [the Afridi] *are a notoriously predatory and warlike people of lean, wiry build, lean eyes and hungry features.*
—H. W. Bellew

Chapter 4

The Khyber

I returned to Peshawar in 1966 on a grant from the Fulbright Commission. I intended to do an ethnographic study of the Naqshbandis to demonstrate the inadequacy of existing anthropological theories to explain Sufi mysticism. Over its one-hundred-year history, anthropology had generated a rich store of theories to explain the variety of religions around the world. But when it came to mysticism, it was woefully reductive. Some anthropologists simply shied away from the subject altogether—the better not to have to explain it. Those who did study Sufis or their orders concluded that Sufis were driven not by a quest for spiritual realization—for it did not exist—but by more mundane political, social, economic, or cultural imperatives. Not surprisingly, very few of the anthropologists who held these theories had ever lived in a khanaqah or had even met a Sufi. Taken together this ethnographic literature represented a new kind of colonialism—intellectual colonialism. Based on my brief experience with Pir Saif ur-Rahman six years earlier, I had concluded such literature was ethnocentric and self-serving.

As my taxi made its way up the Grand Trunk (GT) Road—the five-century-old road built by the Mughal emperors—to the Fulbright House, I noticed little had changed in my absence. Peshawar's character as a Wild West–like frontier town remained intact. Bearded Pashtun men strolled along with their ubiquitous Kalashnikovs and bandoleers slung over their shoulders. Women shrouded in blue burqas skulked furtively along the streets, darting in and out of roadside shops.

Chapter 4

The GT Road itself is a maelstrom of garishly painted buses, bullock carts, cars, huge lorries, and horse-drawn carriages called tongas. In the tonga in front of us, a woman huddled on the back seat caught me staring in her direction and quickly checked to make sure her ankles were not exposed to this intrusive foreigner's eyes.

Mirroring the hurly-burly streets, the buildings were a confused mix of ramshackle wooden kiosks and high-rise office buildings, many of them built with heroin money. The heroin trade was now flourishing in the tribal area. For all the appurtenances of modern life to be found here—a university, a medical college, and an airport—Peshawar remained a medieval place, intensely patriarchal, corrupt, and incorrigibly tribal.

If anything had changed in six years, it was that conditions in Peshawar had deteriorated. Not only had the ongoing civil war in Afghanistan prevented the one million Afghan refugees in the NWFP from repatriating, but Taliban repression there was driving even more Afghans to seek safe haven here. Peshawar was now bursting at the seams with people. The swelling number of refugees made the city a virtual Asian crossroads with Afghan Turkmen, Tajiks, and Uzbeks mixing, uneasily at times, with Punjabis, Pashtuns, and Sindhis.

And there were vehicles, caravans of them, some of them belching thick, asphyxiating clouds of black soot. The mountains, only a few miles from town, were visible only on the rare day of a rinsing rain. It was hard to believe something as sublime as Sufism existed here amidst all the filth, corruption, and danger.

After settling in, I went looking for the glass shop of Habib ur-Rahman, also known as Pir-i piran. It was Habib, with his engaging smile and welcoming green eyes, with whom I had spent the most time on my first visit to the Bara khanaqah. And it was he who had demonstrated the power of Sufism by casting a look at a young student and sending him into fits of ecstasy while pointedly reminding me that my knowledge of Sufism was nil compared to his.

My opportunity to interact with Pir Saif ur-Rahman on that visit six years before had been limited. But it was long enough for the pir to instruct me to work with Habib should I decide to become a Naqshbandi. Habib had been an accountant at a bank in Mazar-i Sharif before the deteriorating political conditions there forced him to migrate to Pakistan in 1986. Like many Afghan Pashtuns, he had taken a job as a small merchant and part-time trader. I was hoping that his shop would still be on the GT Road. Not only did I wish to see him again, but I also hoped he could provide me safe passage through the perilous Khyber Agency to the pir's hospice.

A mile down the GT Road, I found the shop tucked inconspicuously in a rank of dingy auto repair shops. The sign above the shop read, "Ziad Glass: Design Glass, Plan [*sic*] Glass, and Fancy." Habib was not in, but his eldest son, Saifullah, was. He recognized me immediately, embracing me with a bear hug. He said that his father had retired from the glass shop and was now in Afghanistan on other business (Pashtuns were master traders). I imagined Habib, not the merchant, but as Pir-i piran, stopping along the way to see his many disciples, for in addition to being a savvy businessman, he was known for his ability to project awesome spiritual power, as I had witnessed.

Now in charge of the glass business, Saifullah introduced me to his "assistants": three brothers and an aged uncle. Sitting imperiously at his desk, Saifullah brandished a large wad of rupee notes, thumbing through them contentedly. I noticed he was wearing a colorful Sindhi *kollah*, or cap, uncharacteristic for a Naqshbandi Sufi and evidence of what Pir Saif ur-Rahman would view as corrupting Pakistani influence. As we sipped green tea laced with cardamom, I explained in Persian the purpose of my visit: I wanted to go to the Khyber to see the pir.

Saifullah shook his head disapprovingly, "You cannot go there," he admonished. "It's too dangerous for you and besides, you are not Muslim. Why, you don't even have a beard!" This last observation provoked howls of laughter among his staff.

Chapter 4

I explained that I was interested in becoming the pir's disciple. Again he shook his head. I pleaded, and he shook his head again. While this was going on, his brother was moving a large piece of broken glass, the tip of which grazed my arm. It was so sharp that I felt almost nothing. But when I looked down I saw blood flowing profusely from my arm. Everyone rushed to staunch the bleeding. It seemed an inauspicious start.

"Okay. Be here at ten o'clock Friday morning and you can come along," he said grudgingly. The laceration seemed to have weakened his resistance. He told me I should wear a cap and a shalwar kameez.

On Friday morning, I showed up at the glass shop at the appointed hour dressed in a beige cotton shalwar kameez that I had purchased the previous day from the bazaar. The shalwar consists of loose cotton pantaloons tied with a cloth belt, the kameez a long-tailed shirt worn over the pants.

Friday is the weekly religious holiday, and all the shops were closed. The normally chaotic streets were eerily empty. Within minutes, Saifullah appeared around a corner in a truck so small it looked like a toy. True to Pashtun hospitality, I was invited to sit in the cab while his brothers sat in the open bed in the rear.

Bara, where Pir Saif ur-Rahman's khanaqah was located, is less than twenty miles from Peshawar, but dilapidated roads, speed bumps, and periodic police blockades made it seem farther. By the time we got ten miles outside Peshawar, the grimy, crowded city seemed far behind. Cemeteries, brick kilns, and tiny green and white mosques fringed the road. Once outside the city, I was again cruising southwest through the Peshawar plain. The plain is marked by deep crevasses and dry stream beds. Until 1947, local tribes fighting the British had used these gullies as cover for periodic raids on Peshawar. Such fighting was one of the reasons for British India's "forward policy" that pushed its boundaries into Afghan territory to create a buffer zone between itself and the tribal Pashtuns.

The large warning sign indicated we had arrived at the town of Jamrud and the entrance to the Khyber Agency. An unshaven policeman sidled up to the cab and peered in suspiciously. I held my breath. He stepped back and, with a nod of his head, signaled to the attendant to raise the barrier. I let out a sigh of relief. Saifullah laughed and said that because I was with him, we would not be stopped. His white turban was a sign that he was a Naqshbandi coming to the Khyber to see the pir.

The last time I had visited the Khyber, I had vaguely comprehended its danger but not the magnitude of it. Over time I would come to learn more about—and even experience—its unique perils. Ironically, in some ways they were the very reason the pir had settled here.

The Khyber Agency lies in the heart of the Pashtun tribal belt that straddles Afghanistan and Pakistan from the Hindu Kush mountains south to Baluchistan. Roughly the size of Vermont, the Khyber is bordered on the north by the Khyber Pass and on the south by the Orakzai Tribal Agency. To the west is Afghanistan; to the east is Peshawar District, the only "settled" area on the Khyber's borders. The land is rugged with high mountains and barren, stony plains. In the mountains, where the altitude reaches fifteen thousand feet, the climate is alpine with snow blanketing the higher elevations in winter. In summer the plains are impossibly hot and dry with temperatures reaching up to 120 degrees. It is so hot in summer months that electric fans are commonly used outdoors.

Before the coming of Islam in the late seventh century, the region had been Buddhist, part of the Gandhara Kingdom, which ruled central Asia from the sixth century BCE to the eleventh century. Buddhist stone stupas still line the main roads, though plundering has reduced most of them to rubble. By the time Islamic armies arrived in the late seventh century, Buddhism was on the wane and Hinduism was ascendant. It was not until at least the tenth century that Khyber's residents were Islamized. Today, the overwhelming majority of the half million people here are Muslim, with a small number of Hindus and Sikhs, remnant populations from previous conquests.

The population of the tribal belt numbers roughly thirty million, which makes the Pashtun one of the largest ethnic groups in the world. The Khyber is inhabited by the Afridi, one of several subtribes of the Pashtun. If Pashtuns have a well-deserved reputation as warriors, then Afridis are Pashtuns par excellence. Even tribes of the other agencies fear their ferocity. So impressed were the British by their warrior prowess that they enlisted Afridis in their frontier corps such as the Khyber Rifles. The tactic of employing natives to control tribal areas sometimes backfired, however, as Afridi troops were also prone to mutiny.

Throughout history, Afridis have been guardians of the Khyber Pass, the vital gateway from central Asia to India. Virtually every trader and would-be conqueror has been forced to deal with the Afridi, who vigorously resisted outside incursions and periodically raided trading caravans along the Khyber Pass. Legend has it that Alexander the Great did not come through the Khyber Pass in 337 BC because he refused to pay the heavy tolls charged by the Afridi. Neither the Sikhs in the early nineteenth century nor the British after them were able to check their periodic banditry along the pass or their persistent raiding of settled areas.

In retaliation for these intrigues, the British clashed with the Afridi in the First Anglo-Afghan War in 1839. Periodic conflict with them over the next forty years eventually led the British to seek an accommodation. In 1879, by the terms of the Treaty of Gandamak between the British and the amir of Afghanistan, the Afridi and Shinwari agreed to provide safe passage along the Khyber in return for British recognition of their independence and an annual stipend. A modified form of the toll system is still in effect today, with the Pakistani government paying the Afridi on a biannual basis.

The independent status of the Khyber and the other tribal agencies under the British was retained after Pakistan's emergence as a state in 1947. The Pakistan government, unstable in the best of times, has not extended its writ into the tribal areas for fear of inciting an uprising. Today, the Khyber is the oldest of the seven Federally Administered Tribal Areas of the NWFP. (Its official name was changed to Khyber Pakhtunkhwa in 2010.) Neither

Pakistani civil nor criminal law is enforced in the tribal areas, nor are taxes collected. The Pakistani government does, however, maintain a political agent for each district. Based in Peshawar Cantonment, the Khyber political agent arbitrates between feuding clans to ensure tribal peace along Pakistan's sensitive borders.

Some Afridi are pastoral, leading their flocks into the high valleys in spring, returning to warmer places in the autumn. Most Afridis, though, own small farms of two or three acres. Bara Valley, where the pir's khanaqah was located, boasts the richest agricultural land in the Khyber. Most families cultivate subsistence crops, the work being carried out chiefly by women. Men are hardly ever seen in the fields, choosing to supplement their modest farm incomes by working in transport and trading, traditional Pashtun activities. Most of the trading is illicit. Everything from Chinese televisions and shoes to heroin and hashish is smuggled in overland, across central Asia.

The farms around Bara benefit from an extensive network of irrigation canals known as *kanat*, built originally by the Mughals. One of these canals runs right through the pir's hospice, bringing fresh water daily to the interior as well as its fields. Locals revere the Bara River as sacred, especially at the place where the waters are diverted for irrigation. Water distribution follows local custom and is complex. In summer just before the monsoon season, the Bara may be reduced to a trickle, giving rise to water disputes among clans.

The town of Bara is a rude stand of adobe and clapboard stalls straddling the main road. By day, the town is boisterous and noisy with mules, horse-driven carts, buses, and cars pushing slowly through muddy, unpaved, chaotic streets. Clapboard shops of welders, charcoal venders, mechanics, metal workers, and other craftsmen ply their trades close to the road. The bazaar is segregated on the basis of clan, so that one clan may not own or operate a shop in another's precincts. On the west end of town, a large fruit and vegetable market sells produce from the Bara Valley, including that of the Naqshbandi khanaqah.

What makes this scene different from similar ones in the developing world are the myriad illegal activities going on sub rosa. They produce a palpable tension that can erupt into violence at any moment. The corrupt Pakistani police, when not on the lookout for suspicious activity in Bara, are most likely participants in it.

The Afridis in the Khyber are divided into six clans; two other Afridi clans are based just outside the Khyber. Seven of these Afridi clans are represented in Bara District. Among them, the clan known as the Zakha Khel (the term *khel* denotes a lineage) has a well established reputation for ferocity. Its tribesmen were infamous for kidnapping British subjects, a practice observed to a lesser extent by all Afridis and very much in vogue to this day.[1]

Like other Pashtuns, Afridis are Sunnis who adhere to the Hanafi school of law.[2] They claim descent from Qais ibn Rashid, who was said to have been converted to Islam by the Prophet Muhammad himself. Qais ibn Rashid married the daughter of the celebrated General Khalid ibn Walid; she bore him three sons: Sarban, Bitan, and Ghurghust. The Afridi claim descent from Karlani, who is said to have been adopted into the family of Ghurghust. As do all Pashtuns, the Afridi thus identify with a line of descent that takes them to the very beginnings of Islam.

Notwithstanding the Afridi affinity for Islam, the religious law is subordinate to tribal custom. Whenever the shariʿa conflicts with tribal law, the latter will prevail in a judgment. Nonetheless, the Pashtun does not consider himself any less Muslim for this.

Central to all tribal customs is the concept of *ghairat*, or personal honor. Ghairat prevents Pashtuns from subordinating themselves to any system or individual and helps explain the lack of pir veneration among Afridis and the dearth of Sufi centers in the Khyber.

There is an apocryphal story that vividly illustrates the Pashtun view that gives precedence to ghairat over pirs. A holy man went to some of the Afridi in the remote southern part of the Khyber called Tirah, an area that is strictly off limits to non-Afridi. He chastised them for not having a single saint's shrine in their territory. The Afridi wasted no time in coming up with a solution: they killed the holy man on the spot and constructed a shrine over his remains!

Afridi practice of Islam does not go beyond simple observance of basic Islamic practices. Indeed, it is often tinged with a conservatism that makes Afridis receptive to the growing number of fundamentalist groups taking root in the region. This has had serious consequences for the Naqshbandis. The Afridi generally view Sufism as heretical to Islam and thus reject it. Only a few Afridi have been known to embrace Sufism.

Only two Afridi Sufi pirs are known to be living in the Khyber. One is in Tirah. The other, who had been a highway robber before becoming a disciple of Pir Saif ur-Rahman, settled near Landi Kotal, the largest town in the Khyber. Another Afridi Sufi named Sayyid Akbar, who was a Naqshbandi, is remembered for participating in tribal uprisings against the British along the frontier in 1897.

The only time Afridis have followed pirs has been in battle. Such alliances have always been temporary, however.

The absence of Pakistani law notwithstanding, social order is actually highly regulated by a system of tribal norms called *pushtunwali*. Pushtunwali is based on the concept of *nang*, or "chivalry," that stresses values of male autonomy and aggressiveness. Generally, disputes are settled by a tribal council, or jirga, an egalitarian body composed of tribal elders and directed by a khan or malik. Given the leaderless nature of Pashtun society, the khan has no authority over the jirga but acts as a kind of "first among equals," directing and moderating discussion. Decisions by a jirga are usually binding and give the aggrieved party the right to revenge in kind.

If, for example, a man is found guilty of killing another man's goat, then he must allow one of his goats to be killed. If the man refuses to comply, the conflict can quickly escalate. If the decision calls for blood money, it is rarely accepted in the case of murder. In the case of lesser offenses, if the guilty party cannot afford to pay, the law of an "eye for an eye" is followed.

Since revenge is incumbent on every male member of the offended lineage, murder can quickly escalate, drawing the entire group into the feud. The result is that some clans are often in a constant state of conflict, with family against family and clan against clan.

Feuds can persist for decades. One extraordinary case first erupted in 1875, when two men cut off the tail of a horse that belonged to the guest of a khan. Since the act violated Pashtun hospitality, the khan's sons killed two men from the offending lineage. Today, the feud is still going strong with a known total of sixty-one casualties as of this writing.[3]

This unity of pushtunwali and Islam is symbolized in village life by the physical proximity of the mosque and the *hujra*, or tribal guesthouse. These two institutions are usually built simultaneously and often share a wall or courtyard. Generally, each village has its own mosque and is responsible for its upkeep.

The mosques in Bara are usually small and in the "gingerbread" Mughal style of architecture characteristic of the subcontinent: green and white with slender minarets and puffy domes. There are three shrines and two major mosques in the Khyber. One mosque built within the last century, the 'Ali Masjid, commemorates the place where the Prophet's son-in-law, 'Ali, is alleged to have stopped and prayed. The *juma'*, or Friday Mosque, in Bagh in the remote Tirah is the venue for all Afridi jirgas. Despite the proximity of many local mosques, most Khyber Muslims pray in the safety of their homes at night.

Indeed, danger is ever-present in the Khyber. One has to be vigilant at all times, for ongoing feuds could erupt at any time. Not long after my arrival, I made the acquaintance of a young Pashtun named Yar Afzal. He was not a disciple, but because he lived nearby, he often passed the time hanging out at the khanaqah's kiosk, chatting with disciples. One day I saw him with a Kalashnikov slung over his shoulder, something I had not seen before. When I asked him the reason for it, he recounted the following story.

Two men had abducted his paternal aunt and taken her into the nearby hills, where they had raped her. As Yar's father was dead, it fell upon Yar's older brother to avenge the crime. He killed one of the rapists, but was killed in the process. Yar was now obliged to exact revenge from two men: the killer of his brother *and* the rapist still at large. Until the matter was resolved, he said he would keep his Kalashnikov with him at all times. All this the very young man recounted in the most impassive voice, as if he were describing a casual trip into town.

As luck would have it, four weeks later, while in downtown Bara, Yar Afzal came across both men together in the market. The two men had also seen him, but Yar, his Kalashnikov at the ready, fired first. Both of the miscreants were killed. Now that the aggrieved party had settled the score, the affair was considered ended. Typically, the police remain aloof from these tribal conflicts. It is easy to see why.

One factor that serves to mitigate the extent, if not the intensity, of feuds is that most feuds are intraclan. Fighting therefore tends to be confined to a particular village. In similar tribal settings, Sufi shaikhs serve as arbiters in tribal disputes, as the Pir Saif ur-Rahman's father had done in Afghanistan. But because the pir was living as a guest in the Khyber, and among tribals ill-disposed toward Sufism, this was not a role the Afridi would countenance; I never saw Pir Saif called upon to play it.

As a result of the constant friction, neither private property nor roads were safe. Houses were usually fortified as protection against attack or retaliation. If a disciple were caught crossing Afridi land, especially when unveiled women were working in the fields, he could be shot for trespassing. In such a case, no questions would be asked. An anthropologist who studied the Afridi tells how, while on a visit to the Khyber in the late 1950s, the king of Thailand decided to take a photo of some women washing clothes in the river. He stepped out of his car and looked up to see a ring of armed Afridi on the hills around him. It took his official Pakistani escorts considerable time to extricate him from the tense situation. Had he gone so far as to raise the camera to his face, he would surely have been shot.

Likewise, the pir's disciples were always careful not to stray from the gravel road leading to the hospice. Indeed, it was one of the first instructions I was given when I arrived. Once on the property of the khanaqah, disciples never strayed far on the footpaths leading to neighboring farms, even those used by the hospice. Nor did disciples ever attempt to transit the Khyber Agency at night, for fear of being kidnapped or robbed.

Criminals seeking to get beyond the reach of the law often take advantage of a Pashtun custom, *nanawatai*, which requires a host to grant asylum to anyone who requests it, except in the case of rape. Once inside the agency, fugitives customarily enter into a client-patron relationship with their host such as that extended by the Taliban government in Afghanistan, who refused to turn Osama bin Ladin over to the Americans in 2001.

There is also a traditional lively trade in guns, which is a kind of Pashtun national pastime—virtually every Pashtun male carries a rifle. To satisfy the great demand, small weapons factories in the Khyber have for over a century excelled in replicating the latest sidearm or rifle.

One of the legacies of the Soviet-Afghan war is the huge proliferation of automatic weapons in the tribal areas, which has exacerbated conflicts. On any given day, one clan might fire a dozen rockets at its neighbors over a land dispute. A US-government-sponsored program to eliminate from the black market the twenty-five hundred Stinger missiles given to the mujahiddin has been largely unsuccessful; the missiles continue to be traded clandestinely. The head of the Sipah clan of the Afridi in Bara told me that I could easily obtain one. I could even, for the right price, he said, purchase a Soviet tank.

Yet another problem was the growing heroin trade. Poppy was being cultivated in the remote Tirah region of the Khyber. Heroin was being processed in makeshift "bathtub" laboratories in Khyber homes. From Bara it was smuggled through Pakistan and onward to Europe and North America.

Periodically, under pressure from the US Drug Enforcement Agency, the Pakistani government conducted armed raids on suspected heroin labs in the Khyber. One such raid occurred in December 1996, while I was in the Khyber. It was carried out by a regiment of eight thousand soldiers and resulted in the bulldozing of houses where heroin labs were believed to be operating.

In 1979 Afghans began arriving in large numbers in the NWFP as refugees from the Soviet invasion. Within a few years there were over two million Afghans spread more or less equally between the NWFP and the Baluchistan Province. While most refugees moved into camps in settled areas of the NWFP, where they could receive donor assistance and find employment, several thousand had settled in the Khyber Agency, many living in tents.

For the self-determining Pashtun, the act of exiting Afghanistan was essentially a tribally motivated response. They were determined to maintain their traditional autonomy in the face of absorption by a Communist state that did not play by the well-established rules of tribe-state interaction that had prevailed since Durrani's time.

The pir's flight from Afghanistan, on the other hand, was religious in nature. As a Communist state, Afghanistan had ceased to be *dar al-Islam*, "the abode of Islam," and was now *dar al-kufr*, "the house of unbelief." Historically, such migrations reenacted the Prophet Muhammad's own flight from Mecca to Medina in the face of opposition from the leading Quraysh tribe there.

Even though the land for the khanaqah had been a donated by three of his disciples, the pir would not have been allowed to remain in Bara without the consent of the local clans. Afridis gave the pir refuge on the basis of two tribal customs that form the cornerstones of Pashtun social life. As mentioned, one is *nanawatai*, the right of refuge, which must be granted to anyone who requests it. The second is *melmastia*, the granting of hospitality to a guest. As a guest, the pir lived in the Khyber so long as the Afridi tolerated his presence—a condition that would be tested periodically during his time there and eventually exhausted.

Chapter 4

At first glance, the pir's decision to settle in a lawless region populated by hostile tribes, religious conservatives, and drug smugglers may seem ill-considered. Furthermore, Pakistani law prohibits foreign ownership of property in the settled districts as well as the tribal agencies. Thus, his residence, the buildings, and other fixed assets in Bara would never have any permanent, legally protected status. Despite these drawbacks, the Khyber offered a number of unique advantages. It was only forty miles as the crow flies from his birthplace in Afghanistan, providing a familiar setting, linguistically, socially, and geographically. Living in the Khyber also put the pir closer to his disciples fighting in the jihad. His hospice provided the mujahiddin a place to come for spiritual or temporal guidance, or merely to seek respite from the horrors of the war. Perhaps most important, despite the dangers of the Khyber, the khanaqah's rural location insulated him somewhat from the religious conservatism he had encountered in Pakistan's cities.

The Khyber thus provided the pir a liminal place where he could operate much as the teacher of his father's teacher, Hadda-i Sahib, had done in the nineteenth century. After having been conferred with the khalifate by the Akhund of Swat, Hadda went off to establish his own hospice, not in his native region, but in eastern Nangrahar Province, where he created a unique social niche for himself. Like Hadda, Pir Saif ur-Rahman had been able to set the terms of his engagement. Between the political turmoil in Afghanistan and the religious sectarianism of Pakistan's settled areas, he could operate a khanaqah and concentrate relatively unfettered on the spiritual education of his disciples.

The khanaqah was located about eight kilometers northwest of Bara town itself, in the heart of the Bara valley. A large green and white sign posted along the main road announced "Murshid Abad." Nestled amid Afridi farms at the end of a kilometer-long gravel road, the rural setting of Murshid Abad was in stark contrast to the filth and clamor of Bara town. Verdant fields of wheat, corn, and rice stretched in every direction to serene, blue-hazed mountains vaulting in the distance.

We turned off the main road. Along the gravel road, Afridi *qala*, or fortress homes, could be seen here and there. The buildings faced inward so that the outer walls could serve as fortification against bandits and predators. In the fields, unveiled Afridi women pecked away at the earth with hoes. Ahead of us were some Naqshbandis strolling toward the khanaqah, the long tails of their white turbans flapping in the wind.

At the khanaqah we passed through a large metal gate. I was directed to the ablution station and told to wash before seeing the pir, whom I soon learned was generally referred to as Mubarak Sahib within the khanaqah. The performance of ritual ablutions was a requirement for all disciples and visitors entering the khanaqah.

Once these were completed, we walked to the back of the mosque, where we found a rank of several small buildings and the pir's own house. In one room we found him sitting in a folding lawn chair chatting with several disciples, one of whom I was startled to see was foreign. The pir was wearing shiny, square-toed black leather boots. As I never saw those boots again, I assumed they had been a gift from a disciple and were soon given away.

"Oh, oh, oh," the pir intoned when he saw us enter.

Saifullah greeted the pir in the traditional manner: prostrating at his feet and kissing the back of the pir's right hand. The pir did not recognize me. I was not surprised. In a single weekend, he might see more than four hundred persons—disciples and nondisciples—not to mention foreigners who came to the hospice but, for one reason or another, usually chose not to stay. I heard one of the disciples seated against the wall moaning quietly. Saifullah explained to the pir that I had recently arrived in Peshawar and was doing research on the Naqshbandi order. Instantly, the pir beckoned me over and motioned for me to sit as his feet.

"Hu!" he shouted. "Hu, Allah!" The word *hu* means "he" in Arabic and is one of the names of Allah. As he intoned these words, he made a casting motion with his right hand. Seated next to the pir, a khalifa was making motions with his hands as if to cast off something from his body toward me. He alternated this with a lifting motion of his right hand as if to raise something from my lower regions, where his eyes were focused intently. This went on for several minutes. The foreign disciple against the wall told me later that he never saw the pir do this with a non-Muslim.

Repeating the name of Allah is a Sufi practice called *dhikr*. Dhikr derives from the Arabic root *dhakara*, which occurs frequently in the Qur'an in terms of enjoining believers to remember God. Among the many Qur'anic verses cited by Sufis to support this practice is "Remember God with frequent remembrance and glorify Him morning and evening" (33:41). Although used by early Sufis as a means of avoiding distractions and drawing nearer to God, it became an established ritual in all the orders with their development in the twelfth century.

Unique among the orders, the Naqshbandi perform only silent dhikr, meaning that repetition of the word or phrase is not vocalized. Naqshbandis believe the Prophet instructed Abu Bakr in this method while they were secluded in a cave during their migration from Mecca to Medina. As previously noted, the practice was later regularized by Bahauddin Naqshband, who claimed to have received silent dhikr directly from the disembodied spirit of Ghujduwani, an act reminiscent of the Prophet's relationship with the reclusive Uways al-Qarani.

Naqshbandis employ two basic dhikr formulae with many variations. The first, dhikr of the name's essence, entails silent repetition of one of the names of God alone, *Allah* or *Hu*, considered the essence of the divine name and the one being used on me as I sat.

Saifullah told the pir that I spoke Persian.The pir stopped his chanting for a moment to ask me where I was from and how long I planned to be in Pakistan. As we spoke, I was suddenly filled with relief. After my long return journey to Pakistan and then through the perilous Khyber, I was finally in the khanaqah with the pir. I felt at once at home and very far away from my original one.

Abruptly, the pir rose and everyone else in the room rose as well. He walked down the driveway and quietly disappeared through a door that led to his house.

As a foreigner, I needed a permit to enter the Khyber Agency when I wanted to visit the pir's khanaqah. Yet I feared that a formal request would merely produce a formal denial from the NWFP Home Office, permanently barring me from Bara and the pir's hospice. Even if my assumptions were incorrect, I anticipated having to wade through a morass of bureaucratic red tape to obtain such a permit. So I decided to dispense with the permit and enter with disciples illegally, as I had done in my very first visit to the Khyber years before.

The Afridi, however, do not take such incursions into their territory lightly. Typically, they retaliate by kidnapping outsiders—ideally foreigners. The intent is to obtain a compensatory ransom or, in the case of foreigners, to embarrass the Pakistani government in the eyes of the international community. In a few cases, when payment is refused, foreigners have been known to be executed. As the only town on the Peshawar District border, Bara was a chokepoint for weapons trading, criminals, illicit consumer goods, and narcotics. As a consequence, it was a most dangerous place for Pakistanis and foreigners alike.

To minimize the potential for problems, it has long been a policy of the Pakistani government to limit foreign access to the area. Only those foreigners wishing to visit the Khyber Pass or traveling to Afghanistan have been permitted, and then only after obtaining a permit, which entitles one to an armed escort. An incident in July 1996, however, prompted the government to prohibit foreigners from the Khyber altogether. The Afridi had kidnapped a Pakistani income tax agent and were holding him for ransom. Although the commissioner was not mistreated by his captors, apparently the stress of the ordeal was too much for him. He had a fatal heart attack while in their custody. Outraged, the Pakistani government demanded the perpetrators turn themselves in, but the Afridi refused to cooperate. By the time of my arrival in August, the matter was still unresolved and tensions were running high.

Notwithstanding, my strategy of surreptitious entry to the Khyber was successful until my third trip, in September. Saifullah's father, Pir-i piran, had gone missing in Afghanistan. Instead of going to the khanaqah as they did most weekends, Saifullah and his relatives set out for Jalalabad in search of him. With yet no vehicle of my own, I had no means of getting to the khanaqah. Saifullah told me to take a taxi. If stopped by the police, I was simply to say that I was going to see the pir, and I would have no problem. This seemed foolhardy, but Saifullah seemed so sure of himself that I was persuaded to follow his suggestion.

Armed with nothing more than Saifullah's assurances, I hopped into a conspicuous yellow taxi and headed for the Khyber. When we arrived at the frontier, the driver stopped to register his car with the police so that it would be traceable if it were stolen. As we entered Bara, an uneasy feeling came over me, an intuition of imminent danger. My apprehension was heightened by the unusual presence of a large number of police poised at intervals on both sides of the road. They were eyeing every car that passed.

We reached the far end of town, and we had one hurdle remaining, the vegetable market. Once past that we would be out of town and home free.

I never made it.

I happened to glance outside the car and inadvertently caught the eye of a policeman. Out of nowhere a young man with a dirty shalwar kameez and a long bamboo pole appeared. Prancing gleefully alongside the car, he tapped the window with his pole, signaling for us to pull over. Then he disappeared into the crowd.

The policeman approached the taxi and asked what I was doing in Bara. At first I attempted to speak Farsi. I then made a critical error. "Do you speak English?" I asked. His eyes widened as if he had made an astonishing discovery. "English!" he shouted. "English, come with us." The fact that I was wearing a turban and robes immediately raised suspicions that I was a foreign spy, the proverbial blue-eyed devil. During the colonial period, British spies had sometimes masqueraded in the region as holy men.

I was taken to the Bara police station—a dark, shabby, dank place if there ever was one. Once inside, I was angrily interrogated by a surly Bara political agent. Looking me over with my shalwar kameez and turban he summed up his impression, "You look like a Pakistani tribal!" After an hour of questioning, during which he pecked out my responses on an ancient manual typewriter, I was escorted back to the Peshawar Cantonment and interrogated again at the Khyber Political Agency. Nothing I said could dispell their conviction that I was a spy.

As darkness fell, I was expecting to be sent home when one of the policemen, a particularly surly character, gruffed, "Disciple, ha! Now, you wait." I assumed he meant I would be made to wait in his office for a few minutes while they pretended to discuss my fate. But he walked toward his car and sped off. A guard grabbed me by the arm and led me backward toward a square concrete structure. When I saw bars on the windows I realized I was looking at the Khyber Rifles Jail and panicked. I started to object, which made everyone nervous, in particular one elderly tribal, standing a few feet from me, who began waving an old Lee-Enfield rifle very close to my stomach. They concluded that they had an obstreperous prisoner on their hands, and some ancient rusted iron manacles were suddenly produced and fastened onto my wrists. I was summarily thrown in jail. Ironically, the jail had originally been built by the British to incarcerate unruly tribals.

Darkness had fallen. By the light of the dim bulb overhead, I counted twenty men of various ages in a cell barely twenty feet by twenty feet. My cell mates were a motley assortment of drug traffickers, smugglers, Iranian political refugees, and murderers—all apprehended in Bara. There was only one Afridi inmate. He admitted to gunning down three men who had insulted his honor. When I asked him why he did it, he replied with palms outstretched, "It was God's will," conveniently juxtaposing a fatalist interpretation of Islam with Pashtun defense of his honor.

It was the beginning of a five-day holiday weekend, so the Political Agent would not be in the office until the following Wednesday. Since I was being held incommunicado, I was concerned that my situation could deteriorate rapidly, particularly if I got sick. As a precaution, I decided not to eat. On the third day, two of the pir's disciples showed up outside the jail, jubilant at having found me. We talked through a tiny barred window. They said that Saifullah had told the pir that I was coming to the khanaqah. When I did not arrive by the second day, the pir suspected something was wrong and sent some of his disciples out in search of me.

On the morning of the fifth day, exhausted and weak from lack of food, I was summoned before the political agent. I was struck by his polished appearance and Queen's English. He chastised me up and down, telling me to apply for a permit if I wished to visit the Khyber again.

After my ordeal, the pir instructed a Bara police commander to escort me to the Khyber Agency to explain that I was his disciple and to request special dispensation to enter the agency freely. As I suspected, nothing came of this attempt. Indeed, we got only as far as the Bara police station, where I collided head-on with the chief of police, who had been involved in my arrest. He received me coldly. After making me wait three hours for a meeting, he reiterated that, disciple or not, if I were ever again caught in Bara without a permit, he would throw me back in jail—and next time for much longer.

Thus chastened, I applied for a permit that, as I had suspected, took six weeks of exasperating delays and interminable office waits to obtain. Finally, in mid-November 1996, I received a permit to spend weekends at the hospice for a period of three months. After ninety days I would have to apply for another permit.

The process of entering and exiting the Khyber was laborious and time-consuming. Each time I entered, I was given two guards armed with Kalashnikovs who accompanied me to the khanaqah. So clannish is the Khyber that guards were selected on the basis of their affiliation with the clan whose territory we would cross. From the Peshawar line to the Bara police station, I was accompanied by Khyber Khel guards.

Then, from Bara to the khanaqah, I was accompanied by Sipahis. En route, my escorts—invariably teenagers—usually smoked *chars*, a powerful mixture of hashish and tobacco. Forced to ride with stoned guards brandishing automatic weapons, I became more concerned for my safety with each visit to Bara. A few weeks later I learned that in July of that year a Japanese tourist on her way to the Khyber Pass had been shot through the back when the gun of a guard escorting her had gone off accidentally. I grew terrified of the arrangement but was equally terrified about the certain prospect of ending up in jail again if I didn't observe it.

The solution to my dilemma came in December, when the pir, annoyed at seeing armed guards enter the mosque each weekend to collect me, insisted that I forgo formal permission and come directly to the khanaqah with his disciples. The local Afridi residents, he said, had begun to chafe at my highly visible comings and goings, and he wanted me to keep a low profile. If I were always accompanied by at least one of his disciples, no harm would come to me, the pir assured.

In the beginning, each time I entered the Khyber, I lived in virtual terror of being thrown back into jail. But over time, I worked out a system whereby, when I wanted to visit the khanaqah, I had only to telephone one of the khalifas at the hospice—usually one of my roommates—and inform him I was coming. He would then meet me at a tiny roadside mosque outside Bara and accompany me to the khanaqah in my car. In this way, I was able to come to the hospice each Thursday and leave when I wanted.

Invariably, my escort took the opportunity to stop in Bara town to buy groceries. He always instructed me to lock the doors and stay in the car. Afridi passersby would, upon seeing me, usually glare menacingly into the car, clearly disturbed at the presence of a foreigner in their precincts. These moments were always terrifying for me, and I shuddered in fear of being abducted. But as the pir predicted, no harm ever came to me that year, prompting me to wonder about the putative intercessionary powers of Naqshbandi pirs.

The khanaqah is the nest for the bird "purity,"
It is the rose garden of pleasure and the garden of faithfulness.
—Sana'i

According to the Shaikhs, the traveling dervishes should regard the resident ones as superior to themselves, because they go to and fro in their own interest, while the resident dervishes have settled down in the service of God: in the former is the sign of search, in the latter is the token of attainment.
—'Ali al-Hujwiri

Chapter 5
Murshid Abad

On my first visit to Pir Saif ur-Rahman's hospice, I was warmly welcomed, but I was also told not to come back again unless I was prepared to join the Naqshbandi order. The khanaqah, it was made clear, was open neither to non-Muslims nor to scholars simply looking to conduct research or advance their academic careers. It was only for those wishing to commit to the Naqshbandi path.

I had expected as much. I was somehow hoping to divorce shari'a from tariqa, the law from the mystical path. For me, a Westerner, Sufism consisted of the practices leading to experience of the numinous, rhapsodized in the poetry of Rumi and Sa'adi. The formal law, on the other hand, seemed like drudgery, the rote performance of monotonous rituals anthropologists aptly refer to as "normative behavior." If the shari'a was the vessel, then the tariqa was the wine, and it was that intoxicating wine that interested me, not what held it.

More than in any other Sufi order, the conservative nature of the Naqshbandis required one to observe the shari'a to the extreme. Naqshbandi shaikhs from Ghujduwani to Sirhindi consistently maintained that Sufism is not separate from the law; rather, it is part and parcel of it in the way that one's surface skin and internal organs are part of the same body. In short, Naqshbandis regard the law and the path as aspects of an inseparable and organic whole. Religious conversion was not to be taken lightly. Despite having traveled so far with the intention of becoming a Sufi, I wavered. Becoming a full-fledged Muslim was a commitment I was not certain I could make.

Over the next few weeks I struggled with my decision. There were other orders in Pakistan, less conservative than Naqshbandis, even wandering malang ecstatics who, while Muslim, might not be so concerned with the shari'a. But in the final analysis, it seemed that whatever mystical path one chooses to follow entails a highly rigorous discipline. Such are the demands of the spiritual life. So after weeks of agonizing, I decided to take the Sufi oath (*baya'*) of allegiance in the hope that a taste of the wine would eventually make the vessel more appealing. I did not know at the time that the Naqshbandi system included a practice designed especially for those needing spiritual encouragement in the early stages of their apprenticeship.

On a warm September afternoon, I returned to the khanaqah. After evening prayer, one of the khalifas, Malang Sahib, informed the pir that I wanted to take initiation. The pir was seated in his chair, casually conversing with some visitors in the mosque. When he heard the news, he seemed pleased and beckoned me over. He motioned to the roughly forty or fifty disciples in the mosque to take their places. They quickly aligned on either side of his chair, sitting cross-legged, forming an oval that extended to the perimeters of the mosque. The pir instructed me to sit cross-legged at his feet. As I drew my legs underneath me, I wondered how many thousands of times he had done this. He took my right hand firmly in his and instructed me to repeat after him, refrain by refrain, the following formula in Arabic, the liturgical language of Islam:

> I take refuge from reprehensible Satan. In the name of God, the compassionate, the merciful, there is no God but God, and Muhammad is His messenger.
>
> I testify that there is no God but God whose unity has no equal, and I testify that Muhammad is His servant and messenger.
>
> I testify that there is no God but God whose unity has no equal, and He has sovereignty over all and praise to Him who gives life and death and is powerful over everything.

> Praise be to God and praise upon Him, and there is no God but God, and He is great, and there is no might, nor power without God, the great.
>
> Take cover in God. There is no other than He, life, source of the everlasting, and I believe in God, and His angels, and His books, and His messengers, and the Day of Judgment, and the decree of the goodness and the laws of God most high, and in resurrection after death.
>
> I believe in God as He is and in His names, and I accept the testimony of faith confirmed with the tongue and sincerely in the heart.
>
> Be content in God the Lord, and in the Islamic religion and in Muhammad, peace be upon him, and his people.

If I mispronounced a word in Arabic—usually one of the difficult guttural letters—the pir made me repeat it. Ever the perfectionist, he made me repeat certain refrains three times until I got them right. When I completed the oath, he reached down and thrust the extended fingers of his right hand firmly into my heart, intoning "Allah" sonorously three times. The act symbolically linked me to the chain of Naqshbandi initiates going all the way back to the Prophet Muhammad. Sufis say the initiation is more than merely symbolic, however; it confers a powerful spiritual blessing that, without practice, lies dormant in the heart.[1] A copy of the Qur'an was produced, and the disciples took turns chanting verses from it.

The pir then signaled for me to slide to the right, where the most senior khalifa, Sayyid Dawud, was seated. A handsome, regal-looking man in his forties, Dawud instructed me to sit with my back erect and with the tips of my right hand fingers tucked into the palm of my left. Gazing into my eyes with great intensity, he began uttering, "Hu! Hu!" As he repeated this, he lowered his gaze to the area near the base of my spine and made a lifting motion with his right hand. He seemed to exert himself considerably doing this. If my mind wandered or my eyes strayed, he admonished me to refocus. After a half hour, he seemed frustrated with my lack of response.

During the entire time, I could see the center of his heart, beating vigorously underneath his shalwar kameez. Some time later, Dawud rose and moved down the line of khalifas and another took his place.

Meanwhile, the pir and disciples were reciting the Naqshbandi prayers, the *khatm-i khwajagan*. From time to time, he would look over at me while thrusting his palm forward, shouting, "Hu! Hu!" His voice was deep and resonant. After an hour and a half, the session was closed with the communal recital of the khatm-i khwajagan.

My Muslim name would be Ahmad, one of the ninety-nine names of the Prophet.

At midnight, exhausted, I was handed a bedroll and led to a room off one side of the mosque. This room would be my home for the next several months. It was about fifteen by twenty feet with four other disciples living in it. Here we slept, hung out during free time, took our meals, and rested between exercises. Woven with hemp netting, the beds sagged like hammocks. Fortunately, I would sleep on the floor. When I arrived, I expected there would be some resentment toward a fifth person, but instead I was warmly received. I dubbed the room *Utaq-i Farsiwan*, "Chamber of the Persian Speakers," because all of my roommates spoke Persian.

The oldest was "old man Kohistani." Kohistani was a Pashtun from the Kohistan region north of Kabul, the birthplace of Bacha-i Saqqao. Though in his seventies, Kohistani was still surprisingly vigorous. I once saw him on the footpath outside the khanaqah talking to two of the strangest people I had ever seen. Dressed in tatters with a mule in tow, they looked like two fools out of a Middle Eastern folk tale. They were passing by the hospice on their way to Bara and stopped to talk to Kohistani. They were chatting amiably when all of a sudden, I saw Kohistani pick up a large rock and proceed to bash one of the men repeatedly in the head with it. The two staggered off, with one bleeding profusely from the head. I later asked Kohistani what had happened. He refused to tell me. All he would say was that the man was a malang who had said something "very dirty" to him.

Later, when I began to enter the Khyber clandestinely, it was usually Kohistani who would meet me at the checkpoint and accompany me safely to the hospice. Despite his age or maybe because of it, I always felt safe with him. Kohistani looked after my welfare in other ways, too. Once, the pir wanted me to take some of his disciples back to Peshawar. Before I could respond, Kohistani told the pir my car was already full and that it would not be possible to take anyone else. I was surprised at Kohistani's breach of Naqshbandi etiquette. As a rule, disciples do not lie to their pirs. Later I asked him why he been untruthful. "Because they would have ruined your car on these bad roads," he said. For days after, Kohistani took much delight in this innocent bit of mendacity, relating his tale over and over to the other disciples—so much for the anthropologist's canard about the disciple's "blind obedience" toward his shaikh.

I was never quite sure how much of a Naqshbandi Kohistani was. He may simply have been living at the khanaqah because he was old, a penniless refugee without a home of his own.

My other adult roommate was Muhammad Yusuf. Polite and self-effacing, Yusuf was from Herat, once part of the glorious Persian Safavid Empire and still a center of high culture in Afghanistan. As western Afghanistan had long been under Persian influence, Heratis were more cultivated than their Pashtun counterparts. Indeed, virtually every Herati whom I met at the khanaqah seemed more cultivated than other Afghans. Even though Yusuf was a khalifa and a scholar, in our relations he was the perfect egalitarian and always treated me with kindness and respect. He called me his "brother." If I asked him for Persian lessons, he would reach for his Persian reader without giving it a second thought. We often sat on his bed for hours talking about life in Herat before the war.

Yusuf managed the khanaqah bookstore, which was located in an alcove right behind his bed and covered by a worn sheet hung from the ceiling. Usually after prayer sessions, he could be found sitting on the edge of his bed absorbed in a book. If he was not reading, he was in contemplation. Once I walked into the room while he was meditating. When he looked up, I saw tears streaming down his face. Ever courteous, he interrupted his practice to ask what I needed. Embarrassed by my own intrusion into this most private of moments, I shook my head and quietly backed out of the room.

My other roommates were two boys from Nangrahar. Their father, recently widowed, had sent them to the khanaqah to be raised. Whether this was because he was unable to care for them or out of a desire to give them a sound religious education, I did not know. One of the boys, Abdul Haqqiq, was my favorite disciple at the hospice because of his innocence and boyish curiosity about life in America and our Native Americans. Even at his young age he had learned to endure the many privations that his countrymen suffer. He once asked me if America was a bad place to live. No, I said, it is otherwise. "Then will you take me with you?" he pleaded. From my description, America must have sounded like heaven on earth to him.

My roommates kept their entire personal belongings in metal footlockers tucked beneath their beds. These contained their precious possessions: family photographs, an heirloom or two, and a special shalwar kameez for Friday prayer—the meager belongings of impoverished refugees.

The khanaqah had grown considerably in the six years since I had first been there. It was laid out in the manner of an Afridi qala, the buildings facing inward around a courtyard so that the high outer walls served as fortification. When the khanaqah's three large metal gates closed at midnight, it became virtually impenetrable. Other thirteenth-century khanaqahs in the region had been similarly built as protection against Mongol invaders. It was a medieval style of construction that had changed little over the centuries.

Through the visitor's entrance on the left was the mosque, which had been greatly expanded. I remembered it as a dingy pea-green one-room structure. The afternoon I had first walked past it, I turned to steal a glimpse through the side window and saw a large man, whom I would later learn was Saif ur-Rahman. He had been sitting sedately in a chair, his right hand propped on a long wooden staff while all around the room, men were screaming and behaving in the wildest ways.

Six years earlier, everything had had an air of being temporary. But with the prospect of fighting continuing in Afghanistan for many more years, the pir had decided to settle at Murshid Abad for the long term. That meant creating a larger, more elaborate structure to accommodate the growing number of Pakistani disciples. The mosque was now an impressive three-story adobe structure fronted by an arched colonnade.

The ground floor was handsomely carpeted in blue felt. The high ceiling was supported by pillars of white marble from the Khyber's Mullagori mine. Save for the *mihrab*, lined tastefully with beige and blue tiles, the walls of the mosque were windowless and unadorned. The second floor, still unfinished, had another prayer hall to accommodate visitors during festivals such as *'urs*, the annual festival when for three days upwards of ten thousand followers a day may visit the khanaqah to commemorate the death anniversary of Maulana Hashim, the pir's teacher. Labor for the construction of these new facilities was performed by disciples skilled in particular crafts such as plumbing or carpentry.

On each level of the building were several outlying rooms. Some were living quarters for permanent residents or visitors. An important room was a school and day care center for the roughly twenty male and female toddlers residing at the hospice. For disciples with formal responsibilities at the hospice, other rooms served as both bedroom and workplace. In one such room, a disciple ran a store of audiocassette tapes of the pir's sermons and recitations. These rooms were small and, like mine, were shared by several disciples.

The top floor had an open-air common area and a small apartment and library containing several hundred books. The library was managed by a Canadian, a permanent resident of the khanaqah. He was in the process of building an extensive library for the khanaqah. Fluent in Arabic and Urdu, he traveled to the Middle East periodically to collect religious books in Arabic, Persian, and English.

Across from the mosque were two rows of showers, an ablution deck, and several small adobe dugouts for resident disciples. It was in one of these cells that I stayed when I first arrived. They are extremely small, partly subterranean affairs, damp and dark in winter but relatively cool in summer. Some disciples attached newspaper to the walls and ceiling to contain the dust caused by the drying adobe. That first night in the khanaqah I slept on the floor and occasionally in the dark of night felt mice crawling about me.

There was little discernible rank or social order in terms of the housing arrangements. Many senior and elder khalifas shared their tiny cells with visitors, other khalifas, or resident novices. The arrangement was striking by the near complete absence of friction among them.

If a visitor came to the khanaqah for a few days or even months, a place would always be made for him. Despite the cramped conditions, disciples, whether novice or advanced, were always willing to make room for newcomers, as was done for me. On weekends when dozens of disciples visited, some from great distances, they slept and took their meals in the mosque. If need be, they were provided bedding that was stored in large bins in various parts of the compound.

On the north side of the mosque was a large open-air kitchen. At mealtime, huge twenty-five-gallon pots could be seen simmering over roaring wood fires. In the heat of summer the kitchen was an inferno. Here, goats and chickens were butchered and cleaned. Generally, three disciples (a teenager and two khalifas) took turns preparing the meals. Each day an elderly disciple—usually Kohistani—was in charge of purchasing fresh food in the Bara market.

To the west of the mosque, adjoining the back of the pir's house, were two small common rooms (*langars*), one of which contained a small library. These rooms were important, as they were used daily for a variety of purposes: dining, receiving guests, and conducting spiritual exercises.

Across from the langars, separated by a courtyard was a large, covered verandah. When the weather favored, roughly February to November, the pir often sat there with disciples or visitors, especially during holidays and festivals. Once I was eating with a group of mujahiddin who had just arrived from Afghanistan. They looked battle weary and gaunt. We were all eating from one large bowl of rice that contained one small piece of meat, a rare delicacy at the khanaqah. I was eyeing it greedily. Each person eating from the bowl reached in and took a handful of rice, careful not to take the meat. When the bowl was nearly empty, one of the mujahiddin took the meat and handed it to me. When I looked into his hand, I saw only my own shame.

Since some of the visitors were opponents of Sufism who came to debate him, the pir had for a time placed part of his library on the verandah wall behind his chair. Clearly, this was intended to impress upon such visitors the extent of his religious knowledge. He was signaling that he, too, had mastery of the scriptures. The display of books was thus symbolic and contributed to the construction of his public persona. To the rear of the common areas were two vacant apartments, originally built by European disciples who had since relocated with their families to Afghanistan. A stable with six milking cows was adjacent to the apartments. On the north side, a rear gate led to the latrine and the khanaqah's thirty-acre farm.

The khanaqah complex also comprised several outlying homes. The largest was a duplex owned by the most senior resident khalifa. He leased one half to a German family residing at Murshid Abad. On the north side of the pir's house was the modest adobe home of a Nangrahari family of disciples. Father and sons were *dehqanan*, sharecroppers for an Afridi landlord. They worked several acres of land adjacent to the hospice and in Zaka Khel a few kilometers to the west. Still farther on was a large walled compound owned by a wealthy young Afghan khalifa and his family.

Attached to the southeast corner of the khanaqah was the only structure older than the khanaqah itself: the house of an Afridi sayyid family, the pir's disciples who had donated the land for the khanaqah. There were four other houses near the khanaqah, though its residents were not disciples of the pir. I wondered what they thought of the pir and his boisterous spiritual sessions that issued daily from the mosque.

The only area of the khanaqah proper that was strictly off limits was the pir's house. Adjacent to the mosque, it was home to his family of four wives and twenty children, and to some of his children and grandchildren. There must have been thirty persons in the house at a given time.

By restricting access to his house, the pir managed to cultivate a degree of privacy from what was a highly public life. But only a degree, as his house was also the one place in the hospice where female disciples were able to perform spiritual exercises with the pir while maintaining the required segregation (*purda*) from men. So strictly was purda observed that only once did I see a woman entering the pir's house, even though married women from rooms within the hospice went to his house almost daily to work with him. I was stunned to learn very late in my stay that several Afghan disciples who had apartments there were also married. I had never seen their wives. With few exceptions, namely the two pirs believed likely to succeed Mubarak Sahib, even senior visiting khalifas stayed in guest rooms in the mosque.

Overall, the hospice was laid out with a thoughtful and necessary attention to the pir's security. As one approached the hospice from the main road, the first structure one encountered was that of the Afridi family, symbolically signifying the pir's protected status. Next were the public facilities of the khanaqah, the mosque, rooms, and so forth. At the end of the road and last in the sequence of structures was the pir's house, securely ensconced between the mosque and the outlying homes of his disciples. The location of the pir's house, sitting as it did between the mosque and Mecca, also served a powerful symbolic religious function.

A few days after my initiation, I ask the pir's permission, as was customary among disciples, to return to Peshawar. He was listening intently to a tiny transistor radio broadcasting a debate in Peshawar between his disciples and a fundamentalist group. I could not make out what was being said, though it was clearly a heated discussion.

Upon learning that I wished to leave, the pir gave me a reproachful stare. He said that I shouldn't go anywhere until I had learned proper Muslim observance. If I went to a mosque to pray, he said, I would invariably perform the prayers incorrectly and it would redound to his disgrace and the disgrace of the order. He said I must stay and learn how to practice.

"Ahmad, you know, paradise is wonderful," he said with a smile. Nervously, I explained that I had only just arrived and had every intention of learning to practice correctly. I said I would return the next week as soon as I got my affairs in order in Peshawar. He nodded and with a smile bade me farewell. One of the khalifas, a Swiss doctor named Ihsan, remarked approvingly of the pir's caviling, noting I had only been there one day and already the pir was "messing with" me. It was a level of attention that I welcomed as I returned to the khanaqah nearly every week for many months and slowly came to understand how he worked.

Like khanaqahs of the past, the Bara khanaqah was open to all. And so they came on a regular basis: spiritual wayfarers, Muslims seeking personal guidance or a blessing, politicians, clerics, even the pir's opponents. Some Pakistanis came on Friday to pray in the company of a "divine" but were not themselves Sufis. They either did not feel the need or were not prepared to make the kind of commitment required. Disciples came from as far away as Tajikistan and Uzbekistan, usually staying for a few weeks and almost always to benefit from the pir's spiritual blessing power. As word of the pir spread in Pakistan, new disciples came from Lahore, Karachi, Swat, Malakand, and many other Pakistani cities and towns near and far.

Many mujahiddin also came to see the pir. Some had been seriously wounded or maimed in battle. They came into the mosque on makeshift crutches or, if they were lucky, on crude prostheses made by a German charitable organization in Peshawar. They displayed not the least self-pity for their condition. The pir, however, was always visibly shaken to see his disciples in such condition. I came to admire Afghans for their courage and stoicism, so beleaguered they have been over the past few centuries, under siege, by turns, from the British, the Russians, the Communists, and even each other.

There were always disciples who came to the khanaqah for spiritual guidance or to seek counseling for personal problems. Some were Pakistani government officials. Others belonged to a then little-known militia called the Taliban. When the Taliban seized Kabul in September 1994, disciples were elated. When we first heard the news one morning over breakfast, one of the disciples shouted, "We will not stop at the Amu Darya [the river forming the northern border of Afghanistan]. We will go all the way to Bukhara!" This, of course, was a reference to the site of Bahauddin Naqshband's shrine, which is a Mecca of sorts for central Asian Muslims.

The disciple had been speaking out of ignorance. At the time, very little was known about the Taliban, except that they were Afghans who had been educated in madrasas in the refugee camps in the NWFP and Baluchistan. In the beginning, the pir and his disciples viewed them favorably for the simple fact that they represented the triumph of Afghan Islam over feuding mujahiddin parties.

In time, however, Taliban actions caused increasing concern. In areas under their control, there had been reports of improper and inhumane imposition of Islamic law. In one case, a women accused of adultery had been stoned to death on the testimony of a single witness, while the shari'a requires a minimum of three (I regarded both as inhumane). What we would later learn about this still obscure, ragtag militia would portend yet another setback to the pir's mission to return one day to his homeland.

Once some poorly dressed Iraqi students studying in Lahore came to Murshid Abad to meet the pir about whom they had heard much. Although the Iraqis had Sufis, including Naqshbandis, in their own country, judging from their wide-eyed consternation at the disciples' behavior in the mosque, they clearly had never before seen anything like it. Only once during my stay did another Westerner appear at the khanaqah, an Italian. He stayed a few days while deciding whether to take initiation. A chain smoker, he was always sneaking out of the khanaqah to smoke a cigarette. On the third day he left and never returned. When disciples informed the pir, he said, "Let him go," with a disdainful wave of his hand. "He's a drug addict."

Of course, there were opponents of Sufism, usually fundamentalists, who periodically came to debate the pir. Some of them showed up unannounced, and the debates were informal; others were formal, scheduled debates held under the verandah. Whatever the setting, the debates were usually in Pashto and always animated. Whereas his opponents were not well educated and spoke no other languages, the pir spoke Arabic, Persian, and Pashto. During the debate, the pir would quote from this or that text, sending disciples here and there to fetch books so that he could quote from them at length. More than once the pir summoned me to show that his influence extended all the way to America. Some of the debates became heated, and when guests began to raise their voices angrily, everyone became uncomfortable, particularly the pir's bodyguards.

Disciples believed that the pir had a following of more than one hundred thousand disciples, though this was hard to verify. Whatever the actual number, the ways to him were as diverse as his following. Some were following the practice of their fathers, though not necessarily the same pir or silsila; others heard about the pir from friends or fellow worshippers at a mosque. Word of the pir also spread through other sectors of society such as business or government offices and, increasingly, the Pakistani military.

There were disciples, however, who had discovered the pir through less prosaic means, such as in dreams and visions. Muhammad Abid Hussain, from Lahore, was living in Medina when he dreamed of the pir. His Saudi visa having expired, the Saudi government asked him to leave the country. Before departing, he went to the tomb of the Prophet Muhammad. Weeping, he asked for the Prophet's help so that he could continue to visit his tomb. That night the Prophet appeared in a dream saying, "Don't be upset. In your country, there is a pir, Saif ur-Rahman, who is my khalifa. Go and take initiation and sit with him. Sitting [*suhbat*] with him is like sitting with me."[2]

Maulavi Muhammad Arif Akhunzada, of Peshawar, also dreamed of the pir. In the dream, he was sitting in the mosque in the Karak District south of Kohat in Pakistan, where the pir had been invited for lunch. Everyone in the mosque was anxiously awaiting the pir's arrival. Suddenly, an earthquake started to shake the mosque. Arif ran outside to safety.

When the tremors subsided, he went back inside the mosque, where he saw the pir sitting in a snow white chair. Some Qadiris were seated around the chair, relating their own dreams to the pir. The Qadiris said that during the earthquake, they saw Jilani, the founder of the Qadiri order, come out of his grave and sit in the corner of the mosque gazing at the pir's face. Then Jilani put his hand on the ground and the earthquake stopped. Another Qadiri saw Jilani in the sky in the east, in the form of the moon, and the pir in the west in the form of the sun. Interpreting the dream within a dream, a Qadiri said, "The merging of the moon with the sun means that all of Jilani's spiritual powers were transferred to Pir Saif ur-Rahman. Jilani was the greatest saint of his time and Pir Saif ur-Rahman is the greatest of his. In fact, the pir is six times higher than Jilani. Go and study with him."

Abdul Ahad Shah, from Pakistan's Swat Valley, also told of dreaming of the pir. In his dream, he was sitting in a mosque for Friday prayer. After prayer, he looked up to see the pir sitting in the prayer niche, the mihrab. Ahad Shah went over to greet him. When the pir took his hand into his own, Ahad Shah was moved to weep. Then the Prophet Muhammad's voice said, "This is Saif ur-Rahman. He is my disciple. Go and take initiation from him." Shah eventually became a khalifa.

Many other disciples also dreamed of the pir, receiving, Uwaysi-style, spiritual instruction or grace. Qari Abdul Samad, a thirty-two-year-old disciple from Laghman Province in Afghanistan, told me of his own experience. In his dream he was performing the circumambulation of the Ka'aba in Mecca. When he had completed his fourth circumambulation, he saw the pir, who was also performing the ritual. At the sight of the pir, Samad began weeping. The Prophet Muhammad then approached them with grapes in his hand. He handed them to the pir, at the same time instructing Samad to go to the mosque of the Prophet's tomb in Medina, Masjid Nabawi. "There will be a variety of grapes there. Select whatever you want," the Prophet instructed.

As the dream continued, Samad arrived at the mosque to find that the pir was also there. Samad became drawn to his spiritual power. The pir said to Samad that all he had seen was due to the grace of God. Some time after, the pir, apparently cognizant of Samad's dream, told him that the grace Samad had received that evening marked the completion of his education in the Chishti order.

Life at the hospice followed a daily routine. Morning prayer varied with the time of dawn. After prayer, we performed spiritual exercises with the pir for two hours, usually in the mosque. Breakfast followed, usually consisting of black tea and flat bread. Occasionally, there were oranges, though fruit was a scarce commodity. Late morning was free time. Some disciples went off to cultivate the fields or tend the livestock. Others would head off to Peshawar to work or shop. As a novice, I was strictly forbidden from working at the hospice. My only task was to concentrate on my spiritual practice. Afternoon prayer was between 3:00 p.m. and 5:00 p.m. and often followed by more spiritual exercises, as would be the evening prayer. We retired at 10:00 or 11:00 p.m. It was always a full and tiring day.

The eve of the weekly holy day, Friday, was even more intensive. It would begin Thursday afternoon with large numbers of mujahiddin filing in from Afghanistan. So as to spend more time with his mujahiddin disciples, the pir would usually stay in the mosque until very late. With other pirs also coming for the benefit of their own disciples, it was always a spiritually charged time and we all looked forward to it.

When I first visited in the early 1990s, the Thursday session had lasted all through the night until dawn in a kind of spiritual pyrotechnics. However, after my return, I never witnessed any other all-night sessions. When I asked one khalifa why, he said that such all-night vigils had been quite common at one time, but now there were no longer enough pirs to lead them. Pirs, he said, who had managed to survive the Communist pogrom either were too old or had passed away.

As in the private madrasas in the region, education at Murshid Abad was conducted in the traditional manner, highly individualized and informal. Each day a student worked individually with his or her teacher, reading and discussing small portions of a text. Novices were required to begin study of texts on jurisprudence, the systematic elaboration of legal prescriptions of the shari'a. One of the first texts assigned to a novice was *The Light of Explanation and the Salvation of the Spirits* by the Egyptian cleric Shaikh Hassan ibn 'Ammar ibn 'Ali. Written in Arabic in the seventeenth century, the text is a compendium of Hanafi rules for ritual ablution.

On a daily basis about ten to fifteen disciples engaged in such study. Generally, a disciple studied a text with a specific teacher who was a specialist in a particular subject such as calligraphy, Arabic, or theology. When the book was finished, a student could continue with the same teacher or move on to another. In the beginning, I used to sit on a cushion on the top floor of the mosque reading early Sufi texts in Arabic or some of Sirhindi's letters in Persian along with a khalifa. These readings were always intended to drive home a point in one's understanding or practice. Textual study that did not enhance one's personal development and moral edification, one's *suluk*, was regarded as frivolous.

The khanaqah published a few works in Arabic, Persian, Pashto, and Urdu, including books on the history of the Naqshbandi order, hagiographies of saints in the lineage, polemics on Islamic faith, and other books on Islamic tradition. There were also cassette tapes—reproduced on a small cassette recorder—of recitations by the pir of Rumi's magisterial *Mathnavi* and the pir's Persian and Pashto lectures. Since two of the resident foreigners were fluent in Arabic, Persian, and Urdu, from time to time the pir had them translate texts into English or another Western language for the benefit of foreign visitors to the compound.

Life in the khanaqah meant observance of both shari'a and tariqa. While tariqa was wild and ecstatic, shari'a seemed, to me at least, dry and tedious. From the proper form of bathing to eating and sleeping, every detail of life required attention and—in my case—alteration. In terms of one's appearance, this meant growing a beard roughly four inches in length, wearing a turban seven meters in length, donning an immaculate shalwar kameez, *and* observing impeccable hygiene and grooming.

The pir disapproved of long hair and mustaches, though he allowed his uneducated disciples to wear them. Early in my apprenticeship, I conveyed my frustration to the pir about all of the attention to detail that was required. He said, "Ahmad, it is precisely because of the details that this path is a path." Indeed, even early Sufis like Junayd had gone to great lengths to convey that performance of shari'a was not an adjunct to spiritual practice, it was the very organizing principle of it.

An essential aspect of the shari'a was the disciple's exercise of *nisbat*, which means judgment or discrimination in thought and deed. Nisbat was an important means for enhancing the disciple's ability to obtain the pir's grace. One of the cornerstones of nisbat was the observance of the sunna, or prophetic behavior, which the disciple was required to learn in every detail. As the disciple matured in the path through ever more faithful imitation of the Prophet, his behavior became pleasing to the pir. He drew nearer to the pir in a spiritual sense, thereby obtaining his spiritual blessing in greater abundance.

Another requirement of the disciple was *adab*, observation of a strict code of behavior in interaction with the pir. Adab established a relationship between pir and disciple built on respect, obedience, and love. In Letter 292, Sirhindi noted that without adab, spiritual company with the pir would have no effect.[3] Adab required the disciple who visited the khanaqah to first perform ablutions and present himself immediately to the pir. The disciple must bow and kiss the back of the pir's hand. Usually a disciple presented a small token gift at the time. When the pir rose to stand, one also rose. When leaving the pir's presence, one never turned one's back to the pir. The pir was very strict about observance of adab and did not hesitate to educate or correct a disciple when his behavior was *bi-adab*, or incorrect.

Adab, however, never implied blind obedience or submission of the disciple to authority, as Kohistani had demonstrated in his white lie. Rather it was built on the principle of the pir's advanced spiritual realization. A student submitted to his teacher because of the latter's advanced spiritual development.

At the beginning of my stay, whenever I arrived at the khanaqah, I formally shook the pir's hand (instead of the customary kiss) and offered a token gift of fruit. One time, after a long absence from the khanaqah I returned with two kilos of oranges. On the second day of my stay, I was sitting with the pir, waiting for everyone to leave so that I could give him the oranges. When I presented the gift, I was dismayed to see he was not pleased. He then asked me, "Ahmad, where did you get these oranges?"

"I bought them in the market," I said.

"No," he said, "I mean did you bring them from Peshawar, or did you buy them today in Bara?" Somewhat confused by his line of questioning, I said that I had brought them from Peshawar the previous day en route to the khanaqah.

The pir looked at me sternly and said, "When you come to the khanaqah, you come to greet me immediately. This is adab. If you have a gift, you present it to me at that time, not later. If you present it later, it is wasted. It has no effect. It is not adab. Do you understand?"

I replied that I had, although in fact I never really understood what he meant by the act "being wasted." Thereafter, I always made sure to greet him the moment I arrived. Feeling self-conscious, I refused to kiss his hand, however. One day, when I went into the mosque to greet him, I shook his hand, bowed, and began to move on. However, the pir refused to release my hand. Instead, he drew me back.

"From now on," he remonstrated, "when you greet me, kiss my hand—right here," pointing to an area on the back of his hand next to his right thumb. Then he said, "When you come, you give me *something*." I don't care what it is. Even if it is only five or ten rupees, you bring me something. This is adab."

Similarly, adab obligated the disciple to ask the pir's permission (*ijaza*) when leaving the khanaqah. Usually this was a formality, and I never saw him refuse anyone permission. However, he did not hesitate to voice his displeasure if he felt someone was departing too soon. Once I requested permission to leave on the eve of a holiday.

"Where are you going?" he asked, surprised. I stammered that I had to prepare for a trip to Lahore.

"What do you mean? Everything is closed. Really, what do you have to do that is so important? I'll tell you: Nothing. You just want to go home and rest, don't you?" He was right, of course. Life at the khanaqah was extremely taxing—physically and mentally—and I needed to get out regularly to recuperate. Though dissatisfied, he gave me permission to leave nonetheless.

In daily interaction with the pir, adab required the disciple to avoid asking personal or frivolous questions. In fact, the disciple usually spoke only when spoken to, though it was not considered impolite to ask a question. It would have been a flagrantly bi-adab to ask the pir questions about his personal or family life or to make idle chatter. This rule applied not only to novices but to everyone, including his closest khalifas.

I was always astonished by the indefatigable energy and perspicacity with which the pir scrutinized the appearance and comportment of each and every disciple. Each time I arrived, he seemed to take special note of me. And while he was happy to see me, he was usually displeased by my appearance. The first time I returned, he noticed I was not wearing a beard. "Ahmad, what is this?" he asked, holding out his open hands in mock surprise. "You don't have a beard. Where is your beard?"

It had not occurred to me. Facial hair had always repulsed me. I did not want to grow a beard, but I could see this was not going to be optional. The Naqshbandi path involved imitation of the Prophet. If Muhammad had a beard, so would I. A few weeks later, having grown the beard, I decided to trim it to control its growth. When I returned to the khanaqah, I sat in the back of the mosque hoping the pir would not take notice of me. My ploy succeeded for all of fifteen seconds.

"Ahmad, are you shaving your beard?" Sitting so far from him at the back of the dimly lit mosque, I was astonished that he noticed I was trimming it after only a few weeks.

"*Baleh*, Mubarak Sahib," I sheepishly admitted. "*Rish-i man ro mitarasham.*" Then in front of the entire congregation, he held his fist up to his jaw indicating exactly how long a proper Muslim beard should be. And it was not just my beard that did not meet with his satisfaction. Each time I came to the hospice, the pir scrutinized my appearance. My shalwar kameez was too long, my turban too short. And so on.

Once when I went up to shake his hand and obtain his blessing during the festival that marked the end of Ramadan, I inadvertently pricked his hand with a hangnail. It was a small thing, but the pir was visibly angry.

Chapter 5

Ihsan, the Swiss doctor, later told me that he was upset because I had failed to groom myself properly according to the sunna. If the pir was constantly finding fault with me, it was the fault of failing to live up to the Naqshbandi way. He wanted all disciples to be impeccable adherents of the sunna, and he never tired of correcting us. Early on I remarked to a disciple that the pir seemed to be paying special attention to me.

"Everyone says that," he said dryly. He must have heard it a thousand times.

There were enormous expenses involved in running the khanaqah. A visitor to the hospice, for instance, received three meals a day and lodging at no charge. For the many short-term stays nothing was required; those residing long-term were expected to contribute by assuming some of the daily chores. The pir's burden of hospitality was greatest on Thursdays and Fridays, when there were usually one hundred to one hundred fifty disciples present. Electricity was sporadic in Bara—almost totally absent in summer—so a diesel generator powered the mosque during spiritual sessions and prayer. During investiture of the khalifat, the pir often gave cash gifts of two hundred rupees (about five dollars at that time) to disciples. The gift represented a week's wage in Afghanistan.

It was difficult to see how the pir bore these expenses. The absence of an ancestor shrine, so common a feature of dynastic hospices in the subcontinent, deprived the khanaqah of a major source of income. Revenue in the form of donations from disciples was minimal, as most Afghan and Pakistani disciples had little, if any, disposable income. The khanaqah generated a small revenue stream through the sale of literature, incense, and the like.

On Friday mornings after prayer, an open-air bookstall was set up, which offered the order's own publications as well as other books and cassette tapes. Usually, there were no sales. Yusuf usually sat at the book table alone and forlorn, so I would always make it a point to purchase a book from the large selection, some of them about the pir or his edicts.

Then there was the khanaqah's thirty-acre farm, which produced several tons of potatoes, corn, and squash annually. What was not consumed was sold in the Bara market.

Given the meager income that these activities generated, it was remarkable that the khanaqah ran as well as it did and expanded as impressively as it had. It was unlikely that the pir had inherited wealth, for, unlike the clerics in Iran, most Afghan clerics did not have extensive land holdings (a few families did, such as the Mujaddidis and the Gailanis). The pir seemed to rely on wealthy disciples for major infusions of cash when needed. But if such disciples existed, they were never in evidence at the khanaqah. The pir oversaw all of the activities at the hospice—the farm, the khanaqah, and construction projects—with astonishing energy. That he did not delegate these tasks entirely suggested a concern to guard against financial abuse, to which some of his sons and khalifas were prone.

There were two kinds of khalifas in the order. The *mukhlid* was an unconditional khalifa, authorized to teach the spiritual path (*suluk*) and the practice of dhikr. Depending on the means at his disposal and the size of his following, the khalifa may have his own khanaqah. One mukhlid khalifa living at Murshid Abad functioned as the pir's assistant. A few mukhlids from southern Pakistan had a contingent of disciples who functioned as orderlies. An orderly prepared his master's lodging, brought him water for ablutions and food, and otherwise tended to his every need. I never witnessed this phenomenon among Afghans or northern Pakistanis—indeed, that kind of behavior was frowned upon in the khanaqah. But I did witness this among the disciples of the Punjab, suggesting once again the devotional bhakti influence of Hinduism that had so concerned Sirhindi in his day.

Unlike the mukhlid, the *muqayyid* is authorized to teach the dhikr alone; he may not instruct the disciple in any other way. Ostensibly, the first to distinguish the two kinds of khalifas was Ahmad Sirhindi in the sixteenth century. His son, Muhammad Ma'sum, was the first to designate muqayyid khalifas in large numbers, having had over seven thousand. The muqayyid was designated after as little as four or five months of practice, so that there were roughly twenty-five to thirty thousand such khalifas of Saif ur-Rahman in Pakistan and Afghanistan.

To keep track of these deputations, the khanaqah kept a register. Each time a khalifa was invested, a secretary recorded the individual's name, address, and type of investiture in a small notebook. The register verified which khalifas had been properly authorized to teach, thereby warding against fraudulent claims. It also provided a handy reference for Afghans who planned to move or travel to, say, Baghlan Province, of the names of teachers residing in the area.

Upon investiture of the khalifate, each khalifa received a one-page document (*ijaza nama*) elaborately signed in green ink by Saif ur-Rahman authorizing him/her to teach. In a few cases, the pir had given the ijaza to khalifas immediately after taking initiation. By designating so many khalifas, I believe the pir was attempting to counter the perceived decline in moral values and increasing secularization of contemporary life.

Murshid Abad was the seat for all of its satellite khanaqahs scattered throughout Afghanistan and Pakistan. Despite two decades of civil war in Afghanistan, many of these still were still operating, particularly in the north: in Maimana, Mazar-i Sharif, Jalalabad, Herat, and Kabul. Some of the hospices in Afghanistan, however, such as the mother hospice in Dasht-i Archi, had been completely destroyed. The khanaqah in Mazar-i Sharif had many Tajiks and Uzbeks, who periodically came to Bara to benefit from the pir's presence. Interestingly, there were also a substantial number of Sunni Hazara disciples from central Afghanistan, though most Hazara are Shi'a.

Murshid Abad was, then, not the only place where a disciple could formally practice and benefit from the pir's grace. In and around Peshawar were several other centers, each with its own pir and its own coterie of disciples, all linked to the mother hospice in Bara. I often availed myself of them in the hope of connecting with a particular pir and receiving his grace. Disciples having their own pirs was a practice the pir encouraged.

The path led by Pir Saif ur-Rahman was not simply called the "Naqshbandi" or even the "Mujaddidi" but was known as the "Mujaddidi/Saifi." The addition of the term *Saifi* to the Mujaddidi branch of the Naqshbandi order indicated that the pir had founded a new branch of the order. This is a common practice among leading Sufis throughout the

Islamic world, often during periods of great social upheaval. In establishing a new branch, the pir may have also been seeking to distinguish it from the Mujaddidi family line, which had become, by the family's own admission, spiritually defunct. He was also marking a slight departure from certain norms and the introduction of some new spiritual teaching methods.

Over the next several months, I saw Habib, the pir-i piran, frequently. He was always accessible, friendly, and relaxed, whereas Saif ur-Rahman was more formal and, given his office, more imperious. Habib did not have the great burden of being head of this branch of the Mujaddidi order. Less encumbered, he focused on family, business, and his own coterie of disciples. When I saw him for the first time upon my return, he remembered me immediately, shouting in recognition, "Yes, you were the one with the broken leg!" referring to an accident I had just before my departure. One of the khalifas said his remembrance of me was an auspicious sign and urged me to spend time with him.

One day I went to Habib's glass shop and asked one of his sons to guide me to his house located nearby. When I arrived, we chatted politely, and then Habib began *tawajjuh*, the act of transmitting baraka. I started to bob my head as the other disciples did, but he told me to be still. He focused his eyes intently on my heart. After a few minutes I saw his entire body jerk and his back twist as if he had received an electric shock. Several times he winced as if in pain, and it seemed he was probing my interior and absorbing something from within me, some impurity, into himself. My chest was becoming warm and I was eager to continue. After ten minutes, however, his son walked into the room, and Pir-i piran stopped abruptly.

I returned to his house the following week. When I arrived, he was in the sitting room talking to two of his disciples in Pashto. I could make out that he was talking about Sirhindi. Then, beaming with pride, he explained to them that I was in Pakistan on a scholarship working on a study of Sufism. When they left, he began tawajjuh with me, gazing intently at my heart. Occasionally, he would experience an involuntary, violent jolt along the spine. Sometimes he would let go with a "Hu, Allah" and exhale forcefully. We chatted for a while, then he resumed tawajjuh.

At one point, he seemed to have fallen asleep, but his head was rotating in a circular motion, and he was apparently in a deep contemplative state. From time to time, he opened his eyes and focused on my heart. For a while he read a book, written in Persian and published in Turkey, about spiritual messengers; he said it was very good. Watching him read, with his red-hennaed beard and his glasses perched on the tip of his nose, I noticed that at that moment his profile bore an uncanny resemblance to that of the pir.

Later we chatted while lunch was being prepared. When I commented that there was a Turkish Naqshbandi center in New York, he dismissed my remark with a wave of his hand. "Mustapha Kemal," he said disdainfully, implying that the former Turkish President Ataturk's obsession with secularizing Turkey had destroyed Sufism there. We also talked briefly about the Taliban, who had been so much in the news of late. Habib's response was unequivocal. "They know nothing," he said, "about history and things like the French Revolution or even about Afghanistan's own history. They're completely ignorant. How could people like that possibly run a government?"

Pir-i piran was clearly more cosmopolitan than Pir Saif. Many times he had commented that the United States had greatly assisted Afghanistan during the war against the Soviets. He told me he thought that Jimmy Carter had been a weak president but that Ronald Reagan's foreign policy had been helpful to Afghans. He invited me to a Thursday, prayer session at a nearby mosque the following day.

"You come tomorrow," he said. "There are a lot of people there who have powerful tawajjuh and you will get it for sure."

The next day I went to Pir-i piran's house for tawajjuh. When I arrived he was standing in front of his house, smiling. For some reason, he said he could not go with me to the mosque. A large, burly Afghan with a long, pointed beard and a huge smile, Pir Sahibzada, said he would take me there. We crossed the street and headed down a dirt road lined by farm fields. Sahibzada said nothing, and even though I tried to converse with him he did not seem interested in making small talk. We arrived at a village on the other end of the fields.

The mosque was a one-room adobe affair with some rugs and cushions on the floor. On the wall were two scenic posters of Pakistan and a clock. Just as we were about to start, another large man with a wild-looking beard entered. He sat across from me next to Sahibzada, who instructed me to look at the large man's face, signaling the beginning of the session.

During tawajjuh, Sahibzada made wild involuntary movements, jerking, twisting, eyes lolling about in his head, reaching out with his hands toward me, alternately hissing like a snake and moaning. It occurred to me that the jerking was somehow as a result of me, because when he wasn't looking at me he did not make any involuntary movements. The huge man smiled broadly at me, and suddenly I had an irrepressible urge to laugh. I fought to suppress what I thought was inappropriate behavior. Only later did I realize that, by suppressing an instinct to laugh, I might have stifled a breakthough. After about a half hour, another khalifa entered and Sahibzada, appearing tired, let him lead the tawajjuh. When it was over everyone seemed pleased. Despondent, I asked them if I was making progress. They said that they could definitely see that I was.

One day, Pir-i piran phoned me to ask a favor. I was to go to the airport and collect a khalifa who was coming from Paris for his annual visit to the pir. I would be able to distinguish him at the airport terminal by his white turban, Pir-i piran said.

I had assumed the khalifa would be Afghan; indeed when we met I thought he was Pashtun, though this was mostly because of his beard. We were conversing in Persian in the car on the way to Pir-i piran's house when gradually it became apparent from his accent that the khalifa was French. Even more surprising, when we arrived at the house, three Afghan disciples were anxiously awaiting their pir, who was none other than the young Frenchman. Later, as we sat drinking black tea, the Frenchman reached over to one of his elderly disciples, who was jubilant to be sitting with his teacher, and slapped him on the chest. Instantly, the disciple's heart dhikr begin to beat. The disciple purred contentedly like a kitten.

Chapter 5

Despite my time with Pir-i piran, I continued to spend most weekends with Pir Saif ur-Rahman at the khanaqah in Murshid Abad. One day Muhammad Yusuf took me to one of the common rooms there and introduced me to another pir with whom I could work in Peshawar, Ruhani Sahib. We joined Ruhani Sahib and the Pir Saif for lunch. Yusuf had said that Ruhani Sahib projected powerful grace, and as Yusuf focused on his face I noticed Ruhani's head began bobbing up and down rapidly. Next to Ruhani sat a khalifa from Quetta, Abdul Qassim, who would look at me and shout, "Hu, Hu, Hu" so loudly that I thought my ears would burst. Strictly speaking, this was not dhikr, which was always performed silently in the order. Rather, I understood it as an attempt to project baraka vigorously.

These activities went on throughout the conversation and then through dinner. Then the pir asked me if I felt anything. I responded, "No." He then asked me, if I felt nothing, why was my head moving? He was right. My head was bobbing, though I was unable to determine whether it was in sympathy with Yusuf's. The pir laughed.

"Ahmad says he doesn't feel anything," he chuckled, "but his body feels something and he doesn't even know it!" Indeed, my body *was* acting strangely. At night in bed or when I was resting, my muscles twitched incessantly, legs, arms, thighs all fluttering to some kind of internal rewiring. Once when meditating in the mosque with the pir, I briefly saw him as a body of light, emanating light in all directions.

A few weeks later, I was sitting in my room talking with Muhammad Yusuf. I told him I felt I was getting nowhere. He looked at my heart and said, "No, my brother, you are making a lot of progress." I asked how he could tell. He pointed to a mirror hanging on the wall. "It's like that," he said. "When I look at your heart, it's like the mirror."

The following week, accompanied by three bodyguards provided by the Khyber Agency, I went back to Murshid Abad. I arrived just in time for Friday prayer. I was unable to greet the pir formally, so I waited until after prayer to greet him. There must have been a hundred worshippers in the mosque. When he saw me, he beamed, grabbed my now long beard and tugged it. "Ahmad!" he exclaimed. He kept tugging at it and smiling. At last, he liked the beard.

At the start of the session I was told the pir wanted me up front, near him. I was sitting some distance from him and he cried out, "Ahmad! Why didn't you greet me when you arrived? Why did you wait again until after prayer?" Then he reached out and pointing to my heart said, "This is the heart center, right?" I said yes. Then he stuck two fingers into the right side of my chest and pushed very hard. "This is *spirit*," he said. He pushed again, straining inwardly as he did it. Afterward he sat me in front of his khalifa, Dawood, as he tried to transfer his spiritual power to me. After two hours, he stood up and appearing frustrated said, "Oh, this one is weak!"

Later that day, I was in front of the book stall when I heard Ihsan, the Swiss doctor, calling me. He started complaining about some of the Afghans at the khanaqah, warning me to keep my distance from them. Just then the pir's son came up to me and offered to help me get to the khanaqah the next time I came. "You see," Ihsan said later, "they don't offer to help anyone else. Only you. They think you have money. Stay away from them." He said I should be suspicious of the khalifas, for they were the ones most concerned with getting money.

"Does the pir know about this?" I asked.

"In a sense," Ihsan said, "he doesn't want to know, especially where it concerns his own family." Then he started talking about the Barlevi Sufis.[4]

The Barlevis, he said, were the cause of the degeneration of Sufism in Pakistan today. "They don't practice. They just give money to their pirs and expect grace to come of its own accord. They hardly ever see their pir, maybe once in a lifetime."

Ihsan was the intellectual among us foreigners. Tall and gaunt with a stringy beard, he tugged at it pensively when he spoke. He was often very critical of some of the members of the khanaqah, and he always spoke his mind even to the pir. His relationship with the pir was complex. He tended to him as one of his doctors and was a devoted disciple, a khalifa in fact. Yet, on more than one occasion I saw the pir become angry when his name was mentioned. "Ah, he's so critical," the pir would say with a dismissive wave of his hand.

There were perhaps two dozen boys and girls living at the khanaqah, most of them children of the disciples and the pir. They spent their entire time there, studying, performing chores, playing. Boys who had reached the age of puberty were permitted to participate in sessions, though they were accorded low priority, made to sit the farthest from the pir and in the least advantageous places. Few of them showed signs of spiritual awakening. So I was pleasantly surprised one day in the mosque to hear someone behind me frantically pacing back and forth, biting his fist, unable to contain himself. It was my little friend and roommate, Abdul Haqqiq.

Once I saw Haqqiq in the dirt road outside kicking a ball made of rags bound with string. Moved by their meager toys, the following week I brought them a tennis ball. When I handed it to Haqqiq, he was delighted. No sooner had they started playing kickball with it, when old man Kohistani caught sight of the ball. I immediately sensed what was about to happen. He rushed over and stopped the game and picked up the ball. Holding it aloft, he shouted, "Who gave the children this ball?" When I answered that I had, Kohistani proceeded to admonish me about games being *haram*, or forbidden, in Islam. He told me never to bring such corrupting items again into the khanaqah.

If the injunction against recreation seemed extreme, there were also other customs at the khanaqah that gave me pause. One was the practice of *purda*, or segregation of the sexes. Try though I might to attribute it to cultural differences—it is not mandated in the Qur'an—I found the practice unbefitting spiritual life. But the pir had, after all, grown up in the patriarchal Pashtun milieu.

Even though the pir loved his female disciples every bit as much as his male ones, he insisted on strict observance of purda. The custom of observing traditional gender roles was intended to assure not only male dominance but also stability and continuity in family and social life. Nonetheless, to me purda seemed a retrograde and unsustainable practice in a rapidly globalizing world. I was particularly chagrined one day to hear a foreign khalifa lamenting the days when women "knew their place" and stayed in the home to raise a family and maintain the home.

There was also a parochial atmosphere at the khanaqah that was unsettling. Some disciples denigrated other religions as worthless. Once I mentioned to a khalifa that Buddhism, like Sufism, had produced many great saints. With a wave of his hand he said disdainfully, "Buddhism, Marxism, Communism, all of these 'isms' have nothing to offer." Most felt there were no spiritual teachers in the West, despite the migration of dozens of authentic teachers from Zen Buddhist, Hindu, and other spiritual traditions to the United States in recent years. Even Naqshbandis in other countries were dismissed as inauthentic. Only the most learned of the pir's disciples recognized that mystical systems of other major religious traditions shared similar goals if not always similar methods.

My discomfort at some of the customs and attitudes in the khanaqah was exacerbated by the uncomfortable living conditions and the rigors of spiritual practice. Sleeping on the floor in Utaq-i Farsiwan was hard on my weak back. My back was further aggravated by having to sit cross-legged on the hard floor for five hours a day. Because there were so many mouths to feed at the khanaqah, especially during the weekend, food was inadequate and lacked nutrition. By the third day, my desire for meat, fruit, and vegetables was so acute that I couldn't wait to get back to Peshawar to recover for the next weekend.

One day I had a psychological setback. On Friday morning before prayer, I was sitting outside the khanaqah with Abdul Haqqiq, my little roommate. He was helping me read from a small book published at Murshid Abad on the Naqshbandi prayers, the khatm-i khwajagan. When old man Kohistani heard me reading the prayers, I thought he would be impressed. He laughed scornfully.

"Ahmad, what do you think you're doing?" he asked rhetorically. When I told him I was reading the Naqshbandi prayers, he guffawed and said, "Ahmad, you are about as far from the khatm-i khwajagan as you are from America." I looked at him quizzically. Never one to mince words, Kohistani then scolded me, "What are you doing *that* for? You should be doing dhikr, nothing but dhikr, and forget this nonsense." As he walked off, I heard him muttering to himself and shaking his head, "Khatm-i khwajagan. Ha!"

My concerns and frustrations about my failings as a Sufi worsened. If I tried to discuss them with the Afghans, my words would certainly fall on deaf ears. So I decided to talk to one of the foreigners living there, Muhammad Akbar, to learn how he dealt with culture shock and other problems I was having at the khanaqah. Even though he had been there less than a year, Akbar had already become a khalifa and was deeply revered by the other disciples. His transition to khanaqah life was successful. One day after the morning exercises, I went over to him and asked if we could speak.

"Why don't you come for lunch," he suggested.

Around noon I went to his house near the hospice. After taking initiation with the pir, Akbar had moved his wife and two children from Germany to Murshid Abad. I always thought his Teutonic demeanor made him well suited for the kind of wholehearted commitment to the spiritual path required to succeed at the khanaqah.

When I arrived he greeted me warmly and led me into a room lined comfortably with mattresses and cushions. No one used chairs in the hospice, except the pir because of his advancing age and weight. In his mid-forties, Akbar had a large frame and a long grey beard. He was fluent in English but did not speak any of the local languages. This meant there was almost no one at the khanaqah with whom he could converse, outside his own family. Yet he seemed deeply happy there.

Indeed, Akbar was completely devoted to the pir, always at the door in the morning to greet him. As the pir entered the mosque, Akbar would take the pir's walking stick, always kissing the back of his hand before doing so. He had become a khalifa after only five months in Murshid Abad. Once, I was standing in front of the mosque talking to Malang Sahib when Akbar passed by. "Shaikh," Malang Sahib quietly intoned.

I was interested to know how he had come to Murshid Abad. Akbar then related a remarkable story. He always referred to the pir by his title, Mubarak Sahib.

"I used to own a nightclub in Bonn," he said. "I made a lot of money and got rich quickly. Still in my twenties, I had everything a man could dream of: beautiful women, a BMW, a beautiful home, even a vacation home in Spain. I smoked the best cigars and drank the best brandy. I had the best of everything—the best. Sometimes I lit my cigars with rolled up currency just to flaunt my money. But after a few years of living like this, I started feeling dissatisfied. I felt hollow, empty; something was missing."

Akbar paused. Reaching up with both hands, he adjusted his turban.

"I was getting tired of my life," he continued. "I wanted something else, but I didn't know what it could be. I started trying various Western, New Age therapies. One day a friend from college introduced me to Islam. Something in it felt right. I liked the fact that in Islamic countries men pray together five times a day. When I came here, I came for the communal prayers. I didn't know anything about Sufism, or Islam for that matter, and I wasn't Muslim. So you can imagine my surprise when I came here and found Mubarak Sahib and Sufism. It was icing on the cake!"

One of his children entered—a small, redheaded girl—and served us a plate of cucumbers, tomatoes, and onions. After the Spartan conditions at the hospice, I felt as if I were dining in a fine restaurant. Akbar resumed his narrative.

"The beginning was difficult for me. I could not sit on the floor and I had to use a chair in the mosque. I practiced hard, so hard, you can't imagine. I sat in the mosque all day doing dhikr. On the fifth day I got it," referring to the visible beating heart that marks the transcendent moment in Naqshbandi Sufism, the awakening of the spirit.

"Well," I said, "I've been here two months and have only an aching back to show for my efforts. I don't like wearing a beard, either. I can't believe you got the dhikr as fast as you did."

"Not as fast as my wife," he said. He reached up and removed his turban. "The night I took initiation with the pir, I phoned my wife back in Germany to tell her the news. I was shocked by what she told me."

"What?" I asked.

"She said she was at home with the children when a wave of bliss and peace came over her and her heart started beating right through her shirt. Of course, she had no idea what was happening. She didn't know anything about Mubarak Sahib or Sufism. It occurred about the time I was taking initiation. This is how powerful Mubarak Sahib's grace is," Akbar said. "I don't understand it, do you? It's a miracle."

His daughter came in with plates of some grilled kebabs and flat bread. Some plastic cups were produced and she poured us cold water.

Akbar said his wife enjoyed a special connection to the pir that preceded his interest in Islam. This connection was manifested in a series of recurring dreams. The most striking was a dream that presaged their conversion to Islam several years earlier. In the dream, he said, "A flying carpet arrived at our house. We both got on it and the carpet took off in an easterly direction. After traveling a great distance, she looked down and saw a mountainous, arid land with camels roaming the landscape. At that point, the carpet started to descend to a house. In front of the house was standing a man with a large white beard and turban."

Akbar's wife later took initiation with Pir Saif. Her visions and premonitory dreams had since increased.

"In the beginning, I was like you," Akbar said. "I didn't like wearing a beard, so I trimmed it. When Mubarak Sahib noticed, he told me to let it grow. As it grew and I learned how to imitate the Prophet Muhammad, I received so much grace. It was astonishing. What I'm saying makes no sense, I know, but that's exactly what happened. The more I practiced the shari'a, the more grace I received."

"Life is hard here," he admitted, "very hard. But this is the first time in my life that I am truly happy."

Akbar then related another story that he said was by no means unique. The preceding year a German who was not Muslim happened to hear Pir Saif ur-Rahman's voice on a cassette tape, which put him into a state of ecstasy called *jadhba*. Determined to meet the man who had such a profound effect on him, he traveled to Bara. When the pir walked into the mosque and came into the German's physical presence, the latter again went into ecstasy, tearing at his clothing so violently that he lacerated his chest. He stayed in Bara a few weeks, during which time he was invested with the khalifate. He was given contacts back in Germany with whom to follow up for further training when he returned.

"What is it like for you now?" I asked Akbar.

Akbar reached for his turban and ran his hand over the crown of his head. "The grace has disappeared. It's been a while now, some months and . . . nothing. It's been a dry spell. This is a test . . . from God. My faith is being tested now, so I have to be steadfast now during this difficult time. But it's hard. We are being tested in so many ways," he sighed.

Akbar's one-year visa was about to expire, and he was worried that the Pakistani government would not renew it. Concerned by the deteriorating situation in the Khyber, the NWFP home office was no longer renewing foreign visas. An official had told me as much when I obtained my visitor's permit. Akbar's prospects for staying at the khanaqah seemed dim. Still, he was confident that he need only have faith in Mubarak Sahib and his visa would be granted.

Akbar's conversion had been so complete—and the grace he received so abundant—that my complaints would have sounded trivial, and they were. I could only express doubts about my spiritual aptitude. "Don't worry, it'll come. You must focus on the pir. Put your attention on him, open up, and he'll do the rest," he reassured me.

As we rose to leave I headed for the door and caught a glimpse of his wife furtively rushing into the kitchen. Akbar severely reprimanded me, pointing out that when a guest in his house, I must let him lead the way so that I would not see his wife. "Mubarak Sahib is very strict about purda," he said. It had been a good thing, I decided, that I had not raised my concerns after all.

Several weeks later, Akbar received a visa extending his residence in the Khyber for another year.

It wasn't Akbar's pursuit of hedonism but the attainment of it that led him to Islam. It is a typical theme in spiritual life and in Sufism: when the appetite for gratification of carnal or worldly desires—what the Sufis call the *nafs*—is satiated, one comes to the farther reaches of oneself. One experiences a kind of existential exhaustion that can ignite a quest for the spiritual. It happened most famously to the Muslim theologian Al-Ghazali in the eleventh century. Having risen to the most prestigious professoriate in the Islamic world at Baghdad's Nizami madrasa, he underwent a spiritual crisis that led him to abandon his career and eventually become a Sufi. This kind of conversion—unintentional, profound—was not an intellectual act, but existential, a movement of the heart.

Not only had Akbar become a devout Sufi, he had comfortably assimilated Pashtun customs that I found objectionable. His ability to sit cross-legged for long periods of time was an astonishing physical feat for a middle-aged man. Although I admired his accomplishment, Akbar's wholehearted embrace of Islam was not something I felt I could imitate.

Not all disciples were as enthusiastic as Akbar. Another of the foreigners living at the hospice was Ihsan. An Austrian with two medical degrees, he was one of the pir's two attending physicians. He had been living in the Khyber hospice for several years, though initially he had resisted moving there. Like me, Ihsan found certain aspects of the hospice objectionable. Partly for this reason, I could better relate to him and his story.

"I became a disciple of Mubarak Sahib in 1986, but I decided to stay in Austria," he recalled. "The conditions here were too primitive and so are the Afghans. Just look at them!" he scoffed. "They're animals! When I first came here I was repulsed by the conditions. They were much worse than they are now. We had no bathrooms, and we had to defecate in the fields. The khanaqah was small in those days, and it was so crowded you couldn't even sit on the floor. At night we slept shoulder to shoulder on the floor. I awoke in the morning covered with insect bites. I was so repulsed by the conditions, not to mention the food, that I went back to Austria. I thought if I came once a year to see Mubarak Sahib, it would be enough.

"So each year, I came here for four or five weeks. I did the exercises, over and over, each year for six years . . . and nothing happened. Each time I came to Murshid Abad, I felt close to a nervous breakdown and had to run off to a hotel in Peshawar. Nothing was happening to me. Everybody seemed to be getting something but me. I began to doubt I would ever get it. All the disciples around me were having experiences and I was getting nothing. I started to think that I was not cut out to be a Sufi, that this was not my path. I even began to think that perhaps I wasn't cut out for spiritual life." Ihsan tugged pensively at his stringy beard as he talked. "Then one day I was sitting in one of the langars doing exercises with some of the khalifas. The next thing I knew I was on the floor."

When I asked him what he experienced, he said only, "Awe."

Ihsan was so moved by the experience that he decided to move to the Khyber for good. He showed me the dugout in which he had lived during his first year. Adjacent to the woodpile and partly submerged, it had a dirt floor and was windowless. Of all the rooms I saw at the khanaqah this was clearly the worst.

"You must have gotten a lot of grace to live in *that*!" I joked.

"I did," he said, matter of factly. "Now I just sit back and let Mubarak Sahib do it all. It is incredible, like watching a movie."

Ihsan built a small apartment attached to the hospice and took an Afghan wife. The pir selected Ihsan's bride, arranged marriages being the custom in the region. In selecting the proper mate, the pir took into consideration many factors. At first, he had identified a Pakistani girl for Ihsan, but feeling she was not sufficiently educated to be a suitable companion for a polyglot with two medical degrees, he finally settled on an educated Afghan woman.

"Are you happy?" I asked him.

"Very," he said.

I recall his having said the same thing another day while sitting cross-legged on the sofa in my house when one of his teeth suddenly fell out. "Look at me," he said, shaking his head and holding out the tooth, "I am falling apart!" Then almost inaudibly he added, "But I am happy."

Over the past twenty-five years or so, the post-everything (post-modernism, structuralism, colonialism, positivism) attempt to portray "how the natives think" (or thought), or even what they are doing when they do what they do, has come in for a good deal of moral, political, and philosophical attack. The mere claim "to know better," which it would seem any anthropologist would have at least implicitly to make, seems at least faintly illegitimate. To say something about the forms of life of Hawaiians (or anybody else) that Hawaiians do not themselves say opens one to the charge that one is writing out other people's consciousness for them, scripting their souls.

—Clifford Geertz

Anthropology is more like a religion.

—Napoleon Chagnon

Chapter 6

Ascent

Early travelers to the Islamic world were appropriately mystified by the allegiance the disciple paid to his pir and by the behavior of the disciples in the pir's presence. French traveler Arminius Vambery (d. 1913) was one of the first Westerners to record his observations of the Naqshbandis. While visiting Bukhara in the middle of the nineteenth century, he encountered a group of Naqshbandi disciples passing through town.

> When I entered this place, as fate would have it, still farther to enhance the interest of the exhibition, there were passing by, in their weekly procession, dervishes of the order of the Nakishbendi, of whom this city is the place of origin and the principal abode. Never shall I forget that scene when those fellows, with their wild enthusiasm and their high conical caps, fluttering hair, and long staves, danced round like men possessed, bellowing out at the same time a hymn, each strophe of which was first sung for them by their gray-bearded chief.[1]

Vambery was at a loss to explain the nature of what he had seen and the first of many investigators who have been unable to form an accurate understanding of what Sufism actually is.

As Western contact with the Islamic world increased, other observers were even more puzzled by the physical shaking and convulsions of Sufi disciples. In North Africa, French *colons* had a particular interest in the seeming hypnotic hold shaikhs had over their disciples, because Sufi shaikhs were the principal leaders of jihads against them. All along the tribal frontier of Afghanistan, shaikhs also led their disciples in jihads against the British. Unable to decipher the nature of the shaikh-disciple relationship and their strange antics, the Europeans with their superior technological knowledge concluded that it was the irrational behavior of a superstitious and backward people.

After Islamic countries achieved independence, university-trained anthropological investigators picked up where colonial researchers had left off. Research continued to be shaped by the unequal power relations between the two sides. Though Sufis had ceased to be a political threat in the postcolonial period, they still fared poorly in the hands of Western academics. Social scientists—modern, rational—traveled to the Islamic world to investigate the "mystical brotherhoods." Though anthropologists studied different orders and in different regions, the research agenda was almost always the same: ferreting out the latent dynamics that would explain the shaikh's putative sanctity.

Such views of the Sufi privileged the ethnographer's voice over the native one. In place of mystical ecstasies and encounters with the spirit, ethnographers hoisted political, social, and economic explanations—anything but what Sufis said they were doing. Since some of the orders studied were dynastic lineages that had become spiritually defunct and operated simply to maintain family power, prestige, and wealth, what researchers found merely confirmed assumptions about the unregenerate native.

The eminent twentieth-century British anthropologist, E. E. Evans-Pritchard, studied the Sanusi order in Libya, which had waged a spirited, decades-long resistance against the Italian colonization of North Africa. Perpetrating the stereotype of the religious warrior, Evans-Pritchard wrote that the Sufi orders "flourished only among the intellectually backward and in regions where anarchy reigns." The simple Bedouin, illiterate and bellicose, was unfit for religion, Evans-Pritchard said. Therefore, he followed his shaikh—in this case, the reclusive and scholarly Muhammad ibn 'Ali al-Sanusi—in the only way that a simple people can, "personally" and into battle.[2]

Less ideologically driven scholars readily acknowledged an inability to account for certain facts. In his historical account of the Muridis of Senegal, the Irish political scientist Donal Cruise O'Brien believed the order was an adaptation to the social and political upheaval wrought by French colonialism. Those whose lives were displaced by the French conquest found solace in the "traditional bond" between master and disciple, one that provided social belonging and an economic livelihood in the Muridis' cultivation of an important cash crop, the groundnut.

But when Cruise O'Brien turned to the life of the order's saintly founder, Amadou Bamba, he was unable to account for the Muridis' devotion to Bamba: "Their veneration is the more inexplicable as Amadou Bamba seems not to have had any of the flair for self-presentation which accompanies a charismatic appeal."[3] He was equally at a loss to explain how Bamba, despite a life of seclusion and meditation, drew so vast a following that the French were twice compelled to exile him. To Cruise O'Brien and others, it was becoming clear that what drew disciples to the shaikh was something having to do with the shaikh's personality.

The eminent German sociologist, Max Weber, was perhaps the first scholar to attribute a saint's sanctity to something he called "charisma." For Weber charisma was a quality that set certain individuals apart from ordinary men and caused them to be "treated as endowed with supernatural, superhuman, or at least specifically exceptional power." Weber noted that charisma was generally "regarded as of Divine origin," which resulted in the individual's being "treated as a leader."[4] For this reason, he regarded religious charismatics chiefly as social revolutionaries. He characterized charisma as "irrational" and stated that it "repudiates the past, and is in this sense a specifically revolutionary force."[5] As a sociologist, Weber was more intrigued by the social implications of the relationship between the holy man and his follower than by the source and nature of the phenomenon itself. Subsequently, an entire generation of anthropologists would apply Weber's concept of charisma to the Sufi orders they studied.

Other investigators viewed Sufi charisma as little more than the effect of worldly success. Pakistani scholar and social critic, Ahmed S. Akbar, contended that a prominent nineteenth-century Swat valley Sufi, Miangul Abdul Khaliq, was able to build a following simply on the basis of money. "Funds and followers go hand in hand with a charismatic leader and are a vital index to his fortunes. There is a circular and cumulative causation between funds, followers, and charisma."[6]

For the distinguished American anthropologist Clifford Geertz, Sufi sanctity was merely an idea, one that became compelling by virtue of the shaikh's socially powerful position. Acknowledging that "baraka means blessing, in the sense of divine favor," he argued that instead of being a "paraphysical force, a kind of spiritual electricity," as adherents maintained, it was merely a "doctrine" and a "cultural gloss on life."[7]

Another attempt at an explanation was the attribution of the shaikh's power to fanciful tales and stories gullible followers told about him. "Miracles," contended one British anthropologist, "are made every day in cafes and conversations, and it is there that they are created, reproduced, and transformed."[8]

Interpreted in these ways, Sufism becomes an anachronism, a vestige of the backward past that would eventually give way to the enlightened, rational, secular vision of the West. Miracles and extraordinary states are a consequence of the ignorance and poverty of believers, the creation of superstitious minds. Miracles play a role, not in the moral and spiritual development of the disciple, but only in the exercise of religious power and social control.

No doubt many of these theories have been valid at different times and in different social, historical, and geographical contexts. A distortion occurs, however, when these theories are applied a priori or paradigmatically to *all* the orders. Admittedly, such theories were the dominant ones in their day and they allowed little possibility for accepting the truth claims of Sufis. Methodologically, it would also have been difficult for non-Muslims to gain access to Sufi practice and ritual as I did.

Ironically, the inability of Western researchers to grasp the true nature of Sufism was aptly illustrated seven centuries earlier by the Sufi poet Rumi in his cautionary tale of the four blind men. The four were made to touch an elephant. Each was asked to describe it according to the part he had touched. To the one who touched the trunk it was a water pipe, to the one who touched the leg it was a tree stump, and so forth; but no one was able to grasp what the object was in its entirety. The elephant is, of course, the spiritual universe of the Sufis.

The Naqshbandis, like other schools of Sufism, maintain that in addition to sensory and intellectual modes of cognition, a third mode exists: gnosis. Based on the principle that modes of knowing and being are linked, gnosis is attained when the disciple follows a path (*tariqa*) of moral purification and mental contemplation under the initiation and guidance of a spiritual master. The process is intended to undermine narcissistic and exclusive identification of consciousness with self. With the aid of his shaikh, the disciple progresses through more advanced stages and states of consciousness, culminating in realization of the disciple's conscious identity with spirit as the fundamental ground of existence.

For Sirhindi, that realization was almost immediate. In little time, he had traveled far into the Naqshbandi universe and drew on his considerable philosophical and literary skills to map that universe in great detail.[9]

The Naqshbandi spiritual universe begins with its cosmology (fig. 6.1). The world was created by God's eternal and uncreated Formless Essence. Sirhindi maintained that although God created the world, it was entirely distinct from His Formless Essence. Formless Essence gives rise to four levels of manifestation, each level descending from subtle qualities (*latifa*) toward gross material existence.

The first level of manifestation is Oneness, or Essence. It is connected to the Formless Essence by a transitional realm called the Quality of Wholeness, which acts as a bridge between the uncreated and created realms.

The second level of manifestation, Unity, has two dimensions. The higher one, the Unity of Essence, represents the oneness of the divine, whose attributes are undifferentiated. The lower one, the Unity of Being, contains the rudiments of the divine attributes.

In the third level of manifestation, Uniqueness, attributes such as life, power, and knowledge are differentiated. In other words, they begin to take

Chapter 6

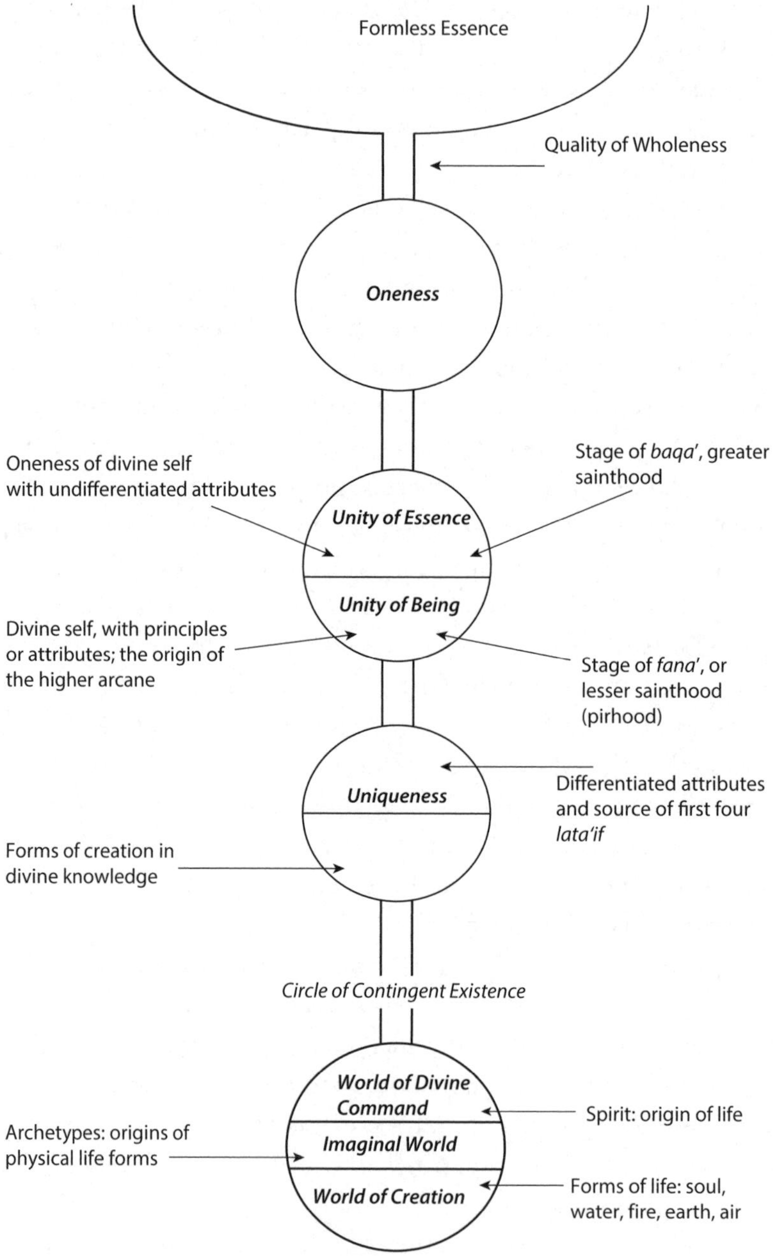

Figure 6.1 The Naqshbandi Cosmology.

on a distinct form of their own. There are also attributes of negation, which actually affirm God's majesty because they deny all imperfections in God (e.g., he has no equal, no beginning or end). The fourth level of manifestation, which contains man and the created world, is called the Circle of Contingent Existence.

On the upper level of the Circle lies the World of Divine Command. The term derives from the Qur'an and has a long history in Sufi thought. It is attributed to such verses as the following: "The Spirit is from the command of my Lord" (17:85). Insofar as the World of Divine Command is linked to the higher levels of manifestation, it is the macrocosm. Its direction is one of ascent, and God's Unity of Essence is the goal or end of the spiritual journey.

On the lower level of the Circle is the World of Creation, the gross physical world, which comprises the four elements and man's nafs, or lower nature. The World of Creation represents the microcosm, and its direction is one of descent.

Between these two worlds lies the Imaginal World. It is a world of ideas or images where abstract forms exist prior to their creation in material form. These abstract ideas are analogous to the Platonic archetypes. They represent a creative as opposed to merely imaginative realm.

As a deeper realm of consciousness, the Imaginal World is the locus of Sufi visions, dreams, and psychic contact with teachers, living and dead. It is how the Prophet Muhammad and Uways were able to commune spiritually at a distance. It is also the level of consciousness where disciples may receive initiations or gnosis from a pir. These events play an important role in spiritual life, providing guidance, spiritual commissions and initiations, and directing disciples to their choice of shaikh.

The two Worlds of Divine Command and Divine Creation, of ascent and descent, macrocosm and microcosm, coincide in humankind. Humans simultaneously inhabit all three dimensions of created existence: body, mind, and spirit.

Chapter 6

Humankind

Creator<------------------spirit---mind---body------------------>Created

World of Divine Command ***World of Creation***

Non-Sufis are aware only of the first two domains: body and mind. Each of these domains has its own modes of perception and relational exchange or association. The body, rooted in time and subject to processes of growth and decay, employs the five senses to mediate the external world. The mind, too, lies in the temporal domain, and its function is to interpret or attach meaning to what the bodily senses convey. It has its own five "senses," which are memory, imagination, thinking, hallucination, and desire. Mind and body cannot perceive divine reality as such, though they do employ symbols to represent it. In other words, because body and mind are subject to temporality, a person cannot access the spiritual domain of his own accord.

Naqshbandis believe that each path has its own unique principle or method for ascent to the divine. The method used by the Chishti order, for example, is based on the principle of going beyond the sense of a separate self. Its methods emphasize activities that provoke ecstasy, such as the spiritual concert and greater submission to the shaikh. By contrast, the Qadiri order aims to undermine self-structures with rigorous ascetic practices such as fasting and long prayer vigils.

Naqshbandis eschew such practices, maintaining that theirs is the best and fastest path to the spirit. Whereas mystical experience is the end point of the other orders, in the Naqshbandi order, the disciple receives a taste of mystical experience at the outset of his or her apprenticeship. Sirhindi called this *indiraj-i nihaya dar bidaya* (inclusion of the end in the beginning). As one khalifa told me, "In the Naqshbandi order you get the grace right at the outset of practice and not at the end like the others." This sudden opening to the transcendent is what Akbar and Ihsan had experienced and what the shaikh and his khalifas were trying to transmit to me.

Naqshbandis do not begin the process of spiritual transformation in the world of creation. To begin the process there would entail a struggle with one's nafs through self-mortification. It is akin to trying to jump over one's knees. While Sirhindi believed that self-mortification could cleanse the nafs, the process alone could not lead to the transcendent World of Divine Command. Spiritual awakening begins with the infusion of baraka in the heart latifa, which is located in the World of Divine Command. Sirhindi claimed that significance of the heart in spiritual discipline was affirmed by Bahauddin Naqshband. The term *naqshband* signifies the shaikh's imprinting or fixing (*band*) the sign of God's name (*naqsh*) in the disciple's heart.

A network of seven subtle centers in the body called *lata'if* (the plural of *latifa*) forms the basis of the Naqshbandi spiritual path. Each latifa opens progressively with the practice of dhikr.

The term *latifa* derives from the Arabic word *latif*, meaning "sensitive" or "subtle." The lata'if were first mentioned by Sufi contemporaries of Junayd. They derive from such Qur'anic verses as the following: "If thou makest utterance aloud, verily He knows the mystery and what is most hidden [arcane]" (20:7). The seven lata'if were first elaborated by the fourteenth-century Kubrawi mystic, 'Ala al-Dawla al-Simnani, who linked them to the seven Prophets of the Qur'an and the seven grades of being that constitute the ascent to God.

The lata'if have been alternately described as subtle centers, sheaths, fields, or bodies. To describe them as subtle centers, however, is misleading, for the lata'if have no real fixed location and could be anywhere in the body. Logically, if they were fixed, they would be bound by the temporal world. The one exception to this may be the heart, which is the only subtle center linked to a particular organ of the body. Indeed, the throbbing of the heart latifa is so visible as to indicate an as yet unknown physical connection to the heart.

While dense matter is subject to the laws of time and space, the lata'if are subject only to the laws of space. The lata'if are local manifestations of a higher realm of the cosmos that lies outside the realm of created things. In providing a framework to facilitate the disciple's reception of divine grace, the lata'if are a spiritual morphology, a framework for the spirit's descent and attachment to the human frame. Naqshbandis maintain that the lata'if form the morphological basis for Sufism found in some form in all Sufi orders and without which it cannot be Sufism.

The lata'if allow one to participate in realms beyond one's individual identity. They represent various levels of being that possess their own inward "senses." However, the thirteenth-century Iranian Kubrawi Sufi Najm al-Din Razi warned not to conflate the functioning of the lata'if with that of the normal senses:

> In the same way that none of the five outer senses can interfere with the functioning of another, hearing being unable to perceive the visible . . . so too none of the five inner senses can interfere with the functioning of another. The intelligence cannot perceive that which is visible to the heart. . . . Thus when those who survey the rationally comprehensible with the gaze of the intelligence wished to survey the world of the heart, the mystery, the spirit, and the arcane, again using their fettered intelligence in ignorance of that which the heart beholds and the other degrees of perception, inevitably their intelligence fell into the trap of philosophy and heresy.[10]

The first five lata'if (fig. 6.2) are located within the World of Divine Command. The last two are located in the World of Creation. The first four lata'if are linked to God's attributes in Uniqueness, from which they receive their baraka. The fifth originates in the Unity of Being. Each latifa is associated with a particular color and a prophet who is believed to have specialized in that particular latifa. Disciples say that the dominant color of each latifa can be seen when the eyes are closed. When two centers are activated at the same time, a mixture of their respective colors appears. Not all disciples experience colors, however, and such experience is thought to occur in an inferior realm of consciousness called the "psychic."

The first latifa is the heart, located two inches below the left nipple; its color is yellow, and its prophet is Adam, the first man. The second, spirit, is located two fingers below the right breast, opposite the heart; its color is red, and its prophet is Abraham. On the left side of the breast, above

WORLD OF DIVINE COMMAND

Latifa	Location	Domain	Prophet	Color
heart	left breast	divine actions, divine attributes	Adam	yellow
spirit	right breast	affirmative attributes	Abraham Noah	red
mystery	left breast	essential attributes	Moses	white
arcane	right breast	negative attributes	Jesus	black
higher arcane	sternum	divine self	Muhammad	green

WORLD OF CREATION

Latifa	Location	Domain
soul	center of forehead	egoic self, passions or soul
physical body	crown of head	the four elements: air, fire, water, earth

Figure 6.2 The Spiritual Morphology of the Naqshbandi/Mujaddidi.

the heart lies the mystery; its color is white, and its prophet is Moses. On the right side, opposite the mystery is the arcane; its color is black, and its prophet is Jesus. The vertical passage between the four lata'if corresponds physically to the sternum and is called the higher arcane; its color is green, and its Prophet is Muhammad, the apex of the World of Divine Command.

The next latifa is the soul, located in the middle of the forehead between the eyes. The last latifa, the *qalab*, corresponds to the physical body and is composed of the four basic elements: water, air, earth, and fire. Each successive latifa both includes and transcends the previous one. Thus, the first four centers are enfolded and completed in the fifth, or higher arcane.

Each latifa has a particular set of moral and contemplative practices required for its mastery to "brighten" it, as one khalifa told me. Heart requires the disciple to cultivate humility and perform long prayers and prayers of repentance. The domain of spirit enjoins the disciple to ignore this world and to fast. At this stage, the disciple may experience visions. In the domain of mystery, the disciple follows the shari'a and is morally steadfast within. In arcane, one is God-fearing and avoids even things that are permissible for other Muslims. The disciple should also recite the divine negation and reject all doubts. One feels God's love at this stage. In higher arcane one follows the inner shari'a and recites personal prayer. At this stage, the disciple gains gnostic wisdom. The higher arcane stage in Unity of Being marks the stage of a *wali,* or "saint."

The higher realm of Unity, Unity of Essence, is the highest stage attainable. For beyond this lies God's essence, which is unattainable but conceivable. Formless essence lies even beyond man's ability to conceive. Humans can come to know only the divine self but never God's Formless Essence.

The last two lata'if, soul and qalab, are rooted in the physical world. Within qalab are four additional lata'if, which have their origin in the four spiritual lata'if. Water derives from spirit, fire from mystery, air from arcane, and earth from higher arcane. The origin of the soul is in the heart. It is always possible for the disciple to backslide, and once achieved no stage is fixed or permanent.

The lata'if are activated by God's original divine effulgence (baraka) through the agency of the shaikh. Baraka is passed down from God to the shaikh via the Prophet Muhammad and the silsila of Naqshbandi preceptors. While many Sufi manuals adduce the specific qualifications of a true shaikh or pir, none is more important to the process of spiritual transformation than his possession of baraka or tawajjuh.

Although these two terms have slightly different meanings, they refer essentially to a pir's emanation of divine grace. Originally the term *baraka* appeared in the Qur'an but only in the plural, signifying "blessings."

In addition to its presence in the body of the shaikh, baraka is also found to varying degrees in the tomb sites of saints and holy men. This explains why historically Naqshbandis have frequented tomb sites and placed importance on constructing and visiting them.

Without a pir's baraka, an aspirant cannot progress, for one's individual actions lie solely within the created world. For this reason, in the Mujaddidi order, the dominant value is tawajjuh, the ability to project baraka. While baraka emanates from khalifas, it emanates most forcefully from the Mubarak Sahib and other pirs. Obtaining baraka is the reason for visiting and residing at the hospice and accounts for the veneration disciples have for the pir. As important as baraka is, no one lays claim to controlling it. Rather, Naqshbandis say baraka originates from God, khalifas and pirs serving as repositories and conduits for its transmission to others.

This, then, is the meaning of the shaikh's charisma. It is not some quality of the personality, but a force that exists independent of the human personality. It is a blessing power that emanates from the physical body. One etymology for the word *charisma*, in fact, goes back to the word *karamat*, or "miracles" in Arabic, of which the shaikh's baraka is deemed the highest.

In the Naqshbandi order, typically a pir first bestows this baraka in the disciple's heart at the time of initiation (bay'a) by placing his four fingers on the heart latifa and pronouncing the name *Allah* three times. At this stage, the disciple is a passive recipient in the process. Afterward, he is given training and instruction (in both the shari'a and tariqa) designed to enable him to attract and become more sensitive to his pir's effulgence. He receives guidance in observance of the prophetic sunna (with the aim of subduing or controlling his nafs); he is also required to progressively perform more advanced spiritual exercises in order to open the lata'if.

In my time with Mubarak Sahib, the pir always began with the heart latifa; one cannot advance on the spiritual path until it is first opened. Thus, the heart is the first and most important latifa. Thereafter, the pir initiated each latifa when he deemed the disciple was prepared to undertake the next step.

Not all such initiations require the pir's physical presence, however. Some occur in the realm of the Imaginal World. One of the pir's khalifas who was also a scholar related the story of a man who, after his first initiation, received initiation in the higher arcane. Surprised the pir had forgotten the four preceding lata'if, the man pointed this out to him. The pir replied, "Don't you remember I gave them to you in a dream?" Upon hearing this, the man suddenly recalled the dream and went into ecstasy.

The term *tawajjuh* comes from *wajh*, or "face" in Arabic, and means "facing" or "confrontation." It was originally used to denote the act of facing Mecca during prayer. The Qur'anic basis of the term is the statement by Abraham, "I have turned my face towards Him who created the heavens and the earth" (6:79). In the Naqshbandi system, *tawajjuh* signifies the khalifa's projection of baraka in order to awaken the disciple's lata'if. Tawajjuh is the principal exercise for awaking dhikr in the disciple's heart. Not only did Pir Saif ur-Rahman perform tawajjuh, but khalifas and even advanced disciples, that is, anyone emanating baraka, may perform it. As an aid to tawajjuh, the khalifa may envision his own heart filled with the Muhammadan light via the silsila of Naqshbandi teachers, which in turn is directed outward toward the disciple. Others simply concentrate their gaze on the disciple's heart latifa or whichever latifa the disciple is working on.

Tawajjuh can take place at any time or place, and there is nothing intrinsically formal about the process. Once I went to the khanaqah at Pabbi Station Noushera to see Ruhani Sahib, who was known for his powerful tawajjuh. Upon greeting me in the parking lot, he smiled broadly and said, "*Insha'llah*, we will get your dhikr going this weekend." Then, reaching over with his right hand, he placed it on my heart and began tawajjuh while we stood waiting for our car to arrive.

Often khalifas perform tawajjuh on the disciple during casual conversation between them. The khalifa may alternate his concentration from one latifa to another in an effort to stimulate them. Whenever possible, the disciple should focus his gaze on the khalifa's eyes or face and eliminate distracting thoughts.

An integral part in awakening the lata'if, tawajjuh also cleanses the disciple of impurities in the form of destructive habits or undesirable behavior, that is, actions not in conformity with the shari'a. During tawajjuh it is not possible for the khalifa to absorb the disciple's destructive habits. However, insofar as baraka is projected outward from khalifa to disciple, it is possible for the disciple to absorb impurities lingering in the khalifa. The one-way nature of the transference notwithstanding, khalifas often experience symptoms of nausea, intense headaches, or fatigue after prolonged periods of tawajjuh. The pir, too, is said to have suffered these unpleasant aftereffects. Indeed, some of his health problems are attributed to the negative effects of tawajjuh.

From the disciple's perspective, it is not so much mentally as physically exhausting. After an hour's practice, I was always so exhausted that I was forced to lie down for an hour. When I communicated my fatigue to a khalifa, he said, "Yes, in the beginning it's like this. I got very tired too. This is the Naqshbandi way—lots of tawajjuh followed by plenty of rest and huge quantities of food."

The essential practice by which the disciple awakens the lata'if is through the practice of dhikr. *Dhikr* derives from the Arabic root *dhakara*, which occurs frequently in the Qur'an as believers are enjoined to "remember" God. Among the many Qur'anic verses cited by Sufis to support this practice is "remember God with frequent remembrance and glorify Him morning and evening" (33:41). Although used by early Sufis as a means of excluding distractions and drawing nearer to God, with the development of the orders in the twelfth century dhikr became a fixed ritual.

Westerners who earlier came into contact with the orders believed dhikr induced a kind of trance state, but the aim is just the opposite. Dhikr intensifies awareness in the disciple. In Murshid Abad, formal dhikr sessions were held two or three times every day for about one to two hours at a time. The only exception was during the month of Ramadan, when, because of the rigors of fasting, the schedule was curtailed.

The disciple must sit cross-legged, his hands joined together, usually the left hand clasping the right wrist. He should not recline against anything or on his hands. He should relax, clear his mind, and open himself to the shaikh's baraka. Ideally, dhikr is performed in the physical presence of a pir or anyone emanating baraka. The optimum position is sitting directly across from and as close as possible to the shaikh. One gazes at his visage while silently repeating the divine name "Allah, Allah, Allah," concentrating on the heart latifa. Additionally, one may picture the name *Allah* inscribed in Arabic on the heart. When not in a pir's physical presence, one may focus on a mental image of him. Representations of the pir in photos or drawings were eschewed because of the Islamic injunction against visual representation of the Prophet.

The pir was always present at these sessions. In fact, during the year I spent visiting Bara, he was not absent for a single one. Apart from formal sessions, dhikr is considered a constant process, and disciples must endeavor to be always in dhikr as the pir was said to be. Dhikr is an ongoing, cleansing process designed to overcome the lower self (*nafs*) and activate the lata'if, thereby bringing the disciple closer to God and thus closer to his innermost nature.

As a technique of contemplation-repetition, dhikr suspends the individual's conscious identity with the mental-egoic self while simultaneously invoking the deeper ground unconscious. *Dhikr* means to "recall" or "remember," precisely because it intends to connect with one's deeper—and higher—identity prior to the body-mind. Dhikr is thus the *act of remembering or recognizing one's original nature*, or "the face you had before you were born," as Zen Buddhists say.

In keeping with the precepts of their lineage, Naqshbandis shun the use of musical instruments or dancing during dhikr, which distinguishes them from many other Sufi orders. The only voluntary movement permitted is a rocking from side to side or other subtle, rhythmic movement of the body used to attune one to the dhikr's inner rhythm. Strictly speaking, there is no spiritual concert as in other orders such as the Chishti. However, during the Thursday evening dhikr, disciples chanted Qur'anic verses and hymns of praise to the pir. They were usually joined by a chorus of five disciples chanting, "Hu, Hu, Hu!" Despite the absence of musical instruments, the effect was very much like a concert. Nonetheless, the rhythmic exuberance generated by such activities was no more than support to dhikr, as evidenced by the fact that many sessions were completely devoid of them.

At the khanaqah, one could always benefit from regular formal dhikr sessions in the presence of the pir. After noon prayer, the pir would take his seat facing the congregation, with his back toward Mecca. With the pir seated at the head, disciples would form an oval stretching out from him. The khalifas (i.e., those with the most baraka) sat on both sides of the pir. If other pirs or senior khalifas were present, they sat closest to Mubarak Sahib. On Thursday evenings, disciples were constantly drifting in so that the oval gradually expanded, eventually reaching the perimeter of the mosque. Disciples faced khalifas for the express purpose of obtaining their baraka. Marbles were distributed to the advanced disciples and to Mubarak Sahib as a device to aid the counting of the Naqshbandi prayers. The qari, who sat to the left of and several persons removed from the pir, would begin chanting verses from the Qur'an as disciples began dhikr. For their part, khalifas would shift their gaze from one disciple to another, usually to those whom they knew or had been instructed to assist. In a few minutes the silence would be broken by several shouts: "Ya'llah!" or "Hu! Allah. Hu!" Others would begin hissing, weeping, and laughing.

As the intensity of a session built, some disciples would rise to their feet. One would be in the corner biting his nails, nervously pacing back and forth, his fist held tight to his mouth as if to suppress some overwhelming inner pain. Another might be on all fours. He would begin crawling toward the pir, moaning and rolling sideways over and over on the floor until he reached the perimeter of the circle, where his movements would subside. One disciple, who might be standing in the middle of the circle, would pick himself up and drop his body sharply onto the hard floor. Over and over he would do this, seemingly oblivious to pain. Some disciples would run full bore around the mosque. Many, though, would still be seated in their cross-legged position, their heads nodding rhythmically. Occasionally their arms would fly up abruptly into the air or their torsos would jerk suddenly, but otherwise those seated were relatively subdued.

Periodically, disciples shifted position by drawing their feet beneath them to recite the prayers silently. Those who were in ecstasy were of course excused from this practice. Such sessions continued for an hour at more or less the same pace. They did not generally build to a crescendo. The pir signaled the end had arrived by lifting his palms up and leading disciples in prayer. If it was not one of the day's formal prayer times, some disciples would leave while others stayed for an additional hour of *suhbat*.

The practice of suhbat is a special feature of the Naqshbandis. *Suhbat* signifies companionship and refers to the spiritual benefit the early Companions received from being in the Prophet's company. During suhbat, the disciples are in the pir's company in an informal setting. Novices were always expected to attend these sessions in order to hasten the awakening of the lata'if. At any time during suhbat, the pir might decide to discuss a particular aspect of the teaching with visitors or disciples. Rarely did the conversation take the form of idle chitchat; it always centered on a particular religious or personal problem or topic. As in formal dhikr, disciples in suhbat silently repeated the name of God while gazing at the face of the pir.

Suhbat sessions occurred on a daily basis for the men, often around the evening meal. About a dozen disciples would gather in the larger of the two langars adjoining the pir's house, seated on mats along the perimeter of the room. They sat facing each other but were angled slightly toward the front of the room, where the pir sat. If khalifas were present, novices sat across from them. Within a few minutes, the pir entered and took his place in his chair at the head of the room.

He was fastidious about the disciples' proper posture while seated, and if someone was angled too far toward the front or leaning against the wall, he instructed him to adjust accordingly. Many times I tried to cheat by using a cushion to support my weak lower back. The pir never failed to notice, motioning with a wave of his hand for me to move from the wall. As many times as I tried this tactic, he never showed that he was vexed with me.

The atmosphere was relaxed, with the pir usually conversing with those sitting nearest him. All the while disciples were in dhikr, repeating "Allah, Allah, Allah" as they gazed at the face of the pir. Some disciples would suddenly shout, "Ya'llah!" or "Hu!" so violently as to send shock waves through the room. Others began rolling on the floor or heaving suddenly. No notice was ever taken of these outbursts, and the conversation continued without interruption.

When dinner was served, those in ecstasy quickly recovered. We might dine on bread, rice, and a little meat followed by green tea. With dinner out of the way, suhbat would resume, this time more intensely. Within several minutes, someone would begin chanting "Hu, Allah!" Soon others joined in. Those who were responding to the pir's baraka would now be on their feet chanting "Hu, Allah! Hu, Allah!" moving toward the pir and back again in unison, like an undulating wave.

Others who were not so inclined continued to sit on the floor. The pir was now smiling, his head gently inclined to his heart side. From time to time, he jerked strenuously to his left side to project his baraka more forcefully. Both sides of his chest, heart and spirit, were beating so vigorously that it was visible through his heavy tunic. Ninety minutes into the suhbat, the pir rose unceremoniously to prepare for the night prayer.

Another kind of suhbat occurred in the mosque, usually on Thursday evenings, when many khalifas attended expressly for the benefit of disciples. Thursday suhbat was the week's longest and most intense, lasting between two and four hours. Khalifas would form a long row at the head of the mosque, with the pir at the center. Usually the most senior khalifas sat closest to the pir. The optimal position for obtaining baraka was sitting directly facing and as close to a khalifa as possible or about a meter away. Since there were usually more than one hundred disciples in the mosque at that time, the remaining disciples would gather behind the head row of disciples, trying to get as close as possible to the khalifas.

The pir would orchestrate the entire session from start to finish, moving disciples here and there, calling forward those overlooked in the back so that everyone had an opportunity to sit at the front row. The pir always gave priority to those whose heart latifa had not yet been activated. For this reason, he made certain to seat novices across from the most spiritually powerful khalifas or himself.

The pir's own relaxed behavior contrasted starkly with the wild ecstasies generated by the suhbat. As several disciples chanted over a microphone set on one side of the mihrab, Mubarak Sahib would smile broadly, tapping his foot and snapping his fingers to the rhythm, completely unbound, no longer merely the stern expositor of the shari'a but now the ecstatic mystic, revealer of the heart's hidden secret. Hallaj, the ecstatic. It was the pir at his most animated. From time to time, he or his khalifas would make a showering motion with their arms to dispense the blessing in greater abundance. Disciples swooned in response. Once, the pir did this while a blind man was seated across from me, his back to the pir. He reacted instantly with a cry that bordered on pain.

The intense mental effort required of the disciple at the beginning was only temporary. For when the heart latifa became activated, it operated automatically with much less mental effort required. Disciples said that it was the pir who placed the dhikr in the heart; the disciple need only open his heart in order for the process to occur.

Once established in the heart, dhikr manifests as a regular beating so pronounced that the organ itself appears to be beating outside the body. Virtually every disciple and khalifa in whom the heart dhikr was activated exhibited this sign. In the pir's case, both sides of his chest beat alternately, heart then spirit and back to heart. In the spiritual sense, Naqshband signifies the fixing, in the purified tablet of the heart, of the imprint of the divine name *Allah* by means of silent and permanent dhikr.

In some cases, the heart latifa opened right during initiation. In a few rare instances, all the lata'if have been known to open simultaneously. Although the vast majority of initiates experienced nothing during initiation, the process was regarded as ongoing even if there were no immediate attendant signs. Typically, with intense practice of dhikr, the lata'if began to open within a year after the disciple took initiation. No one, not even Mubarak Sahib, claimed to know the reason some individuals responded more quickly than others. To some extent, the process depended on close adherence to the shari'a, regular prayer, constant dhikr, and nisbat. Still, some disciples never succeeded in manifesting the dhikr. One of Mubarak's own family members came every fortnight for over a year but never showed any signs. In this connection, Mubarak Sahib said, "I cannot open every heart. You must first believe."

During dhikr sessions, disciples might experience any number of involuntary reactions from vocal outbursts to physical movements. Naqshbandis distinguished between voluntary sounds and movements that were forbidden and involuntary ones that were permissible. Vocal reactions covered a range of sounds from monosyllabic utterances to intelligible words: "Hu!" "Ya!" or "Ya'llah!" Disciples might also groan, sigh heavily, laugh, weep, hyperventilate, or scream. One disciple, who always sat next to me during dhikr, invariably laughed hysterically, an act that would have been considered sacrilegious under any other circumstances. The different responses were attributed to one's essential spiritual nature (*mashrab*).

More dramatic were the physical reactions. Generally, these consisted of uncontrollable jerking of the limbs or sudden spasms in the torso. A few disciples ran around in circles in the mosque or rolled uncontrollably on the floor. One disciple would literally roll all over the mosque for an entire hour, screaming and weeping. Others suddenly took off running through the mosque at full speed, over other disciples. During the annual festival the previous year, one hapless disciple injured himself when he ran directly into the wall of the mosque. When asked why some disciples responded more violently than others, a khalifa said, "It is probably their way of responding to the magnitude of what they are witnessing."

In the beginning I was fascinated by this wild behavior. In time, however, I came to view these dramatic reactions as annoying and disruptive to my own practice, as did others. A Pakistani khalifa, who was also an Islamic research scholar, pointed out that several years ago disciples were more subdued during dhikr than they are today. He attributed the more extravagant behavior to the pernicious influence of Barlevi Sufism of the Punjab.

In the nineteenth century, Barlevi Sufis redefined the relationship between shaikh and disciple. Whereas Sirhindi emphasized rigorous mental and moral discipline supplemented by the shaikh's baraka as the means for spiritual development, Barlevis tended to dispense with personal responsibility entirely, placing sole emphasis on the intercession of the shaikh in order to gain salvation. Reflecting devotional practices of Hinduism, Barlevis believed the shaikh's intercession could be gained through love of the shaikh alone.

In practice, this devotion was expressed in visiting of shrines, writing poetry, attending the annual festival, donating money to the pir, and presumably, the kind of histrionic behavior occurring in the Bara khanaqah. After the arrival of Barlevi Punjabis in Bara, many Afghans were quick to imitate them. Once again, the Indian influence that Sirhindi had struggled against centuries ago had begun to infiltrate the Mujaddidi Sufism that had been preserved unadulterated in Afghanistan's northern hinterland.

As a rule of thumb, those who were most demonstrative in dhikr tended to be the less educated. Low in social status and self-esteem, they engaged in extreme displays in order to gain a standing in the khanaqah they lacked in the world at large. This was partly corroborated by the fact that the better educated Afghans tended to be more sedate, though not entirely. Their movements were confined to a bobbing of the head, a spasm of the torso, or vocal outbursts. Western disciples were the least demonstrative of all in dhikr, perhaps a function of the Western emphasis on individual self-control.

Yet, even while khalifas recognized that some extravagant displays were the result of performance or excessively emotional, because so many somatic reactions were genuine, they followed Junayd's ninth-century admonition not to interfere with the process. Only in rare cases did a disciple become so uncontrollable that he had to be restrained. Moreover, not all involuntary movements were indicative of the awakening of the lata'if. Wild movements were considered indecent and imperfect, taking place in the "psychic," transitional realm between the ego and spirit. Conversely, not all openings of the lata'if were dramatic or ecstatic. A senior Pakistani khalifa told me he had never experienced wild behavior or violent physical reactions in the presence of the pir.

In some disciples, the opening of the lata'if might result instead in a sudden change in undesirable or destructive behavior. Apart from the visible flutter of the heart, neither the pir nor his senior khalifa exhibited any dramatic physical reactions. Senior khalifas might often utter "Ya'llah!"

or emit a heavy sigh, but such generally was the extent of their involuntary reactions during dhikr. This suggests that the spirit's descent initiates a kind of purgative process in the body, which stabilizes with maturing practice.

No one takes much notice of these displays, and any attempt to discuss them is dismissed. Occasionally, the pir would evince a smile of amusement when a disciple, who had shaken his hand, would be thrown violently to the floor, rolling backward so uncontrollably that he seemed as if he were a leaf borne on the wind. However histrionic it may have been, the pir's smile conveyed his pleasure at the outward validation of his spiritual sanctity.

When two or more lata'if became activated, dhikrs borrowed from the Qadiri order were used to stimulate them. The disciple silently recited the name *Allah* while focusing attention on the heart latifa and then "Hu" while focusing on the spirit latifa, alternating so rapidly that the two words merged together. There were many varieties of these dhikrs. Another dhikr employed repetition of "Hu" as the disciple circulated the interior energy vigorously in a circular motion around the lata'if one hundred times. These exercises pointed to the existence of a current of energy in the body when the spirit was awakened. The weeping, shaking, and other involuntary reactions are likely merely the effect of the energy current encountering somatic obstructions as it attempts to establish itself in the body.

When all of the subtle centers were opened, a more advanced dhikr technique, called "the recollection of God though negation and affirmation," was used to stimulate all of them simultaneously. Khidr, the mysterious green one who appears to Sufis in moments when their souls bear witness to the transcendent, is alleged to have instructed Ghujduwani in this technique while Ghujduwani was submerged in water. The disciple was not allowed to undertake the practice until instructed to do so by the pir. The disciple had to set aside at least one hour of solitude in the morning or evening for this practice.

While there were a number of variations on this technique, it consisted essentially of the following: The disciple placed his tongue on the roof of the mouth and was not to exhale through the mouth. Silently pronouncing the divine negation "*la*," the disciple then drew the sound from the area of the navel to the crown of the head. Then, while pronouncing "*illaha*," the disciple directed concentration in a line running from the crown of the head to the right shoulder cap, from there driving the final refrain, "*illa'llah*," forcefully into the heart. The formula was repeated one hundred times and closed with "Muhammad is the messenger of God, messenger of God, and peace be upon Him."

Once the lata'if were completely opened, the disciple had attained the rank of lesser khalifa. According, the Shah Wali Allah, the disciple, having completed his journey through the lata'if, was then dominated by the latifa that was strongest in his nature. One whose heart latifa was dominant, for example, would experience states of ecstasy and longing. Since each latifa corresponded to a particular Prophet, the disciple's spiritual character, or *mashrab*, was said to be *Adami mashrab* or *Muhammadani mashrab*, as in the case of Saif ur-Rahman in contrast to his teacher Maulana Hashim, who characterized himself as *Musoui* (Mosaic) *mashrab*.

After the seven lata'if were opened through dhikr and completely cleansed through "negation and affirmation," with the teacher's permission the disciple undertook the last stage of practice: repetition of the Naqshbandi Contemplations. Originally numbering twenty-four, they were expanded to thirty-six by Shah Rasul Taloqani. The Contemplations are advanced spiritual exercises designed to lead the disciple to the higher realm of Unity. They were performed for an hour, usually after the afternoon prayer, often in the presence of the pir. They were also performed alone at night. The practitioner was cautioned of the pitfalls of falling asleep during the exercise. As with obligatory prayer, the disciple was required to perform ablutions before the contemplations. The disciple remained on a single contemplation for a number of days determined by the pir and could not lessen the time required for each. Nor might he proceed to the next one without the pir's permission. At each stage he was required to inform the pir regarding his experiences.

In the first contemplation, the disciple contemplated Oneness, then he proceeded to contemplate the differentiated attributes. In contemplating the various qualities and attributes of Uniqueness, the disciple's task was to invite baraka from the source of each of the four lata'if by way of the Naqshbandi silsila. The objective was to return each latifa to its origin and thereby achieve its annihilation. Once the disciple had annihilated the first four lata'if, he entered the stage of lesser sainthood. This stage marked pirhood. It was here, in the Unity of Being, that the disciple lost interest in worldly things and experienced the annihilation of the ego, or *fana'*. Admittedly, few Sufis attained this state, as evidenced by all of the competitive jealousies among the khalifas. Sirhindi maintained, however, that this stage was an unstable condition marked by uncontrollable fits of ecstasy. When the remaining higher arcane latifa was annihilated in the Unity of Being, the Sufi then entered the Unity of Essence, the stage of greater sainthood. Greater sainthood was represented in the concept of *wahdat al-shuhud*. The disciple abided in a state of calm and quiet union with God's unity of essence (*baqa'*).

The contemplations performed in greater sainthood also produce benefits in the nafs, leading to a total elimination of bad habits and desires. Thus attained, the baqa' state is analogous to that of the *bodhisattva* in Buddhism: the saint returns to the world transfigured, serving as a moral and spiritual exemplar to awaken others. By virtue of these twin criteria—the overwhelming power of his baraka and his exemplary behavior—Saif ur-Rahman was a living embodiment of this stage. In keeping with his stature as the greater wali, he had returned to the world spiritually transfigured. His sanctity, his charisma, was an embodied spirituality.

Not only did the pir "show the gifts of God to the people," but through the effulgence of his mysterious baraka he dispensed them freely to all who came to Murshid Abad.

If many anthropologists have failed to understand the fundamental nature of Sufism, so, too, do many Muslims and with far more grevious consequences for the pir and his disciples.

The Jews were split up into seventy-one or seventy-two sects; and the Christians were split up into seventy-one or seventy-two sects; and my community will be split up into seventy-three sects.

—The Prophet Muhammad

Islam, they say, is a stumbling block to the progress of the state;
This story was not known before and now it is the fashion.
Forgetting our religious loyalty in all our affairs
Following Frankish ideas is now the fashion.
Alas, in this childish game we came off worst.
What we lost is clear; I don't know what we gained.

—Ziya Pasha

Chapter 7

The Battle for Islamic Tradition

Although in Afghanistan and Pakistan there have always been—and still are—many traditionalists like the pir, including clerics who were not Sufis, there were also many religious leaders who were relinquishing the old traditions. Reform movements in the region appeared as early as the eighteenth century. While there were different kinds of reform movements, each arising in response to a different need, they all shared a common concern over a perceived weakening of Islam in society. During his lifetime, Saif ur-Rahman had to contend with two major types of religious reform: political Islam in Afghanistan and fundamentalism (for want of a better term) in Pakistan. The fact that Naqshbandis were among the founders of these reform movements illustrates both how reform resulted in an eventual rupture with its spiritual (read: Sufi) roots and the effectiveness of the pir's own response to social change.

Since the Prophet's death, reform of Islam has been the subject of an ongoing debate among religious leaders. That debate becomes particularly acute during periods of political and social upheaval or during a perceived decline in the moral status of the Islamic community. There have generally been two major approaches to coping with these crises: revival and reform.

Revival derives from a prophetic utterance that on the eve of every century God would send to the community an individual to renew its religion. Revival signifies an affirmation of the fundamental principles that accumulated during the first millennium of Islam: the Qur'an, the sunna, the four schools of law, mysticism, philosophy, and theology. Together these form the cornerstones of the Sunni Islamic tradition. Whether the concern is the community's moral decline or change in the social and political structure, revival entails no major reformulation of the teachings. It is simply a renewal of practices that have fallen into disuse, not an attempt to reformulate or reconstruct new Islamic responses to change. The idea of revival is contained in the term itself: *tajdid*, "renewal." The person who renews Islam in this sense is a *mujaddid*, as was Sirhindi.

Revival is not an entirely static approach to change. There have been reformulations that gave each revival movement a distinctive intellectual action and framework. Sirhindi, for example, was the first to designate two types of khalifas in the Mujaddidi order, in order to spread the teaching more rapidly and provide wider access to the order's baraka.

Sirhindi's revival philosophy was institutionalized in the Deoband Seminary in India. Deoband was established by clerics and Naqshbandis in 1867, ten years after Britain's devastating suppression of the Great Rebellion. Deoband eschewed politics, even opposition to British colonialism, dedicating itself to educational and scholarly activities. Deobandis turned inward, relinquishing for all time concern with matters of state and colonial politics. The curriculum at the seminary reflected Sirhindi's synthesis of the two main streams of Islamic tradition: textual study and the mystic path, complimentary aspects of a single religious tradition. The Deobandis' abiding concern was to protect, pursue, and transmit the authentic Islamic heritage. To this end, Deobandis, many of whom were Naqshbandis, preached, wrote, offered legal opinions, debated opponents, and acted as spiritual guides to their followers. By disseminating correct knowledge of Sunni doctrine and practice, they sought to restore an Islam weakened and in disarray.

In contrast to revival is *islah*, or "reform." The term *islah* appears frequently in the Qur'an and refers to striving for the moral perfection of individuals. Islah is directly related to the task of the long line of God's messengers whose works are described in the Qur'an. Those who work for islah, called the *muslihun*, are frequently praised in the Qur'an, and they are described as being engaged in the work of God. In its early application, islah meant rejecting Sufism as innovation and advocating a return to the Qur'an and hadith as the only acceptable bases of religious authority.

What makes reform possible is reformers' rejection of the four schools of law. Reformers criticize Muslims who practice *taqlid* (imitation of legal prescriptions) as blind followers of antiquated practices. Reformers feel the old methods are inadequate to deal with the new challenges facing the community. Reformers stress the need for *ijtihad*—or individual interpretation of the Qur'an and the sunna—provided one has sufficient education to do so.

In their attempt to revitalize Muslim educational and legal institutions, early reformers were well aware that they were attacking the traditional structures of society. Yet they felt it was necessary in order to bring about a much-needed social and cultural rejuvenation of the community. To the extent that reformers sought to effect social change, arguments put forth by them deal more with political and sociocultural concerns than with moral and spiritual ones. Thus, while both taqlid and islah seek to revitalize Islam, taqlid does so by reaffirming the existing Sunni heritage; islah, by contrast, advocates changing that very heritage.

Afghanistan had long remained immune to the crises that spawned reform movements in other parts of the Islamic world. For this reason, the pir often referred to Afghanstan as the last true shari'a country in the Islamic world. After the debacle of Amannullah, succeeding rulers had reached a modus vivendi with religious leaders and the tribes that effectively removed Islam as a subject of debate for the next two decades.

But by the mid-twentieth century, creeping secularization prompted some religious figures, including the branch of the Mujaddidi family in Kabul, to adopt an entirely new tactic to defend Islam: Islamism, or political Islam. The Islamist movement began in Afghanistan in 1952 in the faculty of theology at Kabul University. Members of the faculty had studied at Al-Azhar in Cairo, where they came into contact with the Muslim

Brotherhood, whose founder, Hasan al-Banna', was one of the architects of Islamism. *Islamism* was a modern term for a modern phenomenon: the attempt to define Islam as a political ideology in line with the major ideologies of the twentieth century.

Islamists represented an entirely new generation of religious leaders in Afghanistan. Whereas traditional Afghan clerics were educated in the private Deoband and Barlevi madrasas of the subcontinent, Islamists were products of state madrasas. Their roots lay not in private religious networks but in the modern sectors of society. They also owed more to the intellectual ferment of Egypt than to the revival or even the reform movements springing up in the subcontinent. Islamists were urban products of a colonial or quasicolonial environment that looked out at and against the West. Their Western orientation was reflected in the term they used to describe themselves: not *'alim* (religious scholar) but *roshanfikr*, or a new (i.e., Western) kind of intellectual.

Echoing the ideas of the Muslim Brotherhood, Afghan Islamists advocated a form of Islam based on the political ideologies of the West. While some Islamists were sympathetic to Sufism, they rejected revivalism as being an ineffective foil against the West. They felt strongly that the political quietism and religious conservatism of the shaikhs were themselves obstacles to modernization. Islamists thus represented an abrupt departure from traditional Afghan society.

One of the leading Islamists in Afghanistan was Sebghatullah Mujaddidi, the current hazrat, or head, of the lineal branch of the Naqshbandi/Mujaddidis. Like other Islamists, he studied Islamic law at Al-Azhar. From the time he returned to Kabul from Al-Azhar in 1952, he became active in the Islamist movement in Afghanistan, to the detriment of his role in the Naqshbandi tariqa. Sebghatullah refused offers of government jobs, choosing instead to maintain the authority of Islam among the young by teaching at a government madrasa. After the Communist coup in 1978, he went to Peshawar, where he established a new party, the National Liberation Front. From 1989 to 1992, he served as president of the Afghan Interim Government. Afterward, he remained in Peshawar and continued to play a leading role in Afghan politics.[1] He later served in the post-Taliban Afghan government but is now retired.

When I met with Sebghatullah at his home in Peshawar, I was struck by both his deep piety and his dynamic personality. Speaking in impeccable English, he told me he was not a pir, admitting that Hazrat Nur, who died in 1956, had been the last pir in his family. Insofar as Sebghatullah's activities were a departure from the family's traditional role as initiating shaikhs, his political views may have resulted in an ideological division within the family. Signifcantly, after Nur no one in the family line was able to serve as the recipient of the Mujaddidi order's baraka, passed down for centuries from shaikh to disciple. One wonders if Sebghatullah's inability to succeed as pir was a consequence of the very secular influences he struggled against. Whatever the reason, the Mujaddidi family had relinquished the essential part of their Islamic identity passed down since Sirhindi: the mystical.

When I asked Sebghatullah what he thought of Saif ur-Rahman, he was dismissive. "He's no pir. He gives initiation to anyone who comes to his khanaqah. It used to be that a disciple had to wait years to be accepted by a shaikh. What kind of pir is this?" Sebghatullah, apparently, had not considered that the rapid initiation of disciples might be the pir's approach to revival of Islam in troubled times.

Saif ur-Rahman's answer as to secularization was simple: take refuge in the traditions. Yet, to do this, the pir was forced to navigate culturally and spatially outside the modern sectors of society. His early education took place in private Pakistani madrasas, not the modern, state-sponsored madrasas then springing up in Afghanistan's urban areas. His pedagogic training in the Deoband tradition, strong in Pakistan's rural areas, was based almost exclusively on the positive accumulated wisdom gained in the first ten centuries of Islam. As a spiritual disciple and teacher, the pir chose, moreover, to live in northern Afghanistan. Living in the hinterlands placed him beyond the reach of a weak secular state and other modern influences. It also placed him outside the sphere of the powerful Pashtun tribes. Though born a Pashtun, he shunned the role of tribal arbiter often played by Sufis, including his own father. Thus, during the relatively halcyon days in Afghanistan in the first half of the twentieth century, traditionalists went largely unchallenged; the pir was free to pursue his own spiritual development and the development of others in the traditional manner of Naqshbandi/Mujaddidi shaikhs.

In the 1960s, when the larger world outside began to encroach on the relatively stable society of northern Afghanistan, the pir at first seemed to have been beset. When he discovered his brothers' involvement in local politics, he left the country. In Pakistan he first sought counseling from another Naqshbandi, Abdul Salaam. A shaikh in more urban Pakistan, Salaam may have advised him on strategies for dealing with his brothers' activities and the growing influence of the state. When he returned to Kunduz, the pir continued to follow a policy of ignoring the state. Though he was concerned about the social and political changes taking place in the country, his revivalist position narrowly defined the parameters of his activities.

This position, however, did not imply quietism. Even though the pir refused to adapt the teaching to modern forms of political expression, he nonetheless played an important social role in the discourse on reform of Islam. Concerned with addressing the perceived decline of Islam, he maintained that the correct response to modern change was simply to ignore it and to seek refuge within a Sunni mystical tradition reaffirmed by Sirhindi three centuries earlier. For the pir, the very idea of adapting Islam to modern political structures contained the seeds of traditional Islam's demise.

By the late 1970s, the threat to Islam had turned into a full-blown crisis. Communists, first in Afghanistan, then from outside, threatened its very existence. Eventually, the pir responded to this threat by declaring jihad. Even though he joined the mujahiddin parties, they were not parties in the modern sense: they lacked a political ideology, and their organization and affiliation tended to follow old religious lines. They were thus extensions of his religious authority and philosophically in keeping with it.

In the 1990s, yet another equally dangerous foe made its appearance in the region: the Taliban, so named because they were Afghan religious students (talib) who had been educated in the refugee camps in the NWFP and Baluchistan. The schools had been funded by the Saudis during the war against the Soviets and were Wahabi in orientation. As such, the Taliban were ideologically a Saudi-Pakistani phenomenon and not an indigenous Afghan movement. To some extent, the Taliban—that is, radical Islam—can be explained by the failure of both revival and reform movements to stem the tide of outside influence in the region. Insofar as the Taliban were exclusively Pathan, they also represented an attempt to reassert traditional Pathan dominance in Afghanistan after years of turmoil.

After the Taliban took Qandahar in 1994, both Pakistan and Saudi Arabia began supplying arms and assistance directly to the movement. Pakistan was hoping a stable Taliban government would open a secure economic route to central Asia, while the Saudis sought to check Iranian expansionist aims in the region. Once again, Afghanistan had become the battleground for foreign powers.

At first, Afghans, including Naqshbandis, viewed the Taliban with favor. This was largely because the movement had not been involved in the endless feuding—and Western sponsorship—that had so discredited the mujahiddin resistance parties in Peshawar. Nor did the Taliban have ties to the former Communist regime, even though they accepted former Communists within their ranks. Moreover, its call for the restoration of strict shari'a government appealed to Afghans seeking a return to a just Islamic society after years of oppressive—and infidel—Communist rule. On the surface at least, the Taliban appeared to be an indigenous and constructive movement. On the military front, the largely Pashtun Taliban met with little resistance in the tribal areas of the south and east. Once under Taliban control, residents were disarmed, and villages enjoyed peace, stability, and justice to an extent not seen in nearly two decades.

In the khanaqah, disciples from across the ethnic spectrum had enthusiastically supported the Taliban. Indeed, so great was the fervor that the movement began to take on millenarian overtones as disciples spoke of taking their Islamic revolution all the way to Bukhara. Although he refrained from public recognition or outright assistance, the pir did offer moral guidance and support to those disciples within the Taliban government who came to the hospice. He also began to openly express a desire to return to Kabul, suggesting he saw the possibility of a wider role for himself under a shari'a government.

But as the movement grew, it provided a vehicle for many tribal Pashtun youths with no religious training to reassert Pashtun control after the country's domination by a Tajik government. When the Taliban seized Kabul in 1997, the latent tribalism and Wahabism of the movement became more apparent. Once in power, the Taliban began to enact draconian measures such as jailing men without beards, barring women from educational opportunities and the workplace, and banning television and other Western forms of entertainment. As one excess after another came to light, initial enthusiasm in the khanaqah for the Taliban gave way to opposition, particularly among educated disciples, Pashtun and non-Pashtun alike. It also became apparent that the Taliban were anti-Sufi. To some extent, the movement was evolving, becoming more militant and radical over time.

For a time, the pir remained ignorant of the true nature of the Taliban, as we all were. He was unaware of the movement's ideological roots, covert Pakistani and Saudi support, and its growing record of human-rights abuses. This was partly because one of his sons, who was seeking a job in the government, controlled unfavorable news about them. The chief of police in Jalalabad, a member of the Tablighi Jama'at, another reform group that had made trouble for the pir, promised him a job as Minister of Public Works in the new government. It was a relatively unimportant position, but one nonetheless alluring to the pir's son. I wondered whether in fact a Tablighi would have made good on a promise to the son of a Sufi pir or if it was just a ploy of some sort.

Given the regular flow of visitors to the hospice from Afghanistan, efforts to control the information the pir received were doomed to fail.

It must have come as a shock to the pir to learn, as he eventually did, that the Taliban were yet another perversion of Sirhindi's teachings. For the pir always believed that his country was the last true shariʿa country in the world and had looked forward to the day when he could return to the Afghanistan of old.

In Pakistan the pir encountered an entirely different kind of reform from those in his native country, where reform had come late. His principal foe was neither a secularizing government nor Islamists, nor a foreign aggressor, but homegrown Islamic militants. Because of the presence of these groups in Pakistan, armed guards were at the pir's side at all times, even in the mosque, despite its remote location. They also patrolled the premises on a twenty-four-hour basis. The possibililty that an assailant bent on harming the pir could enter the khanaqah almost any time of day created a latent but palpable tension when outsiders were present. Occasionally, the tension would turn to panic when an overzealous disciple would come rushing out of the congregation toward him. At those times, everyone would jump into action, some reaching for their Kalashnikovs, others stepping up to block the way to the pir and shouting orders to step back.

The concern for the pir's safety was particularly acute given the presence nearby of several fundamentalist sects. All of these sects were opposed to Sufism. For some this opposition was benign; for others, hostile. That no one had yet attempted to kill the pir had more to do with the fear of inciting a Pashtun revenge bloodbath in the Khyber than it did any squeamishness on the part of his enemies. If anything had changed since the days of Hallaj, it was that the enemies of Sufism were proliferating—and taking on new forms.

Countering fundamentalists—who were particularly strong in Pakistan—had become one of the pir's major preoccupations since he moved from Afghanistan to the Khyber. He viewed them as far more pernicious than the Islamists. That all of these fundamentalist groups claimed to be Muslim was a disturbing confirmation of Muhammad's prophecy over a millennium ago that his religion would be divided into seventy-three sects. More ironic still, the pir laid the blame for the growing intra-Muslim conflict in the region entirely at the feet of one eighteenth-century Indian Naqshbandi saint, Shah Wali Allah.

Wali Allah was born February 1703. His father, a Naqshbandi in Sirhindi's line, directed Wali Allah's education. He proved to be an exceptional student, completing his religious studies at the age of fifteen. His father died while Wali Allah was still young, leaving him with heavy family and teaching responsibilities.

By Wali Allah's time, the centuries-old Mughal Empire was on the verge of collapse. New challengers to Sunni political power—British, Sikh, Persian, Maratha—were vying for control of the subcontinent. In the uncertain environment, there was continued mixing of Hindu elements with Islam, which had spawned growing discord within the Islamic community. Seeking inspiration for a solution to this disharmony, Wali Allah performed the hajj in 1731. From Mecca he went to Medina, where he spent time visiting shrines and consulting with religious leaders. In both cities, he experienced visions of the Prophet and his Companions. The mystical illuminations he received convinced him of his mission as a restorer of righteousness in his time, much as Sirhindi had been the previous century.

When he returned to India a year later, Wali Allah set out to redirect the social, political, and religious life of Islam in India. He began writing treatises aimed, once again, at bridging the gap between shari'a and tariqa, which he hoped would reunite the Islamic community. Though a spiritual heir of Sirhindi, Wali Allah sought to reform the Mujaddid's teachings, which he felt were based on old traditions. According to the pir, Wali Allah's reforms account for the undoing of Naqshbandi Sufism in the subcontinent, for the minor changes Wali Allah introduced morphed over time into a complete perversion of Sirhindi's teaching. In short, Wali Allah had opened the gates of tradition that led to a floodtide of reform.

Wali Allah was committed to reform, especially in three areas: law, mystical philosophy, and hadith. He believed that because the four schools of law were based on legal decisions formulated during the first three centuries after the Prophet, they were prone to error. In mystical philosophy, unlike the Mujaddid, Wali Allah believed the position of *wujudi*, or "oneness of being," to be legitimate. And from his studies in Mecca and Medina, Wali Allah brought back an emphasis on written hadith as a means of more precisely determining Islamic norms, although he did not reject taqlid entirely. His aim was only to reconcile opposing groups in Islam, including the four schools of law. As reformers came to rely increasingly on scriptural standards to define Islamic identity, however, the approach mutated into a full-blown movement that rejected Sufism and even now continues to divide Muslims in the subcontinent.

Despite Wali Allah's efforts, the excessive, Hindu-like devotion paid to Sufi pirs persisted. By the nineteenth century, Sufism in the Punjab had become completely corrupted by this practice. Lacking true piety or spirituality, the pirs derived their authority solely from family ties with the saintly lineage. Such dynastic Sufism is usually spiritually defunct, lacking in baraka or true pirs. Dynastic pirs lived at the shrines of their saintly ancestors, exploiting family ties for political and economic gain.[2] Because of the considerable local influence of these pirs, Muslim states were quick to harness the shrine-based pirs to the power of the state with offers of land, public office, and honors. When the British arrived, they too established ties to these pirs as a way of establishing control over the rural areas, thus reinforcing the pirs' power and influence.

Frustrated by the continued influence of Hinduism on Islam, Siddiq Khan and Maulana Nazir Hussain founded a reform movement called the Ahl-i Hadith. Ironically, both men were Naqshbandis and among Deoband's leading students. Their families had been brought into the hadith reformist milieu by Wali Allah himself. The Ahl-i Hadith denied the validity of the schools of law and rejected philosophy, theology, and mysticism as well. Endorsing ijtihad, or self-striving, they believed every Muslim was free to arrive at his own interpretation of Islamic behavior based solely on the Qur'an and the sunna. To accomplish its mission, the Ahl-i Hadith built an extensive network of madrasas to teach the Qur'an and the sunna to the exclusion of other sources of religious knowledge.

In addition to their advocacy of ijtihad, from the start the two men exhibited a marked ambivalence to Sufism even though Siddiq was a Naqshbandi. He believed Sufism to be a private matter. He disapproved of the pir-disciple relationship as practiced in its highly devotional form in the Punjab and believed worship at tombs to be un-Islamic. Hussain, who helped establish the movement in the NWFP, also included Sufism in his own teachings. But on the whole the ijtihad movement rejected Sufi esoteric interpretations of the Qur'an and the sunna, as well as mystic claims to the possession of special knowledge.

In its emphasis on a single standard of interpretation based exclusively on the Qur'an and hadith, the movement became more rigid with time. By the twentieth century, Nazir Hussain's students had completely omitted Sufism from their teachings. One of them, Maulana Tahir, undertook missionary work to spread his anti-Sufi teaching in the NWFP. Owing to Tahir's missionary zeal, the Ahl-i Hadith came to be known in the NWFP by the name *Panj Pir* (Five Pirs), the name of Tahir's native village in Northwest Pakistan. The term is deeply ironic, for the village's name commemorates five pirs, underscoring the esteem villagers held at one time for Sufi shaikhs.

After partition in 1947, the growth of Panj Pir schools paralleled the rapid spread of Deoband madrasas (with which they are often confused) in the NWFP and Baluchistan. Deoband schools tended to predominate in rural areas, while the Ahl-i Hadith were stronger in the modern, commercial centers of Pakistan. It was not until the 1950s that Panj Pirs made any inroads into Afghanistan. Indeed, early on, Afghan kings, perceiving the Panj Pirs' doctrines to be a threat, supported missionary activities to defend against them. Amir 'Abdur Rahman had, for example, supervised a group of thirteen clerics to compose a treatise refuting the so-called Wahabi doctrine articulated by an eighteenth-century Arab theologian, Muhammad ibn Abd al-Wahab—and embraced by the Panj Pirs—that laid out the principles of Hanafi law. By the 1950s, however, Pashto-speaking Afghans were studying increasingly in Panj Pir schools in the NWFP.

Initially, Panj Pir missionary efforts in the tribal areas met with resistance. The xenophobic Pashtun tribes persecuted them, often razing their homes in tribal uprisings. But buoyed by financing from Wahabists in Saudi Arabia and their own reformist zeal, the Panj Pirs persisted. Today they are strengthening their hold in settled and tribal areas alike. During my stay in the NWFP in 1996, there were more than two hundred Panj Pir madrasas in the province, each with five hundred to two thousand students.

I met with one of Maulana Tahir's own students, Sayyid Daruf, who headed a madrasa just outside Peshawar. The madrasa was a large, well-appointed facility, atypical of private madrasas in the region. Over a glass of green tea, Daruf told me he regarded the pir-disciple relationship as a form of polytheism and a superstitious vestige of the past. He characterized the pir as a "black magician" who wielded a kind of hypnotic power over gullible individuals to enrich himself. He scoffed at the pir's claim to spiritual power and knowledge, maintaining that such things were reserved for God alone. I had not mentioned that I was Naqshbandi; thinking better than to refute these notions, I thanked him for the tea and politely took my leave.

The pir's conflict with reform movements like the Panj Pir illustrates how he conducted Islamic revival. His approach was shaped both by Sirhindi's revival philosophy and his own perception of the crisis affecting Islam in the region. During the nineteenth century, the Islamic community was more homogeneous than it is today. The British presence actually strengthened Muslim solidarity, as fault lines were drawn between Muslims and non-Muslims, not among Muslims themselves. In the late twentieth century, the conflicting force was not the British but Muslim reform groups; they were insidiously undermining the integrity of Islam from within.

One of the central themes of revival is the call to judge contemporary society. The mission involves judging those Muslims whose practices and beliefs are not in accord with the sunna. Essentially, this entails the act of identifying such Muslims as unbelievers, *kafir*. In the pir's view, there could not be the slightest tolerance of reformist ideas, for that would invite a dangerous dilution of the teachings. While showing tolerance toward laxness in matters of practice, he made no allowance for those who stood in opposition to the traditions:

> The learned of the Ahl-i Sunna are united with regard to the person whose actions are to be called non-Muslim. The person with ninety-nine percent the actions of a non-Muslim and only one percent of those of a Muslim, then that person should be called a believer. But Kharijis, Panj Pirs, and Wahabis with only one-percent of the work of a non-Muslim are unbelievers. . . . Allah save us from them.[3]

In one incident, a khalifa of the pir in Lahore, Haji Abdul Ghaffur, had sent some publicity documents to a printing company for reproduction. The documents contained references to the pir using such Sufi honorifics as "savior" and "pole of the universe." The documents came to the attention of a Panj Pir journalist there, Fazal Rahim, writing under the pen name *Shari'a Yar* (Friend of the Shari'a) for an Afghan weekly newspaper, *Surat*. In a series of articles, Rahim vilified the pir, accusing him of appropriating some of the ninety-nine names of God to describe himself, an act he deemed blasphemous. Rahim argued that, as God's attributes, such terms as *al-karim* (the generous) and *al-rahim* (the merciful) were reserved exclusively for God. (He conveniently ignored the fact that his own name was Rahim!)

Saif ur-Rahman responded to these charges in a book published in Urdu on Islamic faith, *Saifi Edicts*:

> I hear that Shari'a Yar's original name is Fazal Rahim Karim and that Shari'a Yar is his title. He is either a jealous Wahabi, Panj Piri, or related to another perverted sect, or he is ignorant and uneducated. He does not understand or does not want to understand.

> According to a hadith of Muhammad, peace be upon him, to call a person an infidel who is not an infidel but a Muslim, then the accuser himself becomes an infidel. These groups are the enemies of Sufis because they deny the miracles (karamat) of the saints.[4]

Also in *Edicts*, the pir explained the terms he uses to emphasize his subordinate relationship to the transcendent:

> When I write to someone in Arabic, I sign my name '*al-faqir* [the poor] Saif ur-Rahman.' And if I write it in Pashto or Persian, I write '*faqir* Saif ur-Rahman.' I am a poor slave [*banda*] of Allah.[5]

Time and again, he pointed out that God's active attributes are transcendent qualities that are reflected in humans. In another one of his *Edicts*, the pir wrote,

> One of Allah's names is *haqq* [right]. But it is used in relation to many things, in many ways. For example, we say, "he is right, it is your right to do so, the right of a wife, of a husband, and so on. If Wahabis and Panj Pirs think it is *shirk* to share these qualities and characteristics [of God], then there would not remain a single Muslim on earth from Adam up to the present time.
>
> In Kataghan and Badakhshan and Turkmenistan, even in Afghanistan's eight northern provinces, each head of a village is called *arbab*. So the people say that he is the *arbab* of this or that village. In Nangrahar, Kunar, Laghman, Paktia, and throughout Pakistan the head of a village is called *malik*, which is also the qualification of Allah.[6]

In responding to the charge that his claim to possess hidden knowledge was blasphemous, the pir attempted to turn his critic's logic on itself:

> On the one hand he [Shari'a Yar] says that hidden knowledge belongs only to Allah and anyone who claims it is an infidel. Yet on the other he himself employs hidden knowledge for he has not seen me nor the person who had commissioned the printing of this card. Neither I nor Haji Abdul Ghaffur has told him about our beliefs. Until you see bad,

it is better to think good about one of the faithful. Heed the words of Rumi's *Mathnavi*:

> Abandon wrong thinking,
> O' bad thinker.
> Bad thinking is to be called a sin,
> As backbiting is like eating
> The flesh of a human being.
> Sixty years have passed
> But you are still satisfied with it.[7]

In support of his arguments, the pir drew heavily from Rumi's epic poem and other texts of Sunni mystical Islam: the Qur'an, hadith, Hanafi *fiqh*, and Sirhindi's Letters. In his writings and interviews with journalists, he condemned as kafir virtually all Muslims not in accord with the revival teachings of Sirhindi and Sunni Islam.

In defending Sufism against reform groups, the pir also enacted another form of jihad or struggle, *jihad al-da'wa*. An educational form of struggle, it involved an effort to spread Islam among unbelievers by *peaceful* means, usually in speech or writing. Related to this was his practice of *jihad al-tarbia*: the spread of Muslim values and institutions within Islamic society to struggle against corruption and decadence. In waging these two forms of jihad, the pir regularly dispatched his disciples to engage his critics in debate in mosques and public places, just as Sirhindi had done three centuries before.

From time to time, we used to see the pir sitting in the shade of the veranda, his head inclined toward a portable radio on the table at his side. He would be listening to a debate between his disciples and Panj Pirs on the radio. The debates, at times heated, were held at a Peshawar police station to ensure they did not become violent.

The pir also concurred with edicts that condemned reform movements. In these edicts, usually from Sufis or traditional scholars, he restricted his support to those issues that concerned belief, ritual, or personal behavior and ignored conduct of state, an approach that has been the traditional one in the subcontinent. In his struggle with sectarian groups, the pir characterized his position strictly in Sunni revivalist terms: "I am an imitator of Hanafi in law, a follower of Maturidi in theological opinions, and of Sirhindi in mysticism."[8] For this reason, he drew the fault lines sharply between traditional Islam and that of reformers. Reformers were beyond the pale of Islam—kafir.

To refer to the pir's approach as "revivalist" is, in a sense, misleading. It implies a cycle of degeneration and renewal that does not apply to his line of the Mujaddidi order, for his lineage has retained uninterrupted its centuries-old identity and function as spiritual educators. In a world grown increasingly conflicted, secular, and further estranged from its source in the transcendent, he bestowed his baraka to all capable of receiving and benefiting from it.

As some of the mosques in the vicinity of the khanaqah were Panj Pir, the conflict was waged on an institutional level as well. One of the pir's arch enemies was a certain Mufti Shakir, a Panj Pir and former mujahid. Shakir had been expelled from the Kurram Tribal Agency for inciting Shi'a-Sunni sectarian riots. Since arriving in the Khyber, Shakir had developed a substantial following among the conservative Afridi. He set up loudspeakers at his mosque near the khanaqah and broadcast messages denouncing the pir. One of the pir's khalifas described the relationship with such mosques as "a cold war" in which each tried to drown out the other's sermons with loudspeakers. Usually this conflict played out on a Friday with the Naqshbandi and Panj Pir loudspeakers engaging in what sounded like a shouting match, the cacophony reverberating across the valley.

In 1996, the cold war between the two was threatening to turn hot. Fearing they were on the brink of jihad, tribal leaders stepped in, persuading both sides to tone down their inflammatory language. The pir, however, continued to broadcast the Thursday evening sessions, in which the disciples' ecstatic utterances and praises to the pir could be heard a half mile away. He also broadcast the Friday sermon and the calls to prayer—this, in his capacity as imam.

Within the sphere of Pakistani politics, the pir confined his remarks to the religiosity of particular politicians. In an interview with a journalist in May 1996, he boldly described the head of the Awami National Party of Pakistan and all of the party's members as kafir. In an assertion that Islam transcends state, he publicly stated that Pakistan's president and all government officials were legally bound by the precepts of Islam to accept his religious authority. In retaliation for the statement, a Panj Pir journalist writing in a Pakistani newspaper accused the pir of being "a false prophet," further hardening fundamentalist attitudes toward him.

Given the pir's fastidious adherence to tradition, it was not surprising that he resisted siding with other Sufi shaikhs if he deemed that they, too, were at variance with it. He once issued an edict rejecting the edict of a Sufi at the shrine of Golra Sharif near Rawalpindi that prohibited a female of a sayyid family from marrying outside of it. On another occasion when speaking to local journalists, he described a militant order led by Maulana Sufi Muhammad as "a bad tariqa."[9] Even though he endorsed taqlid, the pir allowed for adaptation to social change by employing Sirhindi's concept of "useful innovation." He made it clear, however, that conventional learning has nothing to do with spiritual awakening:

> Though its origin cannot be found in the Qur'an, hadith, or fiqh, it [good innovation] is not against the sunna. For instance, wearing a large turban, eating bread made of filtered flour, constructing tombs to saints, studying math, chemistry, philosophy or medicine, there are so many, but the learning of these subjects is not prohibited or sinful. Imam Rabbani [Sirhindi], may God bless him, has merely said that none of such good innovations is enlightening [viz., invokes the spirit].[10]

After I left Pakistan in 1998, militant fundamentalists strengthened their grip on the Khyber. To what extent this was a result of the flight of the Taliban into Pakistan's tribal areas after the US invasion of Afghanistan in 2001 is unclear.

One fundamentalist leader named Haji Namdar set up his own prisons in the Khyber—naming them after the infamous Abu Ghraib and Guantanamo prisons—to incarcerate Muslims whom he felt were violating Islamic norms by not wearing beards or veiling their women and the like.

Other fundamentalists adopted a new tool for conversion of the masses to their "purer" form of Islam: FM radio stations. Inexpensive to set up and operate, illegal radio stations had been mushrooming in the tribal areas since the 1990s. By 2005, some fifty or sixty illegal FM stations were broadcasting regularly in the tribal regions. These stations were almost invariably operated by madrasas and mosques controlled by fundamentalist religious leaders.

The pir's nemesis in the Khyber, Mufti Shakir, had set up his own FM station in 2004. He started broadcasting messages denigrating the pir's teachings and urging Muslims to follow strict codes of religious and social behavior. Shakir had previously been aligned with Haji Namdar, but the two eventually had a falling out. Shakir, who had long been preaching that the pir was promoting a perverted version of Islam, was now broadcasting the same message over the airwaves. He urged listeners to join his militia and take action "in the true tradition of Islam" against the pir as well as against vices such as drinking, videos, and other forms of Western amusement. His broadcasts were popular with many Afridis, and donations started pouring in. One Afridi woman was so moved by Shakir's preaching on marriage duties that she sold her gold jewelry for three thousand dollars and donated it to his radio station.

Undertaking educational jihad, the pir set up his own FM station the following year. The battle that had once been waged over loudspeakers had escalated to the airwaves. The invective traded by both sides began to bitterly divide Afridi clans as armed Pashtun supporters rallied around their respective leaders.

Even more ominous, Shakir was urging listeners to join his recently formed militia, the *Lashkar-i Islam* (Army of Islam). Led by "amir" Mangal Bagh, an illiterate former truck driver, the militia had begun to forcibly impose a Taliban-style religious code in the Khyber.

Chapter 7

In late 2005, the Lashkar had increased its demands. Shakir and Mangal broadcast a radio message ordering the pir to leave Bara by December 25, 2005, warning of an attack on the khanaqah if the pir did not heed their message.

The pir refused to oblige.

The pir's disciples started to come in from all over the country, vowing to resist at all costs if they were attacked by Shakir's heavily armed militia. Meanwhile, Pakistani authorities, apprehensive about the potential for escalation of the conflict among the tribes, ordered Shakir out of the Khyber. When he refused to leave, the NWFP provincial government dispatched one thousand troops from various regiments, including the Mohmand and the Khyber Rifles.

Meanwhile, the Khyber's Afridi tribal leaders were becoming concerned about the rising level of animosity between the Lashkar and the Naqshbandis. Even though nothing occurred at the December 25 deadline, in early 2006 a jirga of all seven Afridi clans was called to discuss the deteriorating situation. Held in the traditional tribal venue, the Zakha Khel bazaar of the upper Bara valley, the jirga was attended by more than three hundred elders.

The jirga ruled that insofar as the pir and Shakir were both outsiders who had imperiled security in Bara, they should both be expelled. Subsequently, a handful of tribal elders went to Bara to persuade the pir to leave. Since the decision of a jirga was binding and the pir was simply a guest of the Khyber Afridi, he had little choice but to acquiesce.

On February 1, 2006, the pir quit the Khyber for good.

Hailing the verdict as a victory for the Lashkar, Shakir then refused to leave the agency until the pir left Pakistan altogether. "Leaving Bara means nothing. He should be banished from the country," Shakir fulminated. Shakir declared that while "the evil"—an allusion to the pir—would leave, "the good" (Shakir) would stay behind. Under pressure from Pakistani authorities, Shakir moved to the remote Tirah in the southern Khyber in late February.

With the Lashkar militia still intact in Bara, Mangal took over Shakir's FM radio station and resumed broadcasting against the pir. Local animosities continued to fester between Mangal and the pir's Afridi disciples. At one point, the Lashkar attacked and destroyed the Khyber home of one of the pir's disciples. By late March, Mangal decided to eliminate the pir's disciples who had stayed behind in the Khyber. One evening Mangal and his militia showed up in sixteen pickup trucks at the home of a Naqshbandi disciple, Bacha Jan, and ordered him to surrender.

When Bacha refused, the militia opened fire. A battle ensued and lasted throughout the night as the two sides traded fire with mortars, hand grenades, and rocket-propelled grenades. One Pakistani news report said that when Bacha's men ran out of ammunition they surrendered to the militia. They were led to a nearby stream and executed at close range. When it was over, nineteen Naqshbandi men lay dead and their women and children had been taken hostage. Mangal had lost five men.

Three days later, the Khyber Rifles moved in and sealed all roads leading to Bara. Other Pakistani military units from Jamrud and Landi Kotal also moved toward Bara, surrounding Mangal's former headquarters and radio station. Lashkar members surrendered without a struggle. With a single shot, Pakistani troops brought down Mangal's FM antenna. Mangal's home was then razed.

Mangal, however, had escaped to Gugrini in the remote Tirah valley, taking refuge in the caves of the Jamrud hills. There he set up a new FM station and resumed his vitriolic broadcasts. He and his followers also started imposing strict Islamic codes on the local inhabitants, enforcing the wearing of beards and five-times-daily prayer, requiring women to be accompanied by a male blood relative when in the marketplace, and threatening retribution to those who collaborated with the government.

By May, Mangal was threatening to seal off the Tirah if his supporters, who had been arrested in late March, were not released from the Khyber Rifles jail. A month later Mangal returned to Bara, seizing control of the bazaar with several hundred of his forces. They passed out a decree saying they would be establishing a committee to impose penalties on those involved in the sale or drinking of liquor, possession of videos, and other vices.

When the Khyber Rifles reentered the agency, Mangal's militia fled back to the Tirah, taking refuge with the Zakha Khel. In July the government asked the Zakha Khel to turn Mangal over to them. Traditionally unwilling to cooperate with the government, the clan refused. The Khyber Rifles then conducted a sweep of the Tirah, where Mangal and his followers were holed up. Seventy of his militants were arrested along with a large number of the Zakha Khel.

Yet another tribal jirga of 450 elders was convened; they endorsed the NWFP administration's crackdown on Mangal and the Lashkar militia. The jirga also agreed to impose a fine of eight thousand dollars on anyone found harboring Mangal or his followers. Mangal threatened to bring in additional supporters from Afghanistan—possibly referring to the Taliban—and escalate the conflict beyond tribal borders if the administration did not drop calls for his arrest. Eventually he did return to Bara and set up another FM station, prompting yet another sweep of Bara in April 2008 by the Pakistani military. Mangal was rumored to have been killed in a clash with Pakistani police in the Khyber in 2012.

When the pir left the Khyber, he went to Lahore, stopping at the khanaqah of his eldest son at Pabbi Station in Noushera. He had left a mosque in that town twenty years earlier because of problems with fundamentalists, and the situation since then had only worsened. When he arrived in Noushera, a large number of his followers turned out to greet him. Undiminished at seventy-eight years of age, he led the Friday sermon. Then he passed out pamphlets on the Mujaddidi/Saifi tariqa. A few days later, he and his family traveled on to Lahore.

When the pir crossed the Indus River at the town of Attock, he passed—geographically, ethnically, religously—from central into South Asia. History had thus conspired to return him to the land where Sirhindi had led his revival three hundred years before. In exile from Afghanistan for more than twenty years and hemmed in on all sides by hostile reform groups in Pakistan, the pir had remained faithful to his distant mentor Sirhindi. In a way, the lineage had come full circle and remained vibrant and intact.

In Lahore, the pir resumed doing what he had done for decades before and through all the years of his country's vicissitudes: pray, preach, be a moral exemplar and guide, and serve as a living fount of grace to spiritual seekers, not only in his own region but from all over the world. Meanwhile, the world outside the khanaqah was becoming ever more tumultuous and the Islamic community more divided, as group after group morphed into being, attempting to impose its brand of Islam with ever-greater force. Amid the violence, Naqshbandi grace radiated silently, attracting followers to the path as it has for centuries.

Saif ur-Rahman died in his sleep on Sunday morning June 27, 2010. He was eighty-two. Thousands of his disciples flocked to the funeral at the order's khanaqah in Faqirabad, Lahore, to see their shaikh for the last time. Clad in white shalwars and turbans, they formed a line that stretched for hundreds of meters along the dusty road leading to the site. In the mosque's spacious compound, disciples filled the courtyard and stood on rooftops. The pir's body lay perpendicular to the qibla and was wrapped in a white cotton cloth. His face was exposed, as full and vigorous as when he was alive. The cloth was covered with a bright red mantle simulating a bed of roses. It was not the green typically used for Sufi shaikhs. Roses signified the profound heart-love he possessed and awakened in devotees. A large ziyarat has been constructed at the khanaqah where the anniversary of his death (*'urs*) is celebrated each year in June.

So the long odyssey of Haji Saif ur-Rahman, the Pir-i Kunduz—a saint beleaguered by history, misunderstood by academics and maligned even by Muslims but ultimately loved by those who understood him—came quietly to an end.

Among his thirteen sons, he had designated the eldest, Maulana Said Haidri, as his successor.

More excellent than any wise person who achieves the essence of Perfect imitation of his loved one [The Prophet] Muhammad.

—Ahmad Sirhindi

That monarch supreme [Shams-i Tabriz] had shut the door fast;
Today he has come to the door, clothed in the garment of mortality.

—Rumi

Chapter 8
Mubarak Sahib

Who was Mubarak Sahib?

As I think back, the answer to this question is not about the kind of individual he was. By this I mean the pir's personality held no special attraction for me or, I believe, for any of his other close disciples. It is a common fallacy that disciples view the spiritual master with a kind of childlike fascination. In the khanaqah, we did not spend our idle time talking about him in rapt wonder. Nor did we invest his every act with portentous, magical significance. For his part, he did not talk about himself and regarded questions about his personal life and his upbringing as frivolous unless, of course, there was a moral or historical lesson to be derived from it.

In fact, many disciples were quite objective in their assessment of the pir. One said he was a "good cleric, though not exceptional" and not a particularly good writer. He certainly did not publish works of distinguished literary merit as had Sirhindi, Rumi, and many other Islamic mystics. There were even times when he could be the simple, rustic Afghan. He possessed an almost magical regard for Western medicine, as do many Afghans. Medication was a panacea to be taken willy-nilly for any ailment, or for no ailment whatever as a preventive regime. The pir was not immune to this cultural idiosyncrasy, of which his European doctor was constantly trying to disabuse him. He could be politically naïve, too, a common failing of those who traffic in spiritual matters.

That the pir *had* a personality there can be no doubt, but in way that a person has skin: it was incidental to the being that resided within. The "being within" abided in a state of unitive consciousness. It was probably not a state he lived in continuously, a consequence of both phenomenal existence and the mysterious working of grace. The pir dedicated his life to showing others that such consciousness resides in each individual willing to pursue the Naqshbandi path. It is in this sense that he was extraordinary. He showed, as do all spiritual masters, what it meant to be fully human.

To be fully human meant being fully Muslim. At times the pir was the Old Testament lawgiver, the righteous exemplar of the shariʿa. To live in imitation of the prophetic sunna was, for him, the alpha of life. It informed his waking and sleeping activities to such a degree that there was hardly another person existing apart from it. He lived in *imitatio Muhammadi.*

He never forgot the slightest thing said in passing or jest, to be called upon when he needed to make a point. In time, I learned that he said very little not intended in some way to edify or instruct in the sunna. He was an indefatigable ombudsman, chastising disciples for carelessness in their dress and length of turban or beard. He never failed to scrutinize and correct the appearance or comportment of everyone who came within his orbit. Our pants were too long, our turbans too small, our stays too brief. When the pir was introduced to some Iraqi students from Lahore, it was near midnight. While the rest of us were tired and anxious for bed, the pir began to lecture them on the proper dress for a Muslim, raising his right leg aloft to show the proper length of his pants. In one sense, he was instructing them individually. In quite another, I suspected even so small and insignificant a gesture was intended for all of Iraq. Another time he ordered a man out of the mosque who had entered improperly, leading with his left foot instead of his right.

One time an old Afghan man, impoverished and decrepit, came into the mosque during suhbat. He slowly crawled on his belly like a reptile toward the pir, sobbing and moaning. It was a heartbreaking display, and I imagined the man must have just suffered a great loss in the war. I expected the pir to take pity on the wretched figure before him. Instead he chided him for his abject behavior. Later, I was told that this kind of behavior—pir worship—was forbidden by the sunna. It was also the kind of thing that the pir's critics accused him of encouraging in his followers.

Another time, a disciple came to ask him to make an amulet to improve the disciple's relationship with his wife. Whereas the pir freely made them for persons who were ill, in this instance he refused, for such an amulet, according to the sunna, was viewed as meddling in someone's personal affairs.

His daily routine was not just dictated by the sunna; it was the sunna personified. Each day the pir woke before dawn, performed ablutions, and recited twelve supererogatory prayers known as *tahajjud*. He also performed two prayers after every ablution. He then recited an Arabic prayer formula, "I ask forgiveness from God," six hundred and twenty-six times. If he missed this prayer, he would make it up sometime during the day.

Then, with his copper-plated staff in hand, he crossed the narrow drive that separated his house from the mosque to lead the morning prayer. He was always impeccably attired in an immaculate white turban and a colorful khirqa. At this hour he was usually solemn and, except to issue instructions sotto voce, to his attendants he said nothing. Upon entering he would glance at those in the mosque, seemingly making a mental photograph of everyone in attendance. He took his place in front of the mihrab and led us in prayer. After prayer he recited suras from the Qur'an, which he required his disciples to do as well.

After the Sura Yasin was read by the qari, a large white chair was drawn from one side and placed directly in front of the mihrab for one to two hours of exercises. Until late in his life, the pir always sat on the floor with his disciples, but with increasing age and weight, he had begun to use a chair most of the time. He occasionally struggled to his feet when rising, but for the most part remained remarkably agile for a man in his seventies.

During dhikr sessions, the pir was a tireless orchestrator, directing disciples to form a more even circle in front of him, correcting their posture, or calling for adjustment of the lights. On weekends when many more disciples were present, he often ate breakfast in the mosque so as to extend the time for disciples to be in his company for suhbat. If he returned to his house to eat, as he did during the week, he conducted exercises there with his female disciples, who were not permitted in the mosque. When the sun rose, he performed four more prayers.

By late morning, if not at home with visitors or family, the pir could usually be found in one of the langars, or common dining areas, again conducting exercises. The purpose of these informal gatherings was not to socialize, and the conversation rarely took the form of idle chitchat. Occasionally, a visitor came to request a special dispensation from the pir, such as a prayer or counsel. The pir always regarded these sessions as opportunities for the disciple to further his spiritual advancement. Once, when I decided to forgo the session and go for a walk, he upbraided me sharply for missing the session.

Despite the purposeful nature of suhbat, the pir was relaxed, talking animatedly about a variety of issues—trouble he was having with the fundamentalists, how he was betrayed by a disciple, doctrinal points of hadith or fiqh—all the while interjecting his talk with quotes from the Qur'an, Sirhindi's Letters, or Rumi's *Mathnavi*, which was a kind of Persian Qur'an for him. Sometimes he would send an assistant to fetch a text from which he wished to read. His knowledge of the texts was prodigious, and he always seemed to know precisely the page he wished to cite. One time a disciple was reading from the voluminous *Mathnavi* while the pir was talking to us. Whenever the disciple misread a word—which was embarrassingly often—the pir corrected the disciple from the side of his mouth, in such as way as not to break stride in his conversation. We were all ashtonished.

Around lunchtime, the pir returned to his house, where he read three suras from the Qur'an. Then he might spend time with his large family in suhbat with the women. After a short rest, he prepared for the noon prayer, after which he recited more suras. Noon prayer was usually followed by an intense one- to two-hour dhikr session. As with the morning suhbat, the pir was constantly at work during dhikr, directing someone to move closer to him, or others to spread out and make room for late arrivals, giving bay'a to initiates, or chiding those looking around instead of focusing on him or one of the khalifas. Usually, these dhikr sessions were so long that they stretched into the afternoon prayer. He would close a session by reciting, along with the advanced disciples, the khatm-i khwajagan as well as individual prayers to Ahmad Sirhindi, Bahauddin Naqshband, and 'Abd al-Qadir al-Jilani. At the conclusion of dhikr, he returned to his house, where he performed six more prayers and then recited two more suras from the Qur'an.

He returned to the mosque for the evening prayer. Afterward, he called for another session of dhikr. On Thursday night, he ate dinner in the mosque with disciples so that those visiting for the weekend could get as much time as possible in suhbat with him. Dinner was followed by the night prayer. One never knew at what time the night prayer would take place; we were always kept in a state of vigilance until the alert was sounded that he was heading for the mosque, the call "*Salat!*" reverberating throughout the khanaqah. Sometimes the pir would wait until midnight to lead the prayer. After prayer he recited still more suras. Before retiring for the night, he recited the Naqshbandi prayers of contemplation. Three times each year, including the twenty-seventh day of Ramadan, he prayed all night. During Ramadan, he recited the entire Qur'an.

I never saw the pir even once do something that contradicted the teaching or appeared to stem from a personal whim or selfish mood. Even though each disciple was at a different stage of his or her development, the pir's treatment of others was consistently measured by the extent to which they lived up to the teachings. Perhaps, for this reason, he treated the more advanced practitioners more harshly than beginners. Once, one of his most senior khalifas was giving the Friday sermon. Mubarak Sahib was in his house. When he came out to lead the prayer, the pir excoriated the khalifa in front of the congregation for thirty minutes for misquoting the Qur'an. He had been listening intently to the loudspeaker the entire time. His own angry tirade was broadcast over the loudspeakers, too. The khalifa was deeply shamed. There was never any special treatment at the khanaqah or favored treatment for advanced disciples. What Mubarak Sahib said to one, he said to all.

One Friday afternoon, for no particular reason, there was almost no one present for prayer. I later remarked to Ihsan how disheartening it was that more Muslims did not come to the khanaqah. "It doesn't matter," he said.

"Whether there is one disciple standing behind him or one thousand, Mubarak Sahib will still come each day to the mosque and lead the prayer."

During my time with the pir, I did not fully realize what an extraordinary man he was, paradoxically because he was so accessible to me. He was a husband, a father, a farm manager, a community head, an imam and a religious counselor, and a spiritual master. A refugee saint and warrior, he had been driven from his country and witnessed the death or dismemberment of thousands of his disciples. In fleeing to Pakistan, he found little relief. Indeed, his problems only increased as he ran head on into militant fundamentalists. Yet, despite all these hardships, he remained undaunted. He fulfilled his office with an energy that belied his age and a host of ailments that included rheumatism, arthritis, high blood pressure, gastroenteritis, peptic ulcer, sciatica, and migraine headaches.

So much was the pir at the disposal of his disciples, male and female, that it left little time for his family. His youngest children, anxious to see more of their father, often wandered into the mosque during suhbat. By then, the children were already inured to the disciples' bizarre behavior. Standing behind his chair, they would playfully touch the tail of his turban while disciples shook and groaned on the floor in front of him. The pir never displayed any affection or attention to his children at these times, his spiritual work with disciples being uppermost in his mind.

It was not hard to see how the heavy demands of his office and the privileged life his children enjoyed had corrupted some of his sons. The pir, fully aware of their shortcomings, did not hesitate to berate them in front of the congregation as "worthless to me." This indictment was made as much in his capacity as father as in that of a religious leader for their failure to live up to the shari'a. Despite his dissatisfaction with them, he refused to disown them. "What can I do?" he once said, "They are my family." Given his exacting standards, however, their failings must have been a sore point in his life.

Mubarak Sahib owned a vehicle and a fax machine, but he placed no real value on them or on the larger intellectual and scientific world from which they issued. If these modern conveniences had been taken away, he would have felt not the slightest loss. I am certain of that. He was simply not interested in what the West had to offer—not its scientific achievements, and certainly not its intellectual and social achievements.

For the pir, Islam was a complete world, a total way of life. It offered a social and political system, legal injunctions, and intellectual and moral guidelines for a community of believers linked to one another and, ultimately, to God. The path to this life was not to be found in modern progress or scientific discovery. The path was laid down by the Prophet in the seventh century. It was thus to the past that Mubarak Sahib looked, historically, morally, intellectually, and most important, spiritually. The grace he received and transmitted was a living confirmation of the essential rightness of his chosen path. He lived so fully the sunna of the Prophet, within and without, that in reality there was only the living embodiment of the teaching. As someone once described his Japanese Zen teacher, the pir was seamless.

A few years before his death, the pir went to a village in Afghanistan to seek treatment for an ailment. When villagers heard that he was in town, they flocked to his house in the hope of sitting with him in suhbat. Even though he was sick, he sat with his disciples into the wee hours of the morning. His life was one of constant service to his disciples, whom he called "my moral children."

The title *Mubarak Sahib* was not a mere honorific given to a religious authority but an affirmation of a being who bestowed a real, tangible blessing power on all who approached him sincerely and availed themselves of it. He was an impeccable exemplar of his religion and an inexhaustible source of baraka, and disciples said that when he passed, there would be no Naqshbandi pir alive capable of matching his exacting moral standards or the power of his baraka.

It seems paradoxical to revere a man for the fastidiousness with which he imitated a religious ideal and for his inner spiritual realization. For these imply that the person transcended individual existence as the rest of us live it. But that has always been the unspoken, the unutterable, message of the Sufis.

Chapter 8

As the tariqa was to the shari'a, so was there an another side to the stern lawgiver: the mystical ecstatic. Early on, when I complained to a khalifa that the pir was constantly criticizing me, he said, "Don't you understand, he loves you?" Indeed, if I was absent from the khanaqah more than two weeks the pir would, upon seeing me again, inquire as to my health and why I was not coming more often; this, despite the fact that in the intervening period he might have seen more than a thousand individuals and dealt with as many problems.

He was so attentive to each disciple that each felt the object of his special attention. During sessions, he intuitively knew when I wanted to sit up front with the khalifas, even when there were dozens of other disciples in the mosque clamoring for the same attention. At these times, he would beckon me to the front with a warm smile. If he was demanding of his disciples, it is because he worked relentlessly to close the gap between where we were and where we needed to be in order to participate in the ecstatic life of the spirit.

When the pir learned that my departure from Pakistan was imminent, he ordered his closest pirs to sit with me in *tawwajuh* so that I might know his spiritual universe and share my realization with others. He never showed disappointment or disapproval of me, even long after I had lost faith in myself to experience dhikr. He never asked me for a single thing, even though he gave so much of himself. All he asked was that I follow the Naqshbandi path. I know that he wanted me to be his khalifa in America, a task I was unfit to assume, but a goal for which he never lost hope. Perhaps in some small way, this book is a kind of fulfillment of that wish.

Of course, I cannot claim to know the innermost state of any man, least of all a mystic like Mubarak Sahib. There were things he did that were well beyond my ken. Several times individuals—nondisciples—showed up at the khanaqah in a state of what could only be described as possession. Foaming at the mouth, fitful, shaking, they seemed beyond help. After examining them, the pir usually pronounced them to be suffering from physical or psychological afflictions and had them taken to the hospital for treatment.

One time, however, a man came to the pir whom Ihsan insisted was suffering from epilepsy. With wild, feverish eyes and spittle lining the edges of his mouth, the man made bestial whoops like a wounded animal. This time the pir's diagnosis was some sort of psychic possession, and he proceeded to treat him. When the man departed the next day, he was completely healed of his horrific condition and walked off placidly as if nothing had happened. "You think he was suffering from epilepsy or some other disease, but he was possessed by jinn," the pir said to me and Ihsan. "But you people [meaning Westerners] don't believe in such things." The pir had turned the tables on us, and benighted belief was our error, not his.

There is an entire body of esoteric sciences in Sufism that I was told existed, but which I never studied. The pir sacrificed black chickens for supplicants. He created lockets with magic charms and talismans for the weak and the needy, some of whom were disciples but most of whom were simply desperate victims of the war, poverty being their plight as refugees. Whether he was simply trying to give these people moral support or there was more than met the eye, I could not say.

Disciples never talked in the khanaqah about the pir's ability to perform miracles. Such talk was regarded as sensationalist and a distraction from spiritual work on ourselves. For the most part, he did not perform miracles. Sirhindi taught that miracles were not necessary for a saint and advised Sufis to conceal their activities in this regard. In the khanaqah, the one exception to this prohibition was stories concerning the strange workings of the pir's baraka, stories that were not myth—the usual anthropological interpretation—but a reality confirmed every day in the khanaqah.

One such incident occurred near the end of my stay. It was the afternoon prayer and I was sitting at the back of the mosque. The mosque was full. I was despondent that after ten months as a Naqshbandi I had made no progress. Unable to control my sense of failure, I began weeping silently. I was seated directly behind someone, so that the pir—unaccustomed to looking at the congregation during prayer anyway—would not notice me if he were to turn around. As soon as the prayer ended, he immediately turned around and, staring blankly into the crowd, began calling for me.

Chapter 8

"Ahmad, Ahmad, where are you?" he asked. "Are you alright?" He was looking around and still had not found me in the congregation.

At that point, my face dry, I held up my arm. "*Baleh, Mubarak sahib, khailikhub-am, merci* [Yes, I am fine, thank you]," I said.

But I remained distraught. After so many months of immersing myself in the Naqshbandis' rigorous spiritual exercises, I knew I would soon be returning to the United States without ever having tasted that intoxicating wine I had so desperately sought. In a way, I had prepared for years for my spiritual adventure, intensively studying Persian and the history and culture of the region. But the real learning, the spiritual, had eluded me.

Was I too much an academic, too analytical, too critical, too intellectual? Did I erect unconscious barriers to the pir's teaching because it required me to live in the Khyber, which I abhorred?

The great Sufis have said that the first true step in the spiritual path is *ikhlas*, sincerity. This means that one really begins the spiritual journey when and only when one comes to the realization that the demands of the ego for fulfillment through money, career, and other forms of wordly gratification are a fruitless quest, a fool's game. Coming to the end of himself is what made Ismael's conversion to Islam so unqualified, so complete. Only then can one shed the old self and begin to move toward the divine mystery. On the other hand, did not the Naqshbandis offer a taste of the spirit for people just like me as a way of getting us over our lingering egoic attachments? Perhaps I just needed just a bit more time, like Ihsan.

The answers were not clear then, or even now. Indeed, several years later, a deep sense of disappointment still pervades my memory of that special time at the khanaqah. I lived in a spiritual community that needed no intellectual defense, no justification to the world of modern intellectual skeptics or that of backward religious fanatics. We knew who Mubarak Sahib was and what he embodied: the highest human endeavor—the pursuit of the Divine. And we all sought in our own way and in our time to participate in that life.

On my last day in the mosque, I informed the pir of my imminent departure. He suddenly redoubled his efforts to awaken my dhikr. First he drew me close to him, performing dhikr exclusively with me. Then he instructed Pir-I piran to work on me intensively. Taking me to a corner of the mosque, Habib fixed a wild gaze on my heart region, mustering what looked like his total spiritual force to awaken me once and for all. After several minutes, a pain arose in my heart; after a few more minutes it had become so acute that it felt as though a knife were being thrust into it. The pain was so great I had to ask him to stop.

It was our last time together.

Epilogue

Since I left the Bara khanaqah fifteen years ago, there have been many new developments—good and bad. At that time, it seemed as if the pir had finally found a home in the Khyber, a dangerous place to be sure, but also a borderland accessible to Afghans and Pakistanis—and even to outsiders like me. The attack on the Bara khanaqah in 2006, however, was not an isolated incident but symptomatic of a worsening and troubling trend in the region. Indeed, the following year, several independent Pashtun militant groups—including Mangal Bagh's Lashgar-i Islam—organized under the umbrella of the *Tehrik-i Taliban Pakistan* (TTP; Student Movement of Pakistan). Today these groups are stronger, better organized, and, given the fecklessness (and sympathy) of the Pakistani army, they operate with near impunity in the tribal region.

Under the leadership of the TTP, the campaign of terror against Sufis and other minority groups such as the Shi'a has intensified. Over the past decade, the TTP has killed over two hundred tribal elders on suspicion of being foreign spies, attenuating, sadly, the tribal social structure, long a source of stability in the area. While not affiliated with the Afghan Taliban, the TTP does conduct cross-border incursions into Afghanistan and supports the former's fight against the Afghan government and foreign forces there.

For their part, Afghan Taliban now control large portions of the east and south of their country, despite the presence of sixty thousand US troops still in the country. The Taliban are even making inroads into hitherto safe regions such as Bamyan and Mazar-Sharif. Many Afghans fear that with the withdrawal of the last foreign troops in 2014, the Taliban, with the help of their Pakistani allies, will overthrow the Afghan government and restore its medieval form of rule. Such a scenario would obviously be a serious setback for Sufis, not to mention women and the country as a whole.

The Bara hospice is closed now, and the seat of the lineage has moved once again, this time to Lahore, the capital of Pakistan's Punjab Province. While Lahore is the cultural and intellectual capital of Pakistan, its cultural milieu is vastly different from that of Afghanistan or the tribal belt. In the past, Islam has been overwhelmed by the strong cultural influences of the subcontinent, and one wonders how long this lineage can remain a Mujaddidi (i.e., revivalist) one there. For the Mujaddidi, change has invariably led to the transformation of the order and the loss of the grace inherent in it. That other Sufi orders in the Islamic world have successfully reformed raises an important question for the Saifi order: How can an order adapt to its environment while retaining its own inherent grace? Or is the issue that change—however minimal and prescriptive at the outset—sets in motion a process that, once begun, is hard to control?

Despite the Saifi disdain for reform, there has nonetheless been room for modern innovation, as demonstrated by the fact that the order now has its own website and that footage of dhikr ceremonies is available on You Tube.

Of course, the most momentous change for the order has been the passing of Saif ur-Rahman himself. Another great shaikh may well appear in this lineage, but probably not in direct succession. The greatness of a Sufi shaikh is not measured in terms of literary production, social influence, and the like, but chiefly by the power of his baraka. It is what made Sirhindi great as well. Books on Sufism invariably discuss such aspects as the history of the orders, ritual, poetry, theosophy, and hagiography, but relatively little attention is given to baraka. It is Sufism's most defining feature, without which Sufism would cease to be mysticism. Baraka is what makes the spiritual path a truly *transcendent* one. It confirms the lineage's link to the Prophet—and ultimately to the divine Source itself. It is a living link, one that provides access to the transcendent realms the aspirant cannot attain through his efforts alone. Rumi would have been a mere theologian had it not been for the radiant baraka of the strange dervish, Shams-i Tabriz.

Epilogue

In his eloquent ode to his teacher, "Divan-i Shams-i Tabriz," Rumi likened his own teacher's baraka to the transformative power of the sun:

> From the Sun, the pride of Tabriz, behold these miracles,
> For every tree gains beauty by the light of the sun.

The mysterious workings of baraka confirm an important truth about Sufism and mysticism generally: *the body is anterior to the mind*. Looking back, I failed fully to realize this during my stay in Bara. In dhikr ceremonies, I kept waiting to *see* something, to perceive with my mind's eye something entirely new and earth-shattering. While the descent of spirit is indeed earth-shattering, it is not mediated by the mind. It is through the body that the divine Mystery makes it presence known. Uncontrollable shaking, weeping, laughing, and shouting were signs of the physical encounter with spirit, like the wind one never sees save for the grass through which it blows.

I was at first surprised to hear that the pir made his eldest son successor. During his lifetime, whenever disciples speculated as to who would succeed him, his sons were never mentioned. Usually the names of some prominent—and spiritually potent—Afghans and Pakistanis would be mentioned. Cynics will be quick to point out that his decision only confirms the shaikh's concern to maintain wealth and prestige within the family. The pir had indeed left behind a large extended family with no visible means of support, and this, practically, may have played a part in his decision. But there is another reason more in keeping with his organizational abilities and spiritual integrity. During the pir's lifetime, the consensus of disciples was that, when the pir passed away, a Pakistani shaikh would lead the Pakistani disciples and an Afghan shaikh, the Afghans. This split would have reflected the different styles of Saifi Sufism as it has evolved in the two countries. Yet, in designating his son, the pir may well have been concerned to forestall just such a division of the order along national lines at a time of great crisis in the region.

Indeed, weathering the frequent storms that beset this region has, for centuries, made this Sufi lineage an enduring one.

Acknowledgments

I owe a great debt of gratitude to several individuals and institutions without which this study would never have been conducted. Foremost among them are Pir Saif ur-Rahman and his disciples, who gave generously of their time and of themselves, asking only in return that I make a sincere effort to follow the Naqshbandi path. Elsewhere in the field I had so much support that I could not possibly thank everyone. Dr. Azmat Hayat Khan, chair of the Department of Central Asian Studies at Peshawar University, gave generously of his time, and his personal contacts in the region were indispensable. Sayyid 'Umar Mujaddidi, a member of the Mujaddidi family, worked with me painstakingly with many of the Persian texts, responding calmly and thoughtfully to my barrage of questions. He and many other Afghans like him helped sensitize me to the richness of Afghan social, cultural, and religious life. I would never have had the wherewithal to return to Pakistan had it not been for the Fulbright Foundation, which generously funded my research. Thanks also to Dr. Richard Eaton, professor of history at the University of Arizona, who inveigled me to look beyond my preoccupation with spirituality to examine the important social roles the Sufi shaikh plays, which led to chapter 7 of this book. Steve Landrigan made many helpful comments and revisions to an earlier draft and was endlessly supportive in encouraging me to publish this study.

Notes

For full publishing information, please see the bibliography.

Introduction

Epigraph. Sayed Ishfaq 'Ali, *The Saints of the Punjab*, 122.

Epigraph. 'Ali Uthman al-Hujwiri, *Kashf al-Mahjub*, 12.

1. Hamid Algar, discussion with author, University of California at Berkeley, October 1983. Dr. Algar is a specialist on Iran and Sufism and a Naqshbandi practitioner.

Chapter 1

Epigraph. Ibn Anas, *Al-Muwatta* [The Well-Trodden Path], Chapter 15, Hadith #7.

Epigraph. Pickthall, *The Meaning of the Glorious Qur'an: Text and Explanatory Translation*, 5:48.

1. Matt. 5:17.
2. Schimmel, *Mystical Dimensions*, 27.
3. Al-Hujwiri, *Kashf al-Mahjub*, 83.
4. Ibid., 83.
5. Quoted in Ernst, *Shambhala Guide to Sufism*, 52.
6. Ibid., 51.
7. Bukhari, *Hadith*, 3:121.
8. Andrae, *In the Garden of Myrtles*, 14.
9. Quoted in Ernst, *Shambhala Guide to Sufism*, 124.
10. Smith, *Early Mystic of Baghdad*, 69.
11. Ibid., 68–69.
12. Smith, *Rabi'a the Mystic*, 55.
13. Quoted in Schimmel, *Mystical Dimensions,* 38–39.

14. Smith, *Early Mystic of Baghdad*, 256–57.
15. Abdel Kader, *The Life, Personality, and Writings of al-Junayd*, 51.
16. Quoted in Rizvi, *History of Sufism in India*, vol. 1, 59.
17. Massignon, *La passion d'al-Husayn ibn Mansur al-Hallaj*, vol. 3, 50.
18. Ibid., vol. 1, 329.
19. For the definitive study of the life and work of Mansur al-Hallaj see Massignon, *La passion de Husayn*.

Chapter 2

Epigraph. Quoted in Schimmel, *Mystical Dimensions*, 364.

Epigraph. Hanbal, "Manaqib as-Sahaba" [Virtues of the Companions].

1. Trimingham, *Sufi Orders*, 6.
2. Ibid., 10.
3. Maqdisi, *Kitab al-bad' wa al-tarikh*, vol. 5, 148.
4. Trimingham, *Sufi Orders*, 265–66.
5. Bayazid, whose full name was Abu Yazid Tayfur Ibn 'Isa ibn Surushan of Bistam, was fourth in the line to the Prophet after Abu Bakr, Islam's first caliph. Naqshbandis are among a very few Sufi orders who trace their spiritual ancestry to the Prophet through Abu Bakr, who, according to the Sufi al-Hujwiri, represents the contemplative way of Sufism.
6. Quoted in Schimmel, *Mystical Dimensions*, 48.
7. Ibid., 49.
8. Ibid.
9. See Toussulis, *Sufism and the Way of Blame*.
10. Algar, "The Naqshbandi Order," 132.
11. Rizvi, *History of Sufism in India*, vol. 1, 95–96.
12. Ibid., vol. 2, 192.
13. Sirhindi, *Maktubat*.
14. An eighteen-century Naqshbandi, Mir Dard, would call this path *tariqa Muhammadi*.
15. A similar synthesis of shari'a and tariqa had been achieved by the Baghdad theologian al-Ghazali in the twelfth century.
16. The Deoband Seminary, founded in 1867 in a small Indian town of that name in the northeast became a major training center for Sufis and traditional *ulama*.

In the subcontinent, Taliban and other fundamentalist groups are very often mistakenly called "Deobandis."

Chapter 3

Epigraph. Pir Saif ur-Rahman, talk with disciples (Bara, Pakistan, January 1994).

Epigraph. Arberry, *Koran Interpreted*, 6:125.

1. Haji Pachir lived in a subdistrict of Pachir Agam and maintained a khanaqah in Chaparhar that is still operating today.
2. Hadda-i Sahib was a khalifa of the famous Akhund of Swat, the Qadiri Sufi shaikh who had briefly participated in the tribal uprising of 1897. After Hadda was invested as a khalifa in 1835, he moved to the village of Hadda in Nangrahar, where, on the site of an ancient Gandhara Buddhist monastery, he started a mosque and khanaqah.
3. From his base in the Mohmand Agency, Hadda mobilized popular opposition to the growing influence of the British in the tribal areas. In 1897, he and other Sufi pirs led a major uprising against the British that involved Pashtun tribes on both sides of the border.
4. At last report, Haji Pachir's son was running the khanaqah in Chaparhar, though his following today is much reduced in size.
5. A Pakistani Pashtun from Charsadda, Haji Amin was a disciple of a khalifa of Hadda at whose Nangrahar hospice he often stayed when visiting the region.
6. These schools included Mashu Khail, near Bara; Shahab Khail; Bala Manai; and Mazo Grale, in addition to Tahkali Payan. Tahkali Payan's founder, Haji Sahib Turangzai, was also a khalifa of Hadda Haji and a coleader in Hadda's struggle against the British. Turangzai traveled widely in the border areas, attempting to counter the influence of a pro-British Sufi, Mulla Manki, and unite the tribes in jihad.
7. In the village of Babara.
8. Also known as Maulawi Babara.
9. The school where Sandani taught still sits on the western edge of the largest cemetery in Asia and quite possibly the world. The school has been greatly expanded since Sandani's time with study rooms and student lodging.
10. At that time, young Afghan men without a formal university degree were required to perform two years of unpaid military service. Before promulgation of a constitutional law in 1954, the government employed a draft system first introduced by Amir Habibullah in the late nineteenth-century. The system

was dubbed *hasht nafri* (eighth person), as one out of eight men between the ages of twenty and forty was called up for service from village lists maintained yearly by the government. The ratio seems to have varied depending on the army's needs in a given year. In some cases, families wishing to spare their sons military service would pool finances and pay the equivalent of two years' salary in advance for someone willing to enlist.

11. The Sufis are known as *al-qawm* by virtue of hadiths such as the following: "Then they say: 'Lord, amongst them sitting with them is a sinner,' and He saith: 'Him also I have forgiven, for he is among a folk [qawm] whose fellow, that sittith with them, shall not be confounded." In central Asia, Sufis are also known as *Mian*, or "them."

12. In the village of Hisi-i Tagab.

13. With Akhundzada Sahib-i Tagab.

14. Perhaps the exalted title represents the "rhetoric of sainthood" among Sufis that Carl Ernst has identified. See Ernst, *Ruzbihan Baqli*.

15. Despite Taloqani's decision, many of his thirty other khalifas, who were older than Hashim, refused to accept the latter as pir, and a bitter rivalry ensued. Even Taloqani's own son, Ubaidullah Akhundzada, had been passed over. In an attempt to reverse his father's decision, Ubaidullah went to see Hashim in his village of Aibek in neighboring Samangan Province. When Hashim placed his hand over Ubaidullah's chest, he found coldness in all five subtle centers. In this encounter, Ubaidullah seems to have been made aware of his feeble spiritual development, for he subsequently became Hashim's—and later Saif ur-Rahman's—disciple.

16. Not all the land was sold, however. Saif's family, including some of his brothers, reside there today and run a khanaqah.

17. Balkhi, *Tarikh-i awliya'*, 158.

18. Ibid., 162.

19. Ibid., 163. In the absence of a formal *ijaza nama*, this letter is one of several such communications cited as written evidence that Hashim had designated Saif ur-Rahman as his successor.

20. Most of the disciples accepted Saif ur-Rahman as head of the order. However, at least one khalifa, Muhammad Lal, refused. Citing a letter of Sirhindi, he argued that a disciple was permitted to disagree with his shaikh if he felt he had achieved a higher spiritual degree than the other khalifa.

21. In another phenomenon related to Uway's teaching mission, one of Saif's disciples came to him one day to report a vision he had had in which Hazrat Uways appeared. Uways handed the disciple a Qur'an that the Prophet

Muhammad wished him to pass along to Saif ur-Rahman. In a similar mode of spiritual instruction, Saif ur-Rahman's biographer relates the dream of a disciple in which he saw Hashim approaching. Fearing Hashim was going to strike him, the disciple became frightened. Hashim told him not to be afraid. Hashim climbed on the disciple's back and told him to run on one foot. The disciple took off haltingly, but he found himself moving faster. Soon he was running at breakneck speed. When asked the meaning of the dream, Saif ur-Rahman said it was an example of *tariqa qawmi*, the path of the "folk," or Sufis.

22. Aminillah, *Hidayat al-salikin*, 182–83.
23. The Ka'aba is a cubic structure in Mecca that contains a black stone, a meteorite, which has been considered sacred from before the time of Muhammad.
24. See Ernst, *Ruzbihan Baqli*.
25. Roy, *Islam and Resistance in Afghanistan*, 106.
26. Balkhi, *Tarikh-i awliya'*, 164.
27. In the east, where maraboutism was strong, the Sufi orders were not particularly represented. The exception to this was the traditional Mujaddidi family tie with the Sulaiman Khel tribe.
28. Juma Gul was Maulana Hashim's brother.
29. Many years later, when I was conducting interviews at Saif ur-Rahman's khanaqah in the Khyber, several of his khalifas would allude to a scandal during the 1980s, which may have concerned these illicit activities. Whatever the precise nature of the scandal, no one has forgotten, and some disciples still do not trust those who were involved.
30. Balkhi, *Tarikh-i awliya'*, 166.

Chapter 4

Epigraph. Caroe, *The Pathans: 550 B.C.–A.D. 1957*, xv.

Epigraph. Bellew, *An Enquiry into the Ethnography of Afghanistan*, 91.

1. Socially, Afridis are organized into patrilineal descent groups that correspond to territorial boundaries. One or more of these descent groups form the core of a subtribe. Generally, subtribes are clusters of two or three villages consisting of roughly 100 to 150 families. While elders hold achieved status, Pashtuns as a larger group are acephalous—the only recognized head exists within the family. Most marriages occur within the subsection or clan. About one-fifth of these occur between and man and his father's brother's daughter,

the preferred choice of wife for the vast majority of Afridis. Women must strictly observe *purda*, the practice of seclusion from public life. If required to go out in public to shop or visit relatives (which men strongly discourage), they must be completely covered. Increasingly, Pashtun women are voicing their opposition to this custom. Confinement to the home is perceived as a form of bondage from which, owing to the male-dominated nature of Pashtun society, there is no escape.

2. The Hanafi school is the oldest of the four schools of law within Sunni Islam. The other three schools are the Shafi'i, the Maliki, and the Hanbali. The Hanafi school is named after its founder, Abu Hanifa al-Nu'man ibn Thābit (d. 767). It is the oldest of the four and is generally regarded as the most liberal and as the one that puts the most emphasis on human reason. Hanafis are found predominantly in central and south Asia and southeastern Europe.
3. Hart, "The Afridi of the Khaibar Tribal Agency," in *Pakistan*, ed. Akbar S. Ahmed (Karachi: Oxford University Press, 1990), 12.

Chapter 5

Epigraph. Quoted in Schimmel, *Mystical Dimensions*, 232.

Epigraph. Hujwiri, *Kashf al-Mahjub*, 340.

1. This is Martin Lings's contention in *A Sufi Saint of the Twentieth Century*, 73–74. Lings, who had many disciples in Pakistan, was a Sufi and a Shakespeare scholar who had been initiated in the Darqawi order.
2. For a discussion of suhbat, see chapters 5 and 6.
3. Sirhindi, *Maktubat*, 2:292.
4. Barlevism was a late nineteenth-century religious movement that grew out of debates on the nature of God. These debates eventually crystallized around a Sufi shaikh, Ahmad Reza Khan Barlewi. The son of Afghan immigrants to the Punjab, Reza Khan was a Qadiri who spent much of his life attacking Wahabis and the excessive legalism of the Deoband school. His teaching found fertile ground in Sind and the Punjab, areas permeated with Hindu bhakti devotionalism. In relations with their pirs, Barlevis dispense with personal responsibility, stressing enlightenment through intercession of pirs rather than rigorous spiritual exercises and education. Because of the devotion demonstrated by Mubarak Sahib's disciples, the Pakistani press mistakenly refers to him and his followers as "Barlevi."

Notes

Chapter 6

Epigraph. Geertz, *Available Light*, 102.

Epigraph. Chagnon, *Noble Savages*, 32.

1. Vambery, *Travels in Central Asia.*
2. Evans-Pritchard, *The Sanusi of Cyrenaica*, 49.
3. Cruise O'Brien, *The Mourides of Senegal*, 38.
4. Weber, *On Charisma and Institution Building*, 48–49.
5. Ibid., 52.
6. Ahmed, *Millennium and Charisma Among Pashtuns*, 113.
7. Geertz, *Islam Observed*, 44.
8. Gilsenan, *Recognizing Islam*, 75.
9. On the basis of his own spiritual experience, Sirhindi claimed that the true mystic path rested on three mutually interdependent pillars: acceptance of the credal dogma, adherence to the law (*shari'a*), and mystical education (*tariqa*). In synthesizing these elements, Sirhindi maintained he was simply reaffirming the validity of the original prophetic revelation and Muhammad as the spiritual exemplar. Instead of engaging in self-mortification (a common practice of Hindu *sadhus* that had begun to infiltrate Indian Islam), the disciple should cultivate a desire to perform the shari'a and a devotion to the exemplary behavior of the Prophet. In modeling themselves after the prophetic ideal, Mujaddidis believed they were recreating in minute detail the time when the Prophet instructed his own companions. Philosophically, one of the reformulations of Sirhindi's revival concerned his opposition to the doctrine of *wahdat al-wujud*, or "oneness of being." The doctrine defined the relationship between God and his creation. According to the wahdat al-wujud position, creation is illusory, the only reality is God. He alone exists; therefore the mystic must annihilate himself in God. For such annihilation to be possible, however, humans have to be, in some immaterial way, a direct emanation of the Divine, which is anathema in mainstream Islam and even in other schools of Sufism.

    Through the writings of the Persian mystical poets, the doctrine made its way to India, where it found sympathetic ground in the Hindu monistic philosophy of Advaita Vedanta. In some quarters, nourished by Vedanta, the emanationist philosophy of wahdat al-wujud was becoming perilously close to pantheism. For if the Sufi was an emanation of the Divine, then he was a law unto himself and had no need of the shari'a.

To counter the pantheistic tendencies of wahdat al-wujud, Sirhindi employed the philosophy of *wahdat al-shuhud*, "unity of witness," formulated by Ala al-Dawla al-Simnani (d. 1336). According to this doctrine, the entire universe is pervaded by a common existence, an existence at once immanent and transcendent. Beyond this, however, lies the original and uncreated existence of God, which is beyond the mystic's reach. Sirhindi attacked Sufis who declared unitive experience to be the highest and most complete stage of spiritual life, arguing that such a state was incomplete and partly illusory. He maintained that the wahdat al-wujud position actually denied God's oneness and encouraged believers to be lax in matters of law.

On the basis of his claim to have discovered still higher levels of awareness, Sirhindi maintained that Ibn al-'Arabi's philosophy reflected the lesser stage of sainthood, or *fana'*. Echoing Junayd, Sirhindi said that beyond fana' lay the higher stage of *baqa'*, a stage whose heights only a few had ever reached. In baqa' the Sufi returned to the created world transfigured to guide others in the mystic path. Beyond this stage lay the uncreated Oneness of God and His Formless Essence, both of which are unattainable by humankind.

The idea that Oneness and Formless Essence are beyond humankind's reach is at variance with other Sufi theosophical systems, including some other Naqshbandis'. Nor is Sirhindi's argument entirely consistent intellectually, since the concept of *shuhud* is actually a qualified duality believed necessary for realizing divine oneness. Paradoxically, Sirhindi maintained that the ecstatic utterances of Sufis like Mansur al-Hallaj—more in line with the wujudi position—actually affirmed the shuhud philosophy because of his recognition of "only God not I." Nor was his own behavior entirely consistent, as Sirhindi claimed to have surpassed the spiritual state of Abu Bakr, Islam's first khalifa; these claims exposed him to charges of heresy. For this he was chastised by his master, Baqi Billah, and was imprisoned for a time by Emperor Jahangir.

The differences between the two philosophies probably owe more to Sirhindi's desire to rescue Islam in India and prevent it from complete absorption into Hinduism than to any real metaphysical or doctrinal distinction. In this sense his distinctions were probably more theological than ontological; humankind may well be identical to the Formless Essence, only there were serious consequences in saying it, both for Sufis themselves and for the institution of Islam. One of the unintended consequences of Sirhindi's philosophy was that in affirming the necessity of the law it made later Mujaddidis doctrinally intransigent and deeply opposed to even the slightest reform of the teachings.

10. Razi, *The Path of God's Bondsman*, 138–39.

Chapter 7

Epigraph. Abu-Dawud, *Hadith*, 40: 4579.

Epigraph. Pasha, *Terkib-I Bend.*

1. Sebghatullah later went into exile in Denmark. When he returned to Afghanistan after the fall of the Taliban, he served for a time as speaker of Afghanistan's upper house of Parliament and head of the National Unity and Reconciliation Commission. He is now retired.
2. Such shrines can be found today throughout India and Pakistan. The caretaker of the shrine usually charges visitors a small fee for entrance to the shrine.
3. Ur-Rahman, *Fatwa*, 20.
4. Ibid., 18.
5. Ibid., 3.
6. Ibid., 39–40.
7. Ibid., 36.
8. Abu Mansur al-Maturidi (d. 944) was a Hanafi jurist and founder of one of the two Sunni schools of theology, which bears his name. His theology is associated with the Hanafi legal school. Maturidi's doctrine is more rationalist than the other school of theology, Ash'arism. He believed that humankind is obliged and able to gain knowledge of God and to thank him by using reason independent of revelation. *Encyclopaedia of Islam,* 2nd ed., s.v. "al-Maturidi."
9. In November 1994, Maulana Sufi Muhammad, leader of the Nifaz-i Islam, led an uprising in the Malakand area of Swat Vallley Agency against government attempts to replace local shari'a law with uniform civil codes. The Maulana demanded the restoration of Islamic law. Eventually, the government suppressed the uprising, suffering several casualties in the process.
10. Ur-Rahman, *Fatwa,* 38.

Chapter 8

*Epigraph.*Sirhindi, *Maktubat*, vol. 1, 5.

Epigraph. Rumi, *Selected Poems*, xxii.

Glossary

akhund (pl. *akhundan*): An Islamic scholar

akhundzada: A descendant of a religious scholar

'alim (pl. *'ulama*): A religious scholar

amir: A prince, lord, or nobleman; former title of a ruler of Afghanistan

baqa': Literally, "abiding"; the final stage on the Sufi path, in which the seeker abides eternally in God

baraka: Blessing, grace, spiritual power inherent in a saint

bay'a: An oath of allegiance by a disciple to his pir

bid'a: Innovation in religious practice

Chishti: A Sufi order found mainly in the subcontinent, whose founder is Mu'inuddin of Ajmer

dar al-Islam: Muslim territory

dhikr (or *zikr*): A Sufi practice involving repetition of the names of God

fana': Extinction of the self before attaining final union with God

fiqh: Jurisprudence; the discipline of elucidating Islamic law

hadith: Sayings of the Prophet Muhammad based on the authority of a chain of transmitters

hajj: The annual pilgrimage to Mecca required of every Muslim at least once in his or her life

Hanafi: One of four Sunni schools of Islamic law, named after Abu Hanifa

hazrat: Lord; the title applied to Sufi masters of the Naqshbandi/Mujaddidi order

ijaza nama: Written authorization to teach in the name of a Sufi master

islah: The concept of reform in early Islam that emphasized rejection of Sufism and reliance on the Qur'an and hadith as the only legitimate bases of religious authority

ijtihad: Independent legal reasoning based on the Qur'an and hadith

jihad: Holy war in the name of Islam

jihad al-da'wa: Effort to spread Islam among unbelievers by nonviolent means

jihad al-tarbia: Effort to spread Islamic values and institutions within Muslim society

jinn: A subterranean race of good and evil creatures made of smokeless fire who may help or harm humans

jirga: A Pashtun tribal council

kafir: An infidel; non-Muslim

karamat (pl. of *karama*): Miracles, allegedly performed by Sufi saints

khalifa: A successor; one delegated by a Sufi shaikh to teach

khan: A Pashtun tribal leader or chief

khanaqah: A lodge or meeting place for Sufis

khel: The lineage segment, or clan, of a Pashtun tribe

khwajagan (pl. of *khwaja*): A religious title once designating the masters of one of the central Asian schools of Sufism

khirqa: A cloak worn by Sufi masters, of a type believed to have been worn by the Prophet Muhammad.

madrasa: An Islamic religious school

malik: A village chief, often appointed by the government in nontribal areas

maulawi: An Islamic scholar

melmastia: The Pashtun custom of providing hospitality to visitors

mihrab: The prayer niche in a mosque indicating the direction of Mecca

mujaddid: A renewer of Islam sent by God at the beginning of each century

mullah: The religious leader of a village

nafs: The carnal or appetitive self

nang: The sense of shame in an honor culture

pir: A spiritual guide in Sufism

purda: Segregation of sexes by sequestering females

pushtunwali: A Pashtun tribal code of conduct

Qadiri: A Sufi order prevalent throughout the Islamic world, whose founder is 'Abd al-Qadir al-Jilani (d. 1166)

qari: One who recites the Qur'an during ceremonies

qawmi: "The folk," a term used to refer to Sufis

qibla: The direction of Mecca, toward which Muslims face during prayer

qutb: A pole; in Sufism considered to be the head of a hierarchy of saints

Ramadan: The ninth Muslim month, designated as the month of fasting between dawn and dusk

sajjada nishin: The successor to a Sufi pir

salat: Formal prayer performed five times daily

sayyid: A descendant of the Prophet

shaikh: A Sufi master

shalwar kameez: The traditional dress of south Asia worn by men and women, consisting of loose cotton trousers (the shalwar) tied at the waist with a drawstring, and a long shirt or tunic (the kameez) worn over the trousers

shari'a: The entire body of rules guiding the life of a Muslim

shirk: Idolatry

silsila: A chain of Sufis who share spiritual descent from a common founder

suhbat: Companionship; the practice of keeping company with a Sufi pir in order to obtain his spiritual blessing

sunna: The exemplary behavior and conduct of the Prophet Muhammad embodied in hadith

sura: A chapter of the Qur'an

talib: A religious student

taqlid: Legal imitation of one of the four schools of law

tariqa: The mystical path in Sufism; a Sufi order

tawajjuh: Concentration of a Sufi on a disciple as a means of transferring spiritual grace

'urs: A Sufi festival commemorating a saint's death

Wahabi: A follower of the eighteenth-century Arab reformer 'Abd al-Wahab, who emphasized a literal interpretation of the Qur'an and hadith as the bases of Islam; anyone who employs a literalist approach to Islam

wahdat al-shuhud: The metaphysical doctrine of phenomenological monism or unity of witness

wali: A friend of God; a saint

ziyarat: A Sufi shrine

Bibliography

Abdel Kader, Ali Hassan. *The Life, Personality, and Writings of al-Junayd*. London: Luzac & Co., 1962.

Abu-Dawud, Sunan. *Hadith*. University of Southern California Center for Muslim Jewish Engagement. http://www.usc.edu/org/cmje/religious-texts/hadith/abudawud/040-sat.php.

Ahmed, Akbar S. *Millennium and Charisma Among Pashtuns: A Critical Essay in Social Anthropology*. London: Routledge and Kegan Paul, 1976.

Algar, Hamid. "The Naqshbandi Order: A Preliminary Survey of Its History and Significance," *Studia Islamica*, 44 (1976): 123–152.

'Ali, Sayed Ishfaq. *The Saints of the Punjab*. Rawalpindi: Pap Board, 1994.

Aminillah, Maulana. *Hidayat al-salikin*. Peshawar: privately printed, 1996.

Andrae, Tor. *In the Garden of Myrtles: Studies in Early Islamic Mysticism*. Albany: State University of New York Press, 1987.

Arberry, A. J. *The Koran Interpreted*. New York: Simon and Schuster, 1955.

Balkhi, Ali Muhhamad. *Tarikh-i awliya'*. Mazar-i Sharif: privately printed, 1983.

Bellew, H. W. *An Enquiry into the Ethnography of Afghanistan*. Reprint. Karachi: Indus Publications, 1977.

Bukhari, Sahih. "Hadith." http://ahadith.co.uk/sahihbukhari.php.

Caroe, Olaf. *The Pathans: 550 B.C.–A.D. 1957*. London: Macmillan & Co., 1958.

Chagnon, Napoleon. *Noble Savages: My Life among Two Dangerous Tribes: The Yanomamo and the Anthropologists*. New York: Simon and Shuster, 2013.

Cruise O'Brien, Donal. *Charisma and Brotherhood in African Islam*. Oxford: Clarendon Press, 1988.

_____. *The Mourides of Senegal: The Political and Economic Organization of an Islamic Brotherhood*. Oxford: Clarendon Press, 1971.

Ernst, Carl. *Ruzbihan Baqli: Mysticism and the Rhetoric of Sainthood in Persian Sufism*. Surrey: Curzon Press, 1996.

_____. *The Shambhala Guide to Sufism*. Boston: Shambala Publications, 1997.

Evans-Pritchard, Edwin Evan. *The Sanusi of Cyrenaica*. Oxford: Clarendon Press, 1949.

Geertz, Clifford. *Available Light: Anthropological Reflections on Philosophical Topics*. Princeton, NJ: Princeton University Press, 2000.

_____. *Islam Observed: Religious Development in Morocco and Indonesia*. Chicago: University of Chicago Press, 1968.

Gilsenan, Michael. *Recognizing Islam: An Anthropologist's Introduction*. London: Croom Helm, 1982.

Hanbal, Ahmad bin. "Manaqib as-Sahaba." In *The Naqshbandi Sufi Way: History and Guidebook of the Saints of the Golden Chain* by Muhammad Hisham Kabbani and Shaykh Muhammad Hisham Kabbani. Chicago: Kazi Publications, 1995.

Hart, David M. "The Afridi of the Khaibar Tribal Agency." In *Pakistan: The Social Sciences Perspective*. Edited by Akbar S. Ahmed. Karachi: Oxford University Press, 1990.

_____. *Guardians of the Khyber Pass: The Social Organization and History of the Afridis of Pakistan*. Lahore: Vanguard Books, 1985.

Hujwiri, 'Ali Uthman al-. *Kashf al-Mahjub*. Translated by Reynold A. Nicholson. Lahore: Islamic Book Service, 1991.

Ibn Anas, Malik. *Al-Muwatta*. Chapter 15, Hadith 7. http://ahadith.co.uk/maliksmuwatta.php.

Lings, Martin. *A Sufi Saint of the Twentieth Century: Shaikh Ahmad al-'Alaw; His Spiritual Heritage and Legacy*. 2nd ed. Berkeley: University of California Press, 1971.

Maqdisi, Abu Nasr Mutahhar ibn Tâhir. *Kitab al-bad' wa al-tarikh*. 6 vols. Beirut: n.d.

Massignon, Louis. *La passion d'al-Husayn ibn Mansur al-Hallaj, martyr mystique de l'Islam*. Paris: Gallimard, 1975.

Pasha, Ziya. *Terkib-I Bend*. Translated by Bernard Lewis. Raindrop Turkish House. http://www.raindropturkishhouse.org/oklahomacity/58-literature-ziya-pasha.

Pickthall, Muhammad. *The Meaning of the Glorious Qur'an: Text and Explanatory Translation*. New York: Muslim World League, 1977.

Rahman, Saifur. *Ba vujud-i Saifiyya*. Peshawar: privately printed, 1996.

_____. *Fatwa-i Saifiyya*. Privately printed, n.d.

Razi, Najm al-Din. *The Path of God's Bondsman from Origin to Return*. Translated by Hamid Algar. Caravan: Delmar, New York, 1982.

Rizvi, Saiyid Athar Abbas. *A History of Sufism in India*. 2 vols. New Delhi: Munshiram, 1978.

Roy, Olivier. *Islam and Resistance in Afghanistan*. New York: Cambridge University Press, 1990.

Rumi, Jalaladin. *Selected Poems from the Divan-I Shams-I Tabriz*. Edited and translated by Reynold A. Nicholson. London: Curzon Press (reprint), 1994.

Schimmel, Annemarie. *Mystical Dimensions of Islam*. Chapel Hill: University of North Carolina Press, 1975.

Sirhindi, Ahmad. *Maktubat-i imam-i rabbani*. Edited by Nur Ahmad. 3 vols. Karachi: Educational Press, 1972.

Smith, Margaret. *An Early Mystic of Baghdad: A Study of the Life and Teaching of Harith B. Asad al-Muḥasibi A.D. 781–857*. New York: AMS Press, 1973.

_____. *Rabi'a the Mystic and Her Fellow Saints in Islam*. Cambridge: Cambridge University Press, 1928.

Sviri, Sara. "Hakim Tirmidhi and the Malamati Movement." In *Classical Persian Sufism from its Origins to Rumi*, edited by Leonard Lewisohn. London: Khaniqahi Nimatullahi Publications, 1993.

Toussulis, Yannis. *Sufism and the Way of Blame: Hidden Sources of a Sacred Psychology*. Wheaton, IL: Quest Books, 2010.

Trimingham, J. Spencer. *The Sufi Orders in Islam*. Oxford: Oxford University Press, 1973.

Vambery, Arminius. *Travels in Central Asia*. New York: Arno Press, 1970.

Weber, Max. *On Charisma and Institution Building*. Chicago: University of Chicago Press, 1968.

Index

[redacted]

[redacted]